KU-021-437

NEW TITLES FROM AVIZANDUM PUBLISHING

Land Registration

By Kenneth GC Reid and George L Gretton
Avizandum Publishing Ltd; December 2016; **Special Price £95.00 with this leaflet**

The law governing the Land Register of Scotland was substantially recast by the Land Registration etc (Scotland) Act 2012, which came fully into force on 8 December 2014. In addition, the 2012 Act provided for the phasing out of the Register of Sasines, a register of deeds which has been in continuous use for the last 400 years. The Scottish Government's target is for all titles to have migrated from the Register of Sasines to the Land Register by 2024.

These momentous changes are the subjects of the present book. After introductory chapters tracing the history of land registration in Scotland from its beginnings in the sixteenth century until modern times, Professors Reid and Gretton provide a detailed and authoritative guide to the new law as set out in the 2012 Act and in the numerous statutory instruments made under that Act

Nothing So Practical as a Good Theory: Festschrift for George L. Gretton

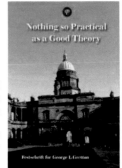

Edited by Andrew JM Steven, Ross G Anderson, John MacLeod
Avizandum Publishing Ltd; November 2017; £40.00

Professor George Gretton's contribution to legal scholarship in Scotland and beyond over the last 40 years has been immense. As a teacher he is held in affection by generations of students. His period of service as a Scottish Law Commissioner from 2006–11 was a distinguished one, which culminated in the enactment of the Land Registration etc (Scotland) Act 2012. He is well known to the Scottish legal profession for his annual conveyancing lectures with Professor Kenneth Reid.

Professor Gretton's interests are varied and wide-ranging. This book, which marks his retirement as Lord President Reid Professor of Law in the University of Edinburgh, is a collection of essays on subject areas of particular interest to him, including obligations, property, succession and trusts. The authors include many distinguished colleagues and friends from academia, the judiciary and legal practice.

Avizandum Publishing Ltd• Registered in Scotland No SC227587• Registered office: 56A Candlemaker Row Edinburgh EH1 2QE
Directors: Margaret Cherry; Elizabeth Thompson   VAT Number GB 801 6271 63

Crofting Law

By Derek Flyn and Keith Graham; February 2017; £125.00: **Special Price £95.00 with this leaflet**

Crofting law has recently been subject to substantial reforms as part of the Scottish Government's land reform programme. Developments include the renaming and reorganisation of the Crofters Commission; the introduction of a registration system for crofts, common grazings and land held runrig in them; and provision for decrofting by owner-occupier crofters. The authors draw on their experience to provide this accessible and practical guide through the complex web of legislation. This text is the first to cover the Crofting Reform etc Act 2007, the Crofting Reform (Scotland) Act 2010, and the Crofting (Amendment) (Scotland) Act 2013.

Civil Jury Trials (3ed)

By Andrew Hajducki; December 2017; £125.00

This is the only book dedicated to the law and practice governing the conduct of a case that goes to civil jury trial in Scotland. The subject is set in its historical context and then covers the progress of a case from choosing the mode of inquiry, through initial procedure and trial, to appeal and review. The use of the civil jury has waxed and waned over the years, but the institution remains an integral part of the administration of justice, particularly in the determination of personal injuries awards. Civil jury trial was reintroduced into the sheriff court in 2015 after a long absence, and a specialised Personal Injuries Court has been established.

Back Issues of the following Annual Volumes of Conveyancing are also available:

Conveyancing 2004	£24.00
Conveyancing 2005	£24.00
Conveyancing 2006	£24.00
Conveyancing 2007	£25.00
Conveyancing 2008	£25.00
Conveyancing 2010	£25.00
Conveyancing 2011	£25.00
Conveyancing 2012	£25.00
Conveyancing 2015	£28.00
Conveyancing 2016	£28.00

Avizandum Publishing Ltd• Registered in Scotland No SC227587• Registered office: 56A Candlemaker Row Edinburgh EH1 2QE
Directors: Margaret Cherry; Elizabeth Thompson   VAT Number GB 801 6271 63

ORDER FORM

Qty	Author	Title	Price	Total
	Reid	Land Registration	£95.00	
	Steven et al	Nothing So Practical as a Good Theory	£40.00	
	Flyn	Crofting	£95.00	
	Hajducki	Civil Jury Trials (3ed)	£125.00	
		FREE POSTAGE in the UK		£0.00
		Total		

Please complete the form below and return together with your payment to:

Avizandum Law Bookshop, 56a Candlemaker Row, Edinburgh EH1 2QE

You may also order by phone/fax **0131 220 3373** or email: **customerservice@avizandum.com**

Delivery information (please complete in block capitals)

Name: _____

Address: _____

Post code: _____   Tel: _____

DX Number: _____

Method of payment

❑   Payment by BACS: Royal Bank of Scotland, Sort Code: 83-19-09, Account No: 00204166,   Account Name: Mrs EA Thompson t/a Avizandum

❑   Please charge to my/our account at Avizandum Law Bookshop

❑   Credit/Debit card: MasterCard/VISA Switch/Maestro

Card number: _____

Security No: _____   Start Date: _____   Expiry date: _____

Issue number (Switch): _____

Name on card: _____

Billing address for card (if different from delivery address):

_____

Post code: _____

❑   Please tick if you wish to receive information from Avizandum by EMAIL
      Your email address:

_____

vizandum Publishing Ltd• Registered in Scotland No SC227587• Registered office: 56A Candlemaker Row Edinburgh EH1 2QE
Directors: Margaret Cherry; Elizabeth Thompson   VAT Number GB 801 6271 63

Avizandum Law Bookshop,
56a Candlemaker Row
Edinburgh
EH1 2QE

Website: www.avizandum.co.uk

Phone/fax **0131 220 3373**

Email: **customerservice@avizandum.com**

Avizandum Publishing Ltd• Registered in Scotland No SC227587• Registered office: 56A Candlemaker Row Edinburgh EH1 2C
Directors: Margaret Cherry; Elizabeth Thompson   VAT Number GB 801 6271 63

CONVEYANCING 2017

CONVEYANCING 2017

Kenneth G C Reid WS

Professor of Scots Law in the University of Edinburgh

and

George L Gretton WS

Lord President Reid Professor of Law Emeritus in the University of Edinburgh

with a contribution by Alan Barr of the University of Edinburgh
and Brodies LLP

Avizandum Publishing Ltd
Edinburgh
2018

Published by
Avizandum Publishing Ltd
25 Candlemaker Row
Edinburgh EH1 2QG

First published 2018

© Kenneth G C Reid and George L Gretton, 2018

ISBN 978-1-904968-90-0

British Library Cataloguing in Publication Data
A catalogue record for this book is available from the British Library.

All rights reserved. No part of this publication may be reproduced, stored in a retrieval system, or transmitted in any form or by any means, electronic, mechanical, photocopying, recording or otherwise, without the written permission of the copyright holder. Application for the copyright owner's permission to reproduce any part of this publication should be addressed to the publisher.

Typeset by Waverley Typesetters, Warham, Norfolk
Printed and bound by Bell & Bain Ltd, Glasgow

CONTENTS

PREFACE

This is the nineteenth annual update of new developments in the law of conveyancing. As in previous years, it is divided into five parts. There is, first, a brief description of all cases which have been reported, or appeared on the websites of the Scottish Courts (www.scotcourts.gov.uk) or of the Lands Tribunal for Scotland (www.lands-tribunal-scotland.org.uk/records.html), or have otherwise come to our attention since *Conveyancing 2016*. The next two parts summarise, respectively, statutory developments during 2017 and other material of interest to conveyancers. The fourth part is a detailed commentary on selected issues arising from the first three parts. Finally, in Part V, there are three tables. A cumulative table of decisions, usually by the Lands Tribunal, on the variation or discharge of title conditions covers all decisions since the revised jurisdiction in part 9 of the Title Conditions (Scotland) Act 2003 came into effect. Next is a cumulative table of appeals, designed to facilitate moving from one annual volume to the next. Finally, there is a table of cases digested in earlier volumes but reported, either for the first time or in an additional series, in 2017. This is for the convenience of future reference.

We do not seek to cover agricultural holdings, crofting, public sector tenancies (except the right-to-buy legislation), compulsory purchase or planning law. Otherwise our coverage is intended to be complete. It has been possible to include a small number of cases from England.

We gratefully acknowledge help received from Alan Barr, Ian Bowie, Neil Campbell, Malcolm Combe, Rebecca MacLeod, Willie MacRae, Roddy Paisley, Hamish Patrick, Lorna Richardson, Andrew Steven, and Neil Tainsh.

Kenneth G C Reid
George L Gretton
14 March 2018

TABLE OF STATUTES

TABLE OF ORDERS

TABLE OF CASES

PART I

CASES

CASES

MISSIVES OF SALE

(1) JAL Fish Ltd Small Self-Administered Pension Scheme Trs
v Robertson Construction Eastern Ltd
[2017] CSOH 70, 2017 SLT 577

An obligation in missives to enter into an overage agreement was held to have been extinguished by negative prescription after five years. The twenty-year prescription did not apply because the obligation could not be said to relate to land. See **Commentary** p 114.

(2) New Ingliston Ltd v City of Edinburgh Council
[2017] CSOH 37, 2017 GWD 9-125

In 2011 Edinburgh Council concluded missives to sell 13.65 acres of land to New Ingliston Ltd (NIL). This was part of a more extensive area which had been compulsorily acquired by the Council to construct the tram line at Edinburgh Airport; in the event, the 13.65 acres had proved not to be needed. Subsequently, the parties were in dispute as to contamination of the site and the Council's responsibility for remedying it. The missives were qualified by a settlement agreement entered into in 2015. Nonetheless, the parties remained in dispute. In this action NIL sought to enforce certain obligations which the Council was said to have undertaken in the missives and the settlement agreement.

The dispute turned on the proper interpretation of the two contracts. In that regard 'it was common ground that the court should adopt the approach enunciated by Lord Neuberger in *Arnold v Britton* [2015] AC 1619 at paragraph 15, applied in Scotland in *@SIPP (Pension Trs) Ltd v Insight Travel Services Ltd* 2016 SLT 131 at paragraph 17' (para 17). The relevant passage from *@SIPP (Pension Trs)* read:

> When interpreting a written contract, the court is concerned to identify the intention of the parties by reference to 'what a reasonable person having all the background knowledge which would have been available to the parties would have understood them to be using the language in the contract to mean', to quote Lord Hoffmann in *Chartbrook Ltd v Persimmon Homes Ltd* [2009] AC 1101, para 14. And it does so by focussing on the meaning of the relevant words ... in their documentary, factual and commercial context. That meaning has to be assessed in the light of (i) the natural

3

and ordinary meaning of the clause, (ii) any other relevant provisions of the lease, (iii) the overall purpose of the clause and the lease, (iv) the facts and circumstances known or assumed by the parties at the time that the document was executed, and (v) commercial common sense, but (vi) disregarding subjective evidence of any party's intentions.

One issue between the parties was the proper interpretation of condition 14 of the missives. This provided for an environmental report to be obtained by the Council. In the event of the report disclosing matters which NIL considered unsatisfactory, NIL could direct the Council to carry out such action as was necessary to remedy the unsatisfactory matters. It was further provided that: 'The Purchaser [NIL] shall have an unfettered discretion to its satisfaction with all matters specified in Condition 14.' Such a discretion, said Lord Tyre, did not extend to determining what remedial works were to be carried out. It was for the environmental report to specify what action was required and then for NIL, in the exercise of its discretion, to decide whether the required action was necessary to remedy the matters that it considered to be unsatisfactory. This left only a small role for the discretion. But 'it accords with commercial common sense to place the decision as to what was "required" in the hands of the environmental expert rather than one of the parties to the contract' (para 19).

Another issue concerned the proper interpretation of clause 5.4 of the settlement agreement. In terms of that clause, if a certain mound of earth was found to be contaminated in terms of the environmental report, then the mound was to be removed at the Council's sole cost and expense. But what meaning was to be given to the word 'contaminated'? Lord Tyre's answer was as follows (para 31):

> The test to be applied, as I have already noted, is what a reasonable person, having all the background knowledge which would have been available to the parties when concluding the settlement agreement, would have understood them to be using the expression 'contaminated' to mean. It is difficult to reach a confident view on this on the basis of the documents alone. For present purposes, however, it is sufficient to reach the following conclusions. I reject the pursuer's contention that the presence of any type of anthropogenic material is enough to amount to contamination. I do so because of the reference in Condition 7.1.8 of the missives to disposal of material stored or positioned on the Property at a tip for 'uncontaminated material'. This, in my view, is a clear indication that in using the terms 'contaminated' and 'contamination' in the missives and in Clause 5.4 of the settlement agreement, the parties had in mind an agent which would preclude disposal of affected material in a manner permissible for material containing inert items such as wood, brick or small amounts of litter. Accordingly, although I find nothing to suggest that the parties had specifically in mind the definition of contamination in BS 10175 (which is a code of practice for investigation of potentially contaminated sites), it seems to me that the reasonable person would have understood the parties to have meant the expression 'contamination' to mean something along the lines of that definition, ie the presence of a substance or agent with the potential to cause harm or pollution.

As the environmental report disclosed the presence of a contaminant with potential to cause harm to human health (benzoapyrene), this was sufficient to amount to 'contamination'. However, a proof would be needed to determine whether the contamination was pre-existing or whether it derived from the Council's ownership of the site and hence was a matter for which the Council was liable.

The overall result was a partial victory – and partial defeat – for NIL.

(3) TMW Pramerica Property Investment GmbH v Glasgow City Council [2017] CSOH 152, 2018 GWD 1-6

The defender concluded missives to sell to the pursuer a new building, comprising office premises, in Bothwell Street, Glasgow. The missives provided for 23 items of remedial work to be carried out by the defender after settlement, divided into two categories ('priority' and 'non-priority'). A retention was made from the purchase price and held in a joint bank account by the parties' solicitors in trust for the purposes set out in the missives. Those purposes were as follows. The remedial work was to be completed by a 'long stop date', separate such dates being fixed for each of the two categories of work. If this was achieved, the retention would be payable to the defender; if not the retention would be payable to the pursuer.

In the event, the works were not completed by the long stop date. That, however, was not necessarily fatal to the defender's claim to the retention. The missives provided that, where the defender had made a substantive start to the works, the defender was entitled to a new, 'deferred' long stop date. This was to be 'such further period of time after the long stop date as the parties agreed (or the independent expert determines) as being reasonable to permit the remainder of those works which have been started to be completed'. As the parties could not agree on a deferred date, the matter was referred to an independent expert. The expert fixed separate deferred dates for each of the 23 items. Once again, the defender seems to have failed to carry out the works. In this action the pursuer sought (i) declarator that it was entitled to payment of the retention, and (ii) decree ordaining the defender to consent to the release of the sums.

The defender's argument was that, in terms of the missives, the expert should have fixed only two deferred dates (ie one for each category of works) and not 23. Hence the expert's determination was vitiated by error of law and fell to be reduced. Hence the pursuer was not entitled to its decree. After detailed analysis of the terms of the missives, the Lord Ordinary (Lord Tyre) accepted this argument. 'The schedule to the missives', he noted (para 20), 'could undoubtedly have been drafted with greater care and clarity. The number of obvious cross-referencing and other errors in it does not inspire confidence that it can be read literally as expressing the parties' common intention.' In interpreting the missives, regard would be had to the well-known guidance by Lord Clarke in *Rainy Sky SA v Kookmin Bank* [2011] 1 WLR 2900 at para 21 that the court must seek to ascertain 'what a reasonable person, that is a person who has all the background knowledge which would reasonably have been available to the parties in the situation in which they were at the time of the contract, would have understood the parties to have meant'. Interpreted in that light, the missives supported the defender's position.

(4) Iftikhar v CIP Property (AIPT) Ltd
[2017] CSOH 148, 2017 GWD 40-609

Property at 35 Argyll Street, Glasgow was sold by roup at a price of £500,000. In terms of the Articles of Roup, the buyer was taken bound to provide to the seller's solicitor KYC (ie 'Know Your own Client') information on or before 15 December 2016, otherwise the seller could rescind. The Articles further provided that:

> 'KYC information' means such information as the Vendor and the Vendor's Solicitors require in relation to the identity of the Purchaser and the source of funds utilised in respect of payment of the Balance of the Price and/or the deposit including, but not limited to, the verification certificate, and initial due diligence form aftermentioned.

Unhappy with the documentation provided by the buyer, the seller rescinded the contract on 22 December 2016, whereupon the buyer raised this action challenging the right of the seller to do so. The buyer sought declarator that the seller was still bound by the contract and that the purported rescission was of no effect.

One issue between the parties was the meaning of the word 'require' in the clause quoted above. The buyer's argument was that it was for the seller to list the documents that it wished to see, and that it was not then entitled to anything else. For the seller it was argued that it was for the buyer to produce such documentation as was needed to satisfy the seller from the perspective of the Money Laundering Regulations 2007, SI 2007/2157 (since replaced by the Money Laundering, Terrorist Financing and Transfer of Funds (Information on the Payer) Regulations 2017, SI 2017/692: see p 73 below). If the seller was not satisfied it could ask for more.

On this point the Lord Ordinary (Lord Bannatyne) found for the seller, for a number of reasons. (i) From both the context and the actual terms, it was clear that the Articles of Roup fell to be construed in the light of the 2007 Regulations. (ii) It did not matter whether the 2007 Regulations governed the transaction. 'The relevant question was whether the reasonable bystander would have understood that the intention was to align the contract with the 2007 Regulations' (para 142). (iii) The buyer's construction was not in accordance with commercial sense. It would require the seller to proceed with the transaction even if the documentation requested proved insufficient and hence even if the result was a breach of the 2007 Regulations.

But even if the buyer's construction of 'require' was correct, the seller was, it was held, still entitled to rescind. The seller had listed certain documents which the buyer was to produce, and the buyer had failed to produce them. In response to this point, the buyer sought to argue that the seller, in terms of the clause quoted above, could only require 'information', and that 'information' did not mean 'documentary evidence' of the kind that had been required by the seller. This was evidently a weak argument and the Lord Ordinary had little difficulty in rejecting it. So narrow a view of 'information' was inconsistent with the content and context of the relevant provisions of the contract. Furthermore (para 132):

> The approach of the pursuer to the construction of the word 'information' renders the clause meaningless and unworkable. If the defender cannot require that a particular form of information is produced ie documentary information, then it is difficult to see that the clause has any content. The defender has an absolute discretion as to when it is satisfied and this suggests that information must be given a wide definition and not the narrow construction contended for by the pursuer. The pursuer's construction does not make commercial sense as it denies to the pursuer the ability to say the form of information which it requires.

In all the circumstances the Lord Ordinary held that the seller was entitled to rescind the contract.

(5) University Court of the University of St Andrews v Headon Holdings [2017] CSIH 61, 2017 GWD 32-507

Various landowners and a developer entered into a joint-venture agreement for the purposes of obtaining planning consent for development of land to the west of St Andrews and of optimising its sale value. Later it turned out that one of the owners (a Mr Headon) held the land on a latent bare trust for another of the owners. On discovering this, the remaining owners raised an action for reduction of the joint-venture agreement on grounds of (i) misrepresentation and (ii) breach of a duty of disclosure. They argued that they would not have entered into an agreement which gave Mr Headon equal rights of participation and control if they had known that he was no more than a bare trustee for another owner. In relation to (ii) they argued that the parties had entered into a partnership, and that accordingly there was a duty of disclosure in respect of the pre-contractual negotiations.

At first instance the Lord Ordinary rejected both grounds and dismissed the action: see [2015] CSOH 113, 2015 GWD 27-464 (*Conveyancing 2015* Case (10)). On appeal, an Extra Division of the Court of Session has now allowed a proof before answer.

The case as to the existence of a partnership was not bound to fail, the Extra Division held, and so the pursuers were entitled to the opportunity to prove it. And if a partnership was found to exist, there was a stateable argument in respect of a duty of disclosure. In the words of Lord Malcolm (para 78):

> A duty of disclosure can arise simply from a fiduciary relationship, for example, trustee and beneficiary, parent and child, and partner to partner. In other cases, the duty arises in advance of a completed bargain because of the nature of the proposed contract, with insurance being a classic example – see *Life Association v Foster* (1873)

11 M 351, Lord President Inglis at 359. When negotiating a standard arm's length commercial agreement, both sides are expected to understand that they must look out for their own interests, and, in general, cannot complain if in due course they learn that the other possessed more accurate information. However, in the case of negotiations to enter a partnership, as with insurance, it is the nature of the contemplated relationship which requires each party to state any known circumstances which could influence the other. Another possible way of looking at this would be to identify a fiduciary relationship once parties enter into such negotiations.

As for misrepresentation, the Lord Ordinary had held that the statements relied on – essentially that Mr Headon 'owned' the land in question – could not be regarded as misrepresentations because they were true. Mr Headon did indeed own the land, albeit in trust. In the view of the Extra Division, this was too narrow an approach. The pursuers' pleadings (para 89):

> go beyond assertions of landownership, and offer to prove that Mr Headon gave the impression that his financial interest in maximising the development value of his company's holding was the same as that of the others, when it was not. In effect, the suggestion is of half-truths, and of being 'economical with the truth', both of which can, depending upon the circumstances, amount to misrepresentations, as indeed can silence in certain circumstances.

On this point, too, a proof before answer was allowed.

TENEMENTS AND OTHER DEVELOPMENTS

(6) Donaldson v Pleace
22 September 2017, Stirling Sheriff Court

The pursuers were the owners of the first-floor flat in a tenement in Stirling; the defender owned the café on the ground floor. The pursuers arranged for repairs to be done to the roof and one of the outside walls. The defender was not consulted. This was an action for payment in which the pursuers sought payment by the defender of the defender's share of the repair bill. It was held that, because the repairs were needed to keep the building wind and watertight, ie for 'shelter', the pursuers were entitled to carry out the repairs on their own initiative and to recover a share of the cost from the other owners by virtue of s 10 of the Tenements (Scotland) Act 2004. See **Commentary** p 128.

(7) Vehicle Control Services Ltd v Mackie
[2017] SC DUN 24, 2017 SLT (Sh Ct) 111

The defender lived with her parents on a housing development in Dundee. The development was subject to a parking scheme operated by the pursuer. Notices at the entrance to the development stated that, except where a residents' permit was displayed in a car, a daily charge of £100 would be made for parking. The defender parked without a permit for 245 days, incurring total charges of £24,500. The pursuer was granted decree in respect of this sum. See **Commentary** p 131.

(8) Apex Property Factor Ltd v BC
[2017] SC GLA 59, 2017 Hous LR 107

Property factors are regulated by the Property Factors (Scotland) Act 2011 and by the Property Factor Code of Conduct: see *Conveyancing 2011* pp 109–16. The former provides, among other matters, for a Register of Property Factors in which all factors must be registered. The latter sets out the manner in which factors should conduct their relationship with those homeowners who employ them. ('Homeowners' is the term used in the legislation. Units in a tenement that are non-residential are not covered by the legislation. We do not know the reason.) All factors must have a system of dispute resolution. In addition, disgruntled homeowners can apply under s 17 of the Act to the Housing and Property Chamber of the First-tier Tribunal for determination of whether a factor has failed to carry out the factor's duties (which will normally be those stipulated in the factor's contract) or failed to comply with the Code of Conduct. If the applicant's case is judged to be made out, the First-tier Tribunal issues a property factor enforcement order (s 19). This cannot be enforced directly by the homeowner, but failure to comply is both a criminal offence and also a ground for the factor being removed from the Register. There is a right of appeal on a point of law from a determination of the First-tier Tribunal (or its predecessor, the Homeowner Housing Committee). Originally this was to the sheriff under s 22 of the Act but since 1 December 2016 has been to the Upper Tribunal under s 46 of the Tribunals (Scotland) Act 2014. The present case was an appeal under the old procedure to the sheriff; the next case is the first appeal under the new procedure to the Upper Tribunal.

Both cases were concerned with the competency to hear applications under the 2011 Act. In this first case, the problem was that, by the time of the application, the factors had ceased to be employed by the homeowners in question. The second case is concerned with the mirror-image issue of where, by the time of the application, the applicants had ceased to be homeowners.

In this first case the sheriff held without difficulty that the application was competent notwithstanding that the factors had ceased to act. Any other conclusion would mean that factors could avoid hostile applications by the simple expedient of resigning.

The case was also concerned with the validity of certain determinations – for example, that the factors had failed to take 'reasonable steps to recover unpaid charges from any homeowner who has not paid their fair share of the costs prior to charging those remaining homeowners if they are jointly responsible for such costs', a requirement of para 4.7 of the Code of Conduct. Instead of following their standard debt-recovery procedure, the factors had simply looked to the other homeowners to bear the shortfall. As with all the other grounds of appeal, this ground was rejected by the sheriff. In the sheriff's opinion the original determination had been 'intelligible' and its reasoning 'compelling' (para 31).

(9) Shields v Housing and Property Chamber
2017 Hous LR 54, Upper Tribunal for Scotland

Section 17(1) of the Property Factors (Scotland) Act 2011 provides that 'A homeowner may apply to the First-tier Tribunal for determination of whether a property factor has failed' in various stipulated respects. In the present case an application to the First-tier Tribunal was rejected on the basis that, while the applicants had been homeowners at the time of the events on which the application was founded, they were no longer homeowners now. Hence, said the First-tier Tribunal, they were ineligible to make an application under s 17(1). The applicants appealed to the Upper Tribunal.

In allowing the appeal, the Upper Tribunal (A F Deutsch) emphasised that it was necessary to take a purposive rather than a literal approach to the interpretation of s 17(1). The Upper Tribunal continued (paras 4 and 5):

> When section 17(1) is considered as a whole it becomes clear that the right to apply to the tribunal is for determination of past failures on the part of the property factor. Once that is recognised it does not greatly strain the language of the subsection to interpret it as requiring only that the person making the application was a homeowner at the time of the failure which is the subject of the complaint ... There is no logical or practical reason why the legislature should have granted to current homeowners a remedy for past breaches while denying the same remedy to persons who happen to have sold their property after the failure occurred. That would be at odds with its policy of making provision for dispute resolution.

SERVITUDES

(10) Dunlea v Cashwell
[2017] SAC (Civ) 12, 2017 SCLR 675

A servitude of access held by the pursuers over the defenders' road was restricted to 'vehicles required in connection with normal residential use of the said plot or area of ground in this title'. It was held that the servitude did not extend to use by construction traffic needed for the conversion into a house of a second building on the pursuers' property which was currently derelict. See **Commentary** p 166.

(11) Pollock v Drogo Developments Ltd
[2017] CSOH 64, 2017 GWD 14-221

The defender had a servitude right for existing services over the pursuers' land. In replacing an existing drainage system with new pipes, the defender departed from the route of the previous system. It was held that the defender was not permitted to change the route. See **Commentary** p 168.

(12) Lane v Irvin Mitchell Trust Corporation Ltd
29 March 2017, Dumfries Sheriff Court

The defenders had a servitude for pedestrian and vehicular access over a private road belonging to the pursuers and which ran alongside one of the defenders' fields. Lying between the tarmac strip of the road and the defenders' field was, in the first place, a grass verge and then a hedge. Access to the defenders' field was taken by means of a gap in the hedge. The current litigation arose when the defenders created a much larger gap by removing 30 feet of hedge. The question at debate was whether they were entitled to do so.

The dispute was analysed as concerning the right of benefited proprietors to alter or improve the burdened property over which their servitude lay. An account of the relevant law can be found in paras 12.123–12.128 of D J Cusine and R R M Paisley, *Servitudes and Rights of Way* (1998). The defenders relied mainly on the decision of the House of Lords in *Alvis v Harrison* 1991 SLT 64, an ever-handy authority for those seeking to argue for an expansive view of servitudes, but also a distinctly controversial one (as to which see Cusine and Paisley paras 14.25–14.30). A wider access point was needed in the interests of certain types of agricultural and construction machinery. Without it there could not be full enjoyment of the servitude. The sheriff (B Mohan) agreed (para 58): the works complained of 'appeared to fall within the limits permitted when exercising an express grant of servitude, judging by the interpretation of such rights in light of the decision in *Alvis v Harrison*'.

There were two further matters which might have been raised but, apparently, were not. One was whether the ground beneath the hedge was part of the road and hence subject to the servitude at all. If the ground was not so subject, there could be no basis for removing the hedge and allowing access over the ground. The other, a point of general application and a difficult one at that, was whether, in cases where a servitude road hugs the boundary of the benefited property, the benefited proprietor is entitled to take access from the road to his property at whatever place or places he chooses.

[Another aspect of this case is digested at p 59 below.]

(13) Fraser v McDonald
18 July 2017, Perth Sheriff Court

In selling a plot of land to the pursuers, the defenders granted two separate deeds. One, in 2008, was a deed of servitude in respect of an access road. The second, in 2011, was a disposition of the plot itself. Although the servitude was constituted by the deed of servitude, it could not come into effect immediately because the defenders still owned both the benefited and the burdened properties. It was thus only on registration of the disposition that the servitude became live: see s 75(2) of the Title Conditions (Scotland) Act 2003.

In terms of the deed of servitude, one plot ('plot A') was the benefited property and the remainder of the land owned by the defenders ('plot B') was the burdened property. But in the event, when the defenders came to grant the disposition to the pursuers they disponed only part of plot A, keeping part back ('the disputed area'). In the present stage of the proceedings, the argument at debate focused on the question of whether, nonetheless, the servitude extended over the disputed area.

The sheriff (Lindsay D R Foulis) held that it did so extend, for two reasons. The first concerned the wording in the pursuers' title sheet which, it seemed, described the servitude as extending between two specified points. This wording seems to have derived from the disposition. The disputed area was located between these two points, so that the servitude as so described extended to the disputed area. Absent any move for rectification, the terms of the title sheet were decisive.

The second reason concerned the proper interpretation of the deed of servitude. It was true that, read literally, the deed included the disputed area as part of the benefited property and not of the burdened property. Hence on a literal reading the servitude did not extend to the disputed area. But in interpreting a deed it was necessary to have regard to the 'general equitable principle in our law that the court will not allow the clear intention of the parties disclosed in a deed to be defeated by a mere inaccuracy or mistake in expression': see *Chalmers Property Investment Co Ltd v Robson* 2008 SLT 1069 at 1073 per Lord Guthrie. In the present case, the parties' clear intention (p 7 of the transcript):

> was to create a servitude of access over the subjects owned by the defenders to enable the pursuers to gain access to the subjects the parties were aware in 2008 the latter intended to acquire but in fact only acquired in 2011, albeit consisting of a smaller area. The definition of burdened property in the deed of servitude falls, in my opinion, within the ambit of the equitable principle as defined by Lord Guthrie in *Chalmers Property Investment Co Ltd v Robson*. It was the land remaining within the ownership of the defenders.

The strength of the first reason is hard to judge without knowing more of the background circumstances and without seeing the precise wording of the A (property) section of the title sheet. That wording appears to have included an express reference to the deed of servitude, which might be thought to limit the servitude to the burdened property as defined in that deed. If not, then consideration would have to be given to the Keeper's 'Midas touch' (ie s 3(1)(a) of the Land Registration (Scotland) Act 1979) in respect of the initial registration, and also to the transitional arrangements in paras 17–24 of sch 4 to the Land Registration etc (Scotland) Act 2012 in respect of a possible deemed rectification occurring on the designated day (8 December 2014). Neither point appears to have featured in the parties' arguments.

The second reason stretches the principle of error in expression further than seems either possible or desirable. In fact there was no error in the description of the burdened property in the deed of servitude because at the time the deed was being prepared it was thought that the disputed area would be included with the property to be sold to the pursuers. It was only when, three years later, a smaller area was disponed to the pursuers that the absence of a servitude over the disputed area became an issue.

We understand that the decision has been appealed to the Sheriff Appeal Court.

(14) Brydon v Lewis
12 February 1958 (debate) and 26 August 1958 (proof),
Edinburgh Sheriff Court

Wishing to repair the gable wall of her ground-floor flat, the pursuer, Christina Brydon, sought to establish the existence of (i) a right of access, arising by operation of law, to carry out the repairs from garden ground belonging to the defenders, and (ii) a right to require the defenders to remove a wooden hut and lean-to which obstructed access to the wall. The pursuer succeeded on both counts. See **Commentary** p 162.

(15) Regency Villas Title Ltd v Diamond Resorts (Europe) Ltd
[2017] EWCA Civ 238, [2017] 3 WLR 644

Last year we drew attention to the decision at first instance in this English case: see *Conveyancing 2016* pp 138–40. That decision has now been largely upheld by the Court of Appeal in a wide-ranging judgment.

The case concerned land, near Canterbury, Kent, used for the purposes of a timeshare development. Originally the land was owned together with an immediately adjacent property which contained sporting and leisure facilities such as tennis courts, a swimming pool, and a golf course. In 1981 the timeshare land was split off. The conveyance conferred on the grantee and its successors and lessees the right:

> to use the swimming pool, golf course, squash courts, tennis courts, the ground and basement floor of Broome Park Mansion House, gardens and any other sporting or recreational facilities ... on the Transferor's adjoining estate.

Later a dispute arose as to whether the right so conferred was merely personal or whether it was an easement (in Scottish terms, a servitude) binding on successors. It has now been held by the Court of Appeal that most, though not all, of the rights in question were easements.

The starting-point of the Court of Appeal was the *dictum* of an English judge in a Scottish case. In *Dyce v Hay* (1852) 1 Macq 305, 312–13, Lord St Leonards said that: 'The categories of servitudes and easements must alter and expand with the changes that take place in the circumstances of mankind.' In Scotland this *dictum* has often been quoted but seldom applied. In *Regency Villas* the Court of Appeal applied it. So far as concerned exercise and recreation, said the court, there had been a major change in the circumstances of man. Already in *In re Ellenborough Park* [1955] Ch 131 the Court of Appeal had held that houses surrounding a private park could have an easement to use the park for walking and for other recreational activities. Today, sport too was a normal and accepted form of exercise (para 54):

> Easements in the modern world must, of course, retain their essential legal qualities. But the views of society as to what is mere recreation or amusement may change, even if the exclusion of such rights were authoritative, which we rather doubt. Physical exercise is now regarded by most people in the United Kingdom as either an essential or at least a desirable part of their daily routines. It is not a mere recreation or amusement. Physical exercise can, moreover, in our modern lives, take many forms, whether it be walking, swimming or playing active games and sports. We cannot see how an easement could either in 1981 or in 2017 be ruled out solely on the grounds that the form of physical exercise it envisaged was a game or a sport rather than purely a walk in a garden. It is also noteworthy that profits à prendre (another incorporeal hereditament, but one that can exist without a dominant tenement) have commonly been held to exist in respect of the right to take game or fish, both of which activities are often (but obviously not solely) undertaken for recreation or sport.

At the same time, however, the essential legal qualities of easements must be observed (para 56):

> In our view, the requirement that an easement must be a 'right of utility and benefit' is the crucial requirement. The essence of an easement is to give the dominant tenement a benefit or a utility as such. Thus, an easement properly so called will improve the general utility of the dominant tenement. It may benefit the trade carried on upon the dominant tenement or the utility of living there.

Against this background the court proceeded to review the various rights granted in the 1981 conveyance. The court had little difficulty with recreation conducted in purpose-built facilities – the tennis and squash courts, putting green, and swimming pool. This was a right in relation to land (the chattels used to play the sport being incidental). And it was a right for the evident benefit of the timeshare property (para 66): 'The utility and benefit to a dominant dwelling or timeshare property of the ability to use a next-door tennis court is obvious to any modern owner. Many country homes these days have their own tennis court or courts precisely as a benefit for the occupants.' Plainly they were easements.

The 18-hole golf course raised in a more acute form a problem which arose to a greater or lesser degree with all of the facilities (para 76): 'We are all familiar with the teams of groundsmen and greenkeepers that such courses need to employ to maintain them to the high standard that players frequently desire.' What would happen if the burdened owner ceased to maintain the golf course? In that case, the benefited owners could step it and do so themselves. This was not in itself a reason for denying the right to play golf the status of an easement.

The court took a different view in respect of the right to use 'the ground and basement floor of Broome Park Mansion House'. This area contained a billiard room, television room, a gym, sunbed and sauna, and a bar and restaurant. But in these cases it was the chattels that predominated, not the land. 'Unlike the empty swimming pool, an empty billiard room is not a billiard room at all' (para 80). These were personal rights and not easements.

This decision marks an important extension of the scope of easements in England and Wales. Might a Scottish court take a similar approach? We would incline to answer that question in the affirmative, given, in particular, the terms of s 75 of the Title Conditions (Scotland) Act 2003. It is true that a servitude of fishing was refused by the Court of Session in *Patrick v Napier* (1867) 5 M 683. But in that case there was a significant distance between the supposed dominant tenement and the river, and hence a corresponding absence of praedial benefit; and besides, as the Court of Appeal emphasised in *Regency Villas*, the status of exercise and recreation is very different today from what it was in earlier times. Finally, we may share with the Court of Appeal (at para 78) the encouragement to be derived from a still earlier Scottish decision, *Cleghorn v Dempster* (1805) Mor 16141, (1813) 2 Dow 40 even if, as Cusine and Paisley point out (*Servitudes and Rights of Way* (1998) para 3.30), the right to play golf which was recognised was in favour of the inhabitants of St Andrews rather than the owners of any particular dominant tenement.

(16) Hamilton v The Scottish Ministers
[2017] CSOH 121, 2017 GWD 31-503

Water outside a definite channel is permitted to drain with the natural inclination of the land, and the owner of a lower property is bound to receive the water which drains naturally from a property which is higher up: see K G C Reid, *The Law of Property in Scotland* (1996) paras 339 and 340. That principle, which is often classified as a 'natural' servitude, was applied in the present case. Water from a field at Lairs Farm, Blackwood, Lesmahagow, Lanarkshire, owned by the pursuer, was ponding rather than draining away naturally. Following a proof it was held that the water drained naturally into the M74 Glasgow/Carlisle trunk road, and that the drainage system on that road had become damaged. As no convincing alternative reason for the ponding could be found, it followed that the ponding was caused by the damage to the drainage system on the M74. The right to drain in accordance with the natural inclination of the land is a *res merae facultatis* and hence imprescriptible under sch 3 para (c) of the Prescription and Limitation (Scotland) Act 1973. The Scottish Ministers were therefore liable to restore the drainage system to full working capacity.

WAYLEAVES

(17) British Waterways Board v Arjo Wiggins Ltd
[2017] SAC (Civ) 15, 2017 GWD 15-240

The pursuer owns the Caledonian Canal. In 1968 the defender (formerly called Wiggins Teape & Co Ltd) entered into a wayleave agreement with the pursuer so as to allow it to construct a mains water pipe under the Canal at Corpach, Inverness-shire, in order to supply the defender's paper mill at Annat. For this there was to be annual payment, adjusted with inflation, and currently amounting to a little over £6,000. The wayleave agreement was to run until 2099.

Arjo Wiggins sold the timber mill to BSW Timber Ltd, and also assigned the wayleave agreement. The issue to be determined was who, after the sale and assignation, had liability to make the annual payments under the wayleave agreement. Had liability passed to BSW Timber or did it remain with Arjo Wiggins?

At first instance the sheriff at Fort William found that, in a question with the pursuer, liability remained with Arjo Wiggins. Only rights could be assigned, not obligations. While obligations could be transferred ('delegated' in the technical sense of that term, from the Latin, *delegatio*), this required the consent of the creditor. See judgment of 12 May 2016 (*Conveyancing 2016* Case (15)).

On appeal by Arjo Wiggins, the Sheriff Appeal Court allowed a proof before answer on the question of whether the pursuer had impliedly consented to the transfer of the obligations under the wayleave agreement to BSW Timber. The factual basis of this argument was said to be the fact that, over a number of years, the pursuer had invoiced and accepted payment from BSW Timber in respect of the annual sums due.

A proof was also allowed in respect of an *esto* argument. If liability under the wayleave agreement remained after all with Arjo Wiggins, the sale and assignation document contained an obligation on the part of BSW Timber to relieve Arjo Wiggins of the cost of the payments to the pursuer. The provision principally founded on was a clause in the assignation in which Arjo Wiggins bound itself to free and relieve BSW Timber 'from all pecuniary and other obligations ... referable to the period prior to the date of entry'. If Arjo Wiggins thus had liability *before* the date of entry, then it might appear to follow that BSW Timber had a corresponding liability *after* the date of entry. Indeed the very fact that Arjo Wiggins' liability was restricted to the pre-entry period seemed to presuppose that the overall effect of the assignation was to make BSW Timber liable for the period thereafter. If that were not the case, there could be no purpose in including the words 'referable to the period prior to the date of entry'.

ROADS, PUBLIC RIGHTS OF WAY AND ACCESS RIGHTS

(18) Loch Lomond and Trossachs National Park Authority
v Renyana-Stahl Anstalt
[2017] SAC (Civ) 11, 2017 SLT (Sh Ct) 138

The Land Reform (Scotland) Act 2003 contains various measures which are designed to preserve and defend the access rights conferred on the general public by s 1. Thus s 3 requires owners of 'land in respect of which access rights are exercisable' to use and manage the land in a way which respects those rights and does not cause unreasonable interference with them. This general duty is supplemented by s 14 which prohibits owners from carrying out various acts where their purpose or main purpose is to prevent or deter anyone entitled to exercise access rights from doing so. The prohibited acts include putting up a sign or notice; putting up a fence or wall; positioning or leaving at large any animal; or taking or failing to take any other action. In the event of a breach of the s 14 duties, the relevant local authority can serve a notice requiring remedial action and, in the event that the notice is not complied with, can carry out the action itself and recover the cost.

Some of the force of s 14 seemed to be removed by the decision of Sheriff Principal Sir Stephen Young QC in *Aviemore Highland Resort Ltd v Cairngorms National Park Authority* 2009 SLT (Sh Ct) 97. In that case the owner of land, shortly before the 2003 Act came into force, erected a fence which obstructed access. Claiming that the erection of the fence constituted a breach of s 14, the local authority served a notice requiring the fence to be removed. The owner sought an order from the court quashing the notice. The order was granted on the basis that the act complained of had taken place before the Act came into force (para 14):

> [W]hen they erected the fence, the pursuers were not the owners of land in respect of which access rights were exercisable, and in any event they could not have erected the fence for the purpose or for the main purpose of preventing or deterring any person entitled to exercise those access rights from doing so since the rights did not then exist. Nor in my view is it correct to characterise the erection of the fence as a continuing state of affairs. It was an act which was completed before Pt 1 of the Act, and with it the access rights in question, came into force, and it is nothing to the point that the continuing presence of the fence has the effect now of preventing or deterring any person entitled to exercise access rights under Pt 1 from doing so.

It seemed to follow from this decision that any obstruction or discouragement to access rights could be kept in place provided it originated in an act performed before the legislation came into force. In particular, established walls, fences, gates and hedges were invulnerable provided only that they could be shown to pre-date the legislation.

That view of things does not survive the decision in *Loch Lomond and Trossachs National Park Authority v Renyana-Stahl Anstalt* which comes close to overturning the *Aviemore* case. The dispute concerned Drumlean Estate in the Trossachs, which was owned by a Liechtenstein entity (an 'Anstalt'), Renyana-Stahl Anstalt. Drumlean Estate consists of about 1,500 acres of land. Most of the Estate was freely open to the public. But public access was denied or hindered to a fenced area of around 150 hectares (about 10% of the estate) at the southernmost point of the Estate. Within this area were a farm and farmhouse and also a red deer population of between 120 and 150. Access from the main road was by two gates both of which were kept locked. There was also a sign warning of wild boar, even though boar were no longer to be found on the Estate.

The local authority served a s 14 notice on the owner requiring the owner to remove the sign and unlock the gates. The notice was challenged on the same grounds as in the *Aviemore* case, namely that both the sign and the gates had been erected before the 2003 Act came into force. Before the sheriff the challenge was successful. Indeed the sheriff seems to have thought that, in so erecting the gates, the owner had succeeded in excluding the application of statutory access rights altogether. On appeal, the Sheriff Appeal Court reversed this decision. *Aviemore*, the court emphasised, was a narrow case. No doubt it was decided correctly on its facts, but it could readily be distinguished. In *Aviemore* the point at issue was whether s 14 was engaged in respect of a one-off act, the erection of a fence, which had taken place before s 14 came into force. Plainly the provision was not engaged. In the present case, however, what was at issue was not a one-off act, but a continuing act, ie the continuing failure of the owner, after the Act came into force, to unlock the gates. The notice in the present case was served not under s 14(1)(b) (the act of putting up a fence) but under s 14(1)(e) (the taking or failing to take any other action).

There was also a wider point which derived from a consideration of the Act as a whole (para 39):

> The sheriff's approach fails to take account of whether the landowner's use of his land is responsible. It fails to recognise that the Act sets out a statutory presumption in favour of access. The access rights are to be exercised in a responsible manner and the Act expects land owners and managers to act in a responsible manner, which anticipates managing land in a way to facilitate access being taken. Responsible use of land in terms of the Act may well entail allowing access to land to which the public previously did not have access. Applying this to the present case the Act imposed a positive obligation on the respondent when the Act came into force, to consider, among other things, whether gates which had previously been locked, should be unlocked so as to enable the access rights created by the Act, to be exercised. In that context, it is easy to see why s 14(1)(e) refers to an omission to take any action.

The fact that something had been done before the Act was not, in itself, a reason for not requiring it to be undone now. Quite simply, the passing of the Act had changed the rules as to what was, and was not, acceptable.

The appeal succeeded too on another matter. The sheriff had held that, even if a s 14 notice could be used in circumstances such as this, it failed the threshold test set out in s 14(1), namely that the acts or omissions complained of must be 'for the purpose or for the main purpose of preventing or deterring' the exercise of access rights. This was because, following a proof, the evidence indicated that the purpose of the locked gates was to protect people, to protect animals, and to protect the farm machinery. Normally an appeal court will not interfere with findings of fact made by the trial judge. But in this case the court thought that the sheriff had gone badly wrong. He had excluded evidence, on grounds of privilege, which ought not to have been excluded; and because of his misunderstanding of the effect of s 14, his assessment of the credibility of the witnesses was flawed. Looking at the evidence afresh the Appeal Court concluded that the main purpose in locking the gates was to deter the public from taking access. Hence the s 14 notice was fully justified, and had to be complied with.

We understand that this decision has been appealed to the Inner House.

(19) Trustees of the Grange Trust v City of Edinburgh Council
[2017] CSOH 102, 2017 GWD 23-387

This case concerned a six-foot strip of land which, at one time, lay between Comely Bank Road in the Stockbridge area of Edinburgh and playing fields belonging to the Edinburgh Academical Club. The strip was owned by Trustees on behalf of the Club. In 1912 the Trustees and the Club entered into a contract with the City of Edinburgh Council in which they agreed to relinquish their rights in the strip to allow widening of the public road; in exchange the Council would demolish the existing boundary wall and erect a new wall on the line of the playing fields. There was no conveyance of the strip to the Council, but the road was widened as planned. Recently, the Council has demolished the wall. Its *solum* is of value in view of a plan to develop playing fields fronting on Comely Bank Road for retail, leisure and restaurant use. Potentially the *solum* is a ransom strip and one which the Trustees are keen to take advantage of.

In this action the Trustees sought (i) an order requiring the Council to rebuild the wall, failing which payment of £185,569.20 being the estimated cost of rebuilding, and (ii) a declarator that the Council could use the *solum* only for the erection of a wall, as agreed in 1912. In the event, the action was dismissed due to absence of title to sue: it was held that the action required to be brought by the Club, as well as by the Trustees, since the Club had been a co-contractor. But the Lord Ordinary (Lord Boyd of Duncansby) gave some indication of his views on the merits of the case.

If the Council's rights were merely those conferred in 1912, then its position would have been weak. But since then the road had been listed and the wall was included in the listing. Therefore, argued the Council, the Council held a whole series of powers in respect of the *solum* which derived from the Roads (Scotland) Act 1984. That argument does not appear to have been challenged, and the case focused on the question as to whether the *solum* of the wall was part of the road. The Lord Ordinary thought that the fact of listing was not conclusive, and also that, in the ordinary case, a boundary wall marks the end of a road and is not included as part of it. Nonetheless, s 28 of the 1984 Act empowers roads authorities to construct walls and fences for the purpose of safeguarding persons using the road, and the role of the wall as protection also seemed to have been in the minds of the parties in 1912. If, therefore, the wall did perform a safeguarding function, as to which the Lord Ordinary would have allowed a proof before answer, it 'might be possible to conclude that the boundary wall did form part of the road and hence was properly listed in the list of public roads' (para 39).

STATUTORY NOTICES

(20) Hussain v Glasgow City Council
[2017] CSIH 69, 2017 SLT 1321

In April 2011 Glasgow City Council served work notices in terms of s 30 of the Housing (Scotland) Act 2006 on the owners of all the flats at 196 Langside Road, Govanhill, Glasgow. The works that were required to be done were extensive, including repairs to the roof, windows, chimney heads, stonework and pointing, gutters and downpipes, drainage, timbers in the roof space, walls and ceilings.

No doubt to the Council's surprise, the repairs were not carried out by the owners within the 21-day period prescribed by the notices. In the event, they were to take four years to complete. The work was carried out by the Council, but on the basis that grant assistance would be available to the owners. The standard grant was 50% of the cost but with a further 25% being available on a means-tested basis. Mr Hussain, the owner of one of the flats in the building, secured a grant of 75%. Only 25% of his share required to be met by Mr Hussain.

From the outset it was made clear by the Council that payment of the balance of 25% by not later than the time of agreement of the final account was a condition of the grant. If payment was late, or not made at all, the grant would automatically fall and the owner would be liable for 100% of the cost. Mr Hussain failed to pay any of the £21,260.89 which fell to him as his share of the cost, whereupon the Council withdrew the grant. Mr Hussain petitioned for judicial review of the imposition of the condition as to payment.

Section 71(4) of the Housing (Scotland) Act 2006 allows local authorities to provide grants and other forms of assistance 'on such terms as the authority thinks fit'. At first instance the Lord Ordinary (Lord Mulholland) concluded that the condition imposed as to prompt payment was one which was authorised by s 71(4) and other provisions in part 2 of the Act: see [2017] CSOH 1, 2017 SLT 231.

On appeal, an Extra Division of the Court of Session has taken a different view. The issue, said the court, was not a narrow one of textual interpretation but whether, looking at the Act as a whole and the purposes for which the grant was given, the condition attached to the grant was for a purpose connected with the grant rather than for some ulterior purpose or, to put it another way, whether the condition fairly and reasonably related to the grant. This approach derived from, for example, the speech of Lord Rodger in *Stewart v Perth and Kinross Council* 2004 SC (HL) 71 at para 55. If matters were viewed in this way, the Council's condition could be seen to be *ultra vires* (para 24):

> The grant, if made, is made for housing purposes. In a case such as the present it is made because owners of buildings, or of flats within buildings, do not have the means to carry out and pay for the repair and renovation works which the council, on the basis of its own expert advice, considers necessary. We could understand conditions being imposed which sought to regulate the quality of the works to be undertaken, or required certification by the council before grant monies were released, or something of that sort. There might be any number of detailed conditions relating to the availability or application of the moneys advanced by way of grant. But the condition here relates to payment by the petitioner of his own money, not grant money. It relates to payment by the petitioner to the council of sums spent by the council on the repairs, sums which are not and have never been covered by the grant. It is seeking to use the promise of a grant, and the threat of its withdrawal, as a stick with which to force the petitioner into compliance with his obligations as regards the expenditure not covered by the grant. In our opinion this goes well beyond what is legitimate.

Worse than that (para 25), the condition seemed 'intended as a kind of sword of Damocles, hanging over the owner of the property to encourage him to pay the sum due from him for his share of the cost of the repairs. But, if activated, the effect goes much wider than enforcing payment of the sums already due; it takes away the whole of his grant'.

COMPETITION OF TITLE

(21) McDade v Hill
8 December 2017, Lands Tribunal

For conveyancers of a certain cast of mind (such as ours), this case is a delight. By a disposition recorded in the Sasine Regiater on 18 January 2002, the Trustees of the late Sir Robert Duncan Sinclair Lockhart acting under a trust disposition and settlement of 13 December 1916 disponed (among other property) the residue of the Cambusnethan Estate, Lanarkshire, to Patrick McDade, Maureen Allan and John Thomas Sexton. No consideration was disclosed in the disposition, and only simple warrandice was granted. The description of the property conveyed is exceptionally enjoyable:

> ALL and HAILL the lands and barony of Cambusnethan … all lying within the Sheriffdom of Lanark all unite erected and incorporated in ane haill and free barony called the barony of Cambusnethan by ane Charter under the Great Seal in favours of James Lockhart of Castlehill brother of the said Dame Martha Lockhart dated the Twenty sixth day of July Sixteen hundred and Ninety five years …

The description continued by enumerating a number of attractively-named properties such as Crindledyke, Branchillburn, Herdhill and Burnhouse. This was followed by no fewer than 88 exceptions, so how much of the Estate was left to be conveyed by the disposition must be open to question.

The dispute concerned a plot of ground comprising 1.53 hectares and lying to the south-west of Castlehill Road. It had been the subject of competing and unsuccessful attempts by the grantees of the 2002 disposition, and also by Robert Hill and William Dale Hill, to persuade the Keeper to register their title in the Land Register. The plot lay between two other properties owned by the Hills who were not, they emphasised, title raiders (para 20). Eventually, the Hills were able to obtain a registered title to the plot, albeit with exclusion of indemnity, following the granting and registration in 2014 of a disposition of the plot by the granters of the 2002 disposition, ie the Trustees of the late Sir Robert Duncan Sinclair Lockhart. The disposition contained a virtuoso clause of deduction of title, enumerating the links to the last recorded title, which had been in 1820. The Lands Tribunal could not disguise its admiration, describing the deed as 'an impressive piece of conveyancing' (para 29).

The present application was the response of the 2002 grantees to the 2014 disposition. Invoking the jurisdiction of the Lands Tribunal under s 82 of the Land Registration etc (Scotland) Act 2012, it sought a determination of the accuracy of the Hills' title to the plot. That in turn depended on what had been conveyed by the 2002 disposition. It was contended for the 2002 grantees that the disposition had conveyed the plot of 1.53 hectares, and hence that the later disposition by the Trustees to the Hills was *a non domino* and ineffective. This view of matters was resisted by the Hills.

It was held by the Lands Tribunal that there was no inaccuracy. The description of the Lands and Barony of Cambusnethan in the 2002 disposition was tied to a Charter under the Great Seal of 1695. But title research had shown that the plot was not acquired by the Lockhart family until 1820. It was not, therefore, part of the Barony in 1695 and hence was not carried by the 2002 disposition. The 2002 grantees had no title to the plot.

It is worth saying a little about what would have happened if the opposite conclusion had been reached, ie if the plot had, after all, passed under the 2002 disposition. The Land Registration etc (Scotland) Act 2012 replaced the Land Registration (Scotland) Act 1979 on 8 December 2014. As the registration of the Hills' title occurred in the early months of 2014, it was governed, just, by the 1979 Act and hence by the Midas touch. Accordingly, on registration the Hills would have become owners, notwithstanding the absence of title in the granters. Their triumph, however, would have been short-lived. On 8 December 2014 the transitional provisions contained in sch 4 of the 2012 Act came into effect. The result of these provisions would have been to restore ownership on that day to the 2002 grantees. This is because (i) the Register was (bijurally) inaccurate in showing the Hills and not the 2002 grantees as owners, and (ii) due to the exclusion of indemnity, the Keeper could have rectified the Register had she chosen to do so. Even after the restoration of ownership, of course, the Register would have remained inaccurate in showing the Hills as owners, and so would still have stood in need of rectification. But this would now be a 2012 Act inaccuracy (ie an actual inaccuracy) and not a 1979 Act inaccuracy (ie a bijural inaccuracy). The procedure to be followed in a case such as this is clearly and helpfully set out in a Lands Tribunal application from last year, *Highland Ventures Ltd v Keeper of the Registers of Scotland* 2016 GWD 22-403 (discussed in *Conveyancing 2016* pp 186–89).

(22) Miller v Smith
[2017] SAC (Civ) 26, 2017 GWD 28-444

In 2004 a house at 39 Third Avenue, Auchinloch, near Lenzie, Lanarkshire, was bought by the appellant's son. Two-thirds of the price was contributed by the appellant and her late husband, and the arrangement was that the appellant and her husband could live in the house, rent-free, for the duration of their lives. Although this arrangement was not constituted or recorded in writing, its terms were accepted by all the parties to this litigation. It was also accepted that the arrangement might be categorised as an improper liferent. Strictly, though, an improper or (trust) liferent required that the house was being held by the son in trust for his parents, and the appellant so argued. That characterisation, however, seems not to have been accepted by the respondents and would have needed to be proved in the event that the case had proceeded as far as a proof. Whether there was sufficient evidence to establish a trust, as opposed to a mere contractual arrangement, is unknown and may perhaps be doubted.

The initial purchase in 2004 was followed by a series of further conveyances. First, the son (and, in the appellant's view, trustee) disponed the house to his daughter by his then partner. The daughter then disponed the house to her mother, ie the son's partner. Finally, the mother, by now no longer in a relationship with the son, disponed the house to her brother. No consideration was paid for any of these transfers. All involved knew of the arrangement with the appellant and her husband, and indeed the appellant and her husband continued to live in the house throughout. At the time of the litigation the appellant was still in occupation, although the current owner (the brother of her son's former partner) had raised proceedings for recovery of possession.

In this current litigation the appellant sought reduction of the three dispositions granted since 2004. If successful, the effect would be to return ownership to her son and hence, on the appellant's view of things, to the trustee under the trust. In that way the improper liferent could then continue to run. The action was defended by the former partner of the appellant's son and by the former partner's brother, the current owner.

The appellant's argument was based largely on the rule against offside goals. The disposition by the son/trustee to his daughter was in breach of the improper liferent. As the daughter was in bad faith, in the sense that she knew of the liferent, and in any case was a donee, the disposition was voidable at the instance of the appellant, the trust beneficiary. And as the daughter held on a voidable title, so all of those acquiring through her, being likewise in bad faith and donees, also held on a voidable title. Hence all three dispositions could be reduced.

This argument was rejected by the Sheriff Appeal Court. The facts, as the court noted, were close to those in *Wallace v Simmers* 1960 SC 255. In that case the purchaser of a farm was held to be unaffected by a contract entered into by the seller, and known to the purchaser, whereby relatives of the seller were entitled to live rent-free in a farm cottage. The Sheriff Appeal Court's conclusion was as follows (para 23):

> There is a distinction between the facts of *Wallace v Simmers* … and the instant case, because in the instant case the dispositions are said not to have been granted for value. We have however concluded that even although the dispositions are not granted for value, where the agreement between the appellant and her late husband only establishes a personal right between the appellant and the third respondent, this does not give a basis to reduce the subsequent dispositions, granted by the fourth and second respondent respectively. This is because the personal right against the third respondent is enforceable only against him and does not, even where the subsequent transactions are not for value, give the appellant the right to reduce the subsequent transactions.

This was, however, a harder case than the Sheriff Appeal Court appears to have realised, and in a number of respects its reasoning seems unsatisfactory. Here we mention two. First, it cannot be right that the appellant failed because her right against her son was only a personal one. All offside goals cases involve rights which are only personal. The reason for the decision in *Wallace v Simmers* was not that the right of the occupier was personal, but that the right was not one capable of being made real. In other words, it was not a personal right for the acquisition of a real right in the property, such as ownership or lease. Rather, it was a personal right which had nowhere further to go. That, of course, was equally true in the present case: the appellant had nothing more to hope for than the improper liferent that she already had.

Secondly, the appellant's case was based on breach of trust and not, as in *Wallace v Simmers*, on breach of contract. That may well make a difference although the law here is undeveloped: see K G C Reid, *The Law of Property in Scotland* (1996) para 691. Yet the distinction appears to have been overlooked by the court, and hence the chance to develop the law – so important a function of appeal courts in a jurisdiction as small and with so few cases as Scotland's – was lost. As might be expected, the issue of transactions by trustees which are in breach of trust and *ultra vires* was considered by the Scottish Law Commission in the course of its recent review of trust law: see *Discussion Paper No 138 on Liability of Trustees to Third Parties* (2008) paras 2.27 and 2.32, and *Report No 239 on Trust Law* (2014) para 13.21. In the first of these papers, the Scottish Law Commission gave the law as being that, except where s 2 of the Trusts (Scotland) Act 1961 applies – and it does not apply to gratuitous transactions such as the ones litigated in *Miller v Smith* – an *ultra vires* transaction by trustees is 'voidable at the instance of the beneficiaries if it was gratuitous or the third party was in bad faith' (para 2.27). This, of course, was precisely the argument of the appellant in *Miller v Smith*. This rule, thought the Law Commission, was a good one insofar as it applied to gratuitous transactions and they recommended that it should not be changed (para 2.32):

> Gratuitous *ultra vires* transactions are and should remain challengeable as the trustees have no power to give trust property away except as directed by the trust deed. To make gifts unchallengeable would weaken the position of the beneficiaries to a very considerable extent.

With this last sentence the unsuccessful appellant, faced with eviction in old age from her home, would presumably be in emphatic agreement. It may be added, however that she is perhaps not without a remedy against her son, depending, of course, on what rights, if any she could prove against him.

(23) Russell v Russell
[2017] CSOH 137, 2017 GWD 34-531

John Russell and Elizabeth Russell owned a flat at 263 Cumbernauld Road, Denniston, Glasgow, currently worth about £45,000. In 2004 they signed a disposition of the flat to themselves in liferent and to their granddaughter in fee. The judgment does not mention whether the disposition was registered, but we assume that it was. The judgment does not say whether the disposition was gratuitous, but it seems almost certain that it was. The two disponers died successively in 2005 and 2006. A son of the disponers (and thus it seems an uncle of the disponee) raised the present action to reduce the disposition on the ground that, at the time of execution, both of the disponers had become incapax. The action was raised in February 2014. (The reason for the long delay is not known to us.) The action was eventually successful, and the reported judgment was about expenses. In a most unusual move, the court held that the defender's solicitor should be personally liable for part of the expenses of the action.

Dispositions by one family member to another are fairly common. Sometimes other family members feel disgruntled, and may even challenge the disposition, on various grounds. In the previous year there were three such cases: see *Conveyancing 2016* pp 20–22. The prudent conveyancer, when involved in a proposed gratuitous disposition by an elderly person, will be cautious. We wonder whether more guidance from the Law Society of Scotland might perhaps be useful. We note that the Law Society of England and Wales and the British Medical Association have a joint publication, currently in its fourth edition, called *Assessment of Mental Capacity: A Practical Guide for Doctors and Lawyers* (edited by A Keene).

One of the issues in the case was that the conveyancing file had disappeared. The Lord Ordinary, Lord Boyd of Duncansby, said (at para 46): 'Mr Renfrew [who acted for the disponee] was not obliged to keep the conveyancing file; the 10 years referred to in Mr Heaney's submissions [Mr Heaney was the pursuer's counsel] is merely a recommended time for destruction of conveyancing files and has no other status.' We offer no comment.

One final remark. In this action the Keeper was called as a defender. That was once common practice. Since the Land Registration etc (Scotland) Act 2012 came into force it is, in normal cases at least, inappropriate. In the normal case the Keeper has no interest in being a party to an action of reduction. If the action is successful she will simply give effect to the decree: see K G C Reid and G L Gretton, *Land Registration* (2017) para 6.12. Thus a pursuer who calls the Keeper as a defender is acting pointlessly and even runs the risk of being found liable in expenses.

(24) O'Neil v O'Neil
[2017] SC GLA 40, 2017 GWD 22-361

This is another case in which a disposition by an elderly and now deceased parent in favour of one or more children is challenged by one or more other children, this time unsuccessfully.

The late Mrs Martha O'Neil had four sons: David, John, Michael and James. In May 2010, aged 80 and in poor health, Mrs O'Neil disponed her house in Foinaven Drive, Glasgow, to John and Michael. No consideration was paid. Mrs O'Neil died less than two years later. David, who had assisted his mother with the purchase of her house and who, he averred, had reason to expect to inherit a share of her estate, raised the present action for reduction of the disposition on grounds either of undue influence or of facility and circumvention.

The action was dismissed. The pursuer's pleadings, said the sheriff (Alan D Miller), were lacking in specification and failed to set out a relevant basis for reduction. They relied too much on inference and too little on the averment of specific facts and events.

More precisely, in respect of the case for undue influence (paras 24–26):

> The extent of the case as pled is that the disposition marked an unexplained change from Mrs O'Neil's previously expressed intentions; that the defenders must have persuaded her to give effect to this change of intention; that they did so with the intention of benefiting themselves and dis-benefiting the pursuer; and that Mrs O'Neil's change of heart came about because they took advantage of their familial relationship, and because they resided along with Mrs O'Neil to exert influence over her. Taking at face value the averments of previous expressions in the pursuer's favour, there is no doubt that the execution of the disposition was both unexpected, and highly unfavourable to him. But that in itself is no ground for reduction … Essentially, the pursuer's case is to infer from the alleged change of heart, together with the defenders' familial relationship with the deceased, that Mrs O'Neil must have given way to malign influence by the defenders. In doing so it seems to me he is trying to add 2 + 2 to make considerably more than 4. He makes no averments at all about the character of the relationship between Mrs O'Neil and the defenders, such as whether she had in fact trusted and confided in them to any extent previously. There is nothing to support the bare averment – at best an inference – that the defenders played any part in persuading Mrs O'Neil on this or indeed any other matter. There is nothing to suggest that any such influence was 'undue'.

Other facts that emerged from the pleadings provided a challenge to the pursuer's inference of undue influence. The disposition was consistent with a subsequent, and unchallenged, will by Mrs O'Neil in which she left everything to John and Michael. Furthermore, 'while the extent and quality of legal advice and assistance may well be unknown to the pursuer, it is incontrovertible that a solicitor was involved in the preparation and execution of the disposition' (para 27).

The case as pled in relation to facility and circumvention was no stronger. To establish such a case it was necessary to show facility, circumvention, and lesion. The averments in respect of the first of these were particularly bare (paras 39 and 40):

> [A] party cannot set up a case of facility simply by describing the general condition of the person whose will was allegedly circumvented … Secondly, I take that while physical state or indeed life circumstances are certainly not irrelevant to the question of facility, the crux of the issue is the impact on the person's will-power and judgment. Ultimately, as Mr Davies [counsel for the defenders] argued, 'facility' is mental facility, however it may be caused. And thirdly, it is essential to lay a basis for evincing facility that is correlated to the date and circumstances of the disputed transaction. Here, the pursuer's case on record for his mother's facility consists of a list of her physical health conditions, a reference to her age, and a 'believed and averred' statement that she was thus rendered facile. This seems woefully inadequate and leaves crucial questions unanswered.

LAND REGISTRATION

(25) Munro v Keeper of the Registers of Scotland
2017 GWD 17-277, Lands Tr

The title sheet of a plot of land contained an area which, the Keeper accepted, was actually part of a neighbouring plot of land. But while the inaccuracy was manifest, the Keeper concluded that she was prevented from rectifying it by s 81 of the Land Registration etc (Scotland) Act 2012. This prevents rectification by the Keeper where an inaccuracy is in the course of being cured by positive prescription. In such a case, rectification is permitted only of consent or where the inaccuracy is judicially determined. This was an application for such judicial determination. See **Commentary** p 179.

[Another aspect of this case is digested at p 59 below.]

(26) Veen v Keeper of the Registers of Scotland
2017 GWD 17-276, Lands Tr

In 1976 the Church of Scotland General Trustees sold the former manse at Laggan, Newtonmore, Inverness-shire, to a Dr Richardson. The feu disposition described the property by (i) plan, (ii) a traditional verbal description of the boundaries, and (iii) area. The first and second of these were consistent and disclosed an area of about 1.02 acres (= about 0.413 hectares). The third, however, gave the area as being 1.65 acres (= about 0.668 hectares). The purchaser occupied the property as described in (i) and (ii). The feu disposition was a split-off deed, and the Church of Scotland General Trustees remained in possession of the remainder.

Almost 30 years later, in 2005, Mr and Mrs Veen bought the property from Dr Richardson's executor. The transaction induced first registration. In registering the property, the Keeper followed the boundaries given in (i) and (ii). In accordance with normal practice, no statement as to area was given. (Under the Land Registration (Scotland) Act 1979 s 6(1)(a) the area of a plot of land had to be stated in a title sheet only if it was 2 hectares or more. The Land Registration etc (Scotland) Act 2012 has no provision on this issue. The Land Register Rules etc (Scotland) Regulations 2014 reg 12 provide that the area must be stated if greater than half a hectare. But the title sheet was made up in 2005, ie under the 1979 Act.)

In 2010 the Veens applied to the Keeper for rectification of the Register, asking that the title sheet should say that the area was 1.65 acres. The application was refused. Several years later there was an appeal against that decision. (The property had since 2010 passed to two of their children, who were thus the parties involved.)

The Lands Tribunal held that the Register was not inaccurate. The well-established rule was that where, in a deed, there is a discrepancy between boundaries and measurements, the former prevails. The feu disposition thus conveyed just over an acre of land and not the 1.65 acres given as the area. The cadastral map was therefore correct in showing this smaller area. See **Commentary** p 177.

There was also, as the Tribunal noted, a further problem about the appellants' position. The unit comprised about 1.02 acres. If the area were now to be stated as 1.65 acres, then the boundaries as shown in the title sheet would, as a consequence, have to be changed – in other words extra land would have to be added. But where would this extra land come from? It was true that the Church of Scotland General Trustees owned the surrounding land. But precisely which part of that land could be used to make up the (non-existent) 'shortfall' in area, and on what basis? But the appellants never got as far as that problem, since the title sheet was accurate anyway. The Tribunal observed that if the Keeper were now to add a statement as to area, it would be the figure of about 1.02 acres, not 1.65 acres.

The appellants were not legally represented, and it seems unlikely that a lawyer would have advised bringing what was evidently an appeal without merit. Expenses were awarded in favour of the Keeper.

RESIDENTIAL RIGHT TO BUY

(27) Cassidy v Trafalgar Housing Association Ltd
2017 GWD 26-433 Lands Tr

The Housing (Scotland) Act 2014 s 1, read with the Housing (Scotland) Act 2014 (Commencement No 1 etc) Order 2014 (SSI 2014/264), abolished the residential right to buy with effect from 1 August 2016. Valid applications already lodged on or before 31 July 2016 were unaffected by the abolition. Unsurprisingly, there was an eleventh-hour rush of applications to buy, a number of which ended up before the Lands Tribunal during 2017.

The first of these cases with which we deal, *Cassidy*, involved a scramble to meet the deadline. Section 63(1A) of the Housing (Scotland) Act 1987 says that 'where the landlord is a registered social landlord the tenant shall, when serving on the landlord the application to purchase, give the landlord a certificate issued by the local authority', the certificate to be that no arrears exist of council tax or water and sewerage charges. In this case the tenant wished to buy the property that she rented, deciding to do so only a few days before the deadline. Her problem was that there were substantial arrears of council tax. She rushed to pay these off, making two payments on 27 July and 29 July. She delivered her application by hand on Saturday 30 July, but at that time was still awaiting the certificate from the local authority. The certificate was received on Monday 1 August (which seems commendably fast work) and she rushed it round on the same day to the landlord.

The landlord rejected the application on the ground that it had not been a valid application since it had not included the necessary certificate. That would not have mattered had it not been for the 2014 Act. But the effect of that Act was that on 1 August 2016 the right to buy no longer existed, subject only to valid applications lodged on or before 31 July. No such valid application had been received.

The tenant appealed to the Lands Tribunal, but without success. The legislation was clear. The tenant had done her best to catch the train, but had reached the platform too late.

(28) EK v City of Edinburgh Council
27 September 2017, Lands Tr

Mrs K applied to buy her public-sector tenancy of a property in the Gilmerton area of Edinburgh, doing so on 28 July 2016, just before the final abolition of the right to buy. She was, however, in arrears of both rent and council tax and therefore (see the previous case) was not in fact entitled to buy. Accordingly the landlord rejected the application. Where a landlord refuses an application that must be done within one month: s 68(1) of the Housing (Scotland) Act 1987. Mrs K said that she had never received the refusal letter and that accordingly, founding on *East of Scotland Water Authority v Livingstone* 1999 SC 65, she was entitled to buy. The landlord led satisfactory evidence that the letter had been posted timeously via the recorded delivery service and had not been returned as undelivered.

Section 7 of the Interpretation Act 1978 provides:

Where an Act authorises or requires any document to be served by post (whether the expression 'serve' or the expression 'give' or 'send' or any other expression is used) then, unless the contrary intention appears, the service is deemed to be effected by properly addressing, pre-paying and posting a letter containing the document and, unless the contrary is proved, to have been effected at the time at which the letter would be delivered in the ordinary course of post.

(For the equivalent provision for modern Holyrood legislation, see s 26 of the Interpretation and Legislative Reform (Scotland) Act 2010.) The Tribunal thus accepted that it was open to Mrs K to plead non-delivery, but that the burden of so proving fell on her. She did not satisfy the Tribunal in this respect. Accordingly her appeal to the Tribunal failed. At paras 47 and 49 the Tribunal said:

The onus of proof is upon the applicant to show that the notice was not delivered within the time at which it would have been delivered in the ordinary course of post, in that it was not delivered at all. We are satisfied that the item was properly addressed, paid for and posted, thus giving rise to a presumption of service. We are not prepared to accept the applicant's assertion that she did not receive the notice without that position being supported by other evidence. We did not consider that she was a straightforward witness in that she tended to engage in fencing with counsel, for example, by asking questions instead of answering them. We did not hear from the other member of the applicant's household to confirm how household post was dealt with or what might have happened. It is of course statistically possible that the item got lost in the Royal Mail system, and this possibility was conceded by Mr Jackson. [Mr Jackson was the Council's 'mail services assistant'.] But we do not think that goes far enough to satisfy us that this was what occurred … In these circumstances we find that the applicant has not discharged the onus of proof by satisfying us, in terms of the second limb of s 7, that she did not receive the notice of refusal. Accordingly the presumption that service was effected is maintained.

(29) Ahmed v Glasgow Housing Association Ltd
21 November 2017, Lands Tr

Where a tenancy was taken of 'new-supply social housing' the landlord could give a 'notice of limitation' whereby the right to buy would be excluded. In this case Ms Ahmed and Mr Khan took such a tenancy in March 2016 and immediately applied to buy the property. The landlord asserted that a notice of limitation had been given. The tenants denied that they had been given it. The case went to the Lands Tribunal, and much of the case was devoted to that disputed factual question. Eventually, however, the case was decided on another point: the landlord had failed to send a notice of refusal timeously and accordingly was bound to sell. The relevant deadline here was two months in terms of s 68(2) of the Housing (Scotland) Act 1987, rather than the one-month period, applicable to the previous case.

(30) Oakley v North Ayrshire Council
2017 Hous LR 13, Lands Tr

The applicant sought to buy the property in West Kilbride, Ayrshire, which he rented from the local authority. But since 2008 the area had been designated as a 'pressured area' in which the right to buy was suspended. Accordingly the Tribunal refused the application, despite the sympathy it felt. It commented (paras 4 and 5):

> The applicant is the latest of a number of disappointed tenants who have seen their applications – no matter how otherwise meritorious – refused by their landlords because of pressured area status and who have applied to the tribunal in the hope of having these refusals set aside. However, as has been explained in the cases of *Caven v Irvine Housing Association* [2016 GWD 23-433, *Conveyancing 2016* Case (33)] and *Clark v South Ayrshire Council* [2016 GWD 32-578, *Conveyancing 2016* Case (32)], that is not something the tribunal can do. We acknowledge that this will be a disappointing result for the applicant. Number 4 Ardrossan High Road is the only home of which he has meaningful memories and where he lived with his mother for some 30 years before her untimely death. As the applicant says, had his mother had any foreknowledge of her early death she would probably have passed the tenancy to him much sooner and he would have been in a position to exercise the right to buy before it came to be suspended. That did not happen, however, and in those circumstances the law simply does not allow people in the position of the applicant to insist on their former right to buy nor does it give this tribunal any discretion to overturn the respondents' refusal to sell. The application must, therefore, be refused.

(31) Chaudhry v South Lanarkshire Council
2017 GWD 12-190, Lands Tr

Mr and Mrs Chaudhry sought to buy the property (in Hutchison Street, Hamilton, Lanarkshire) that they rented from the local authority. The application was refused by the landlord on the basis that they had become tenants on 13 June 2011, which was after s 141 of the Housing (Scotland) Act 2010 had come into force (1 March 2011). Section 141 removed the right to buy for new tenants: see *Conveyancing 2010* pp 51–52. Mr Chaudhry asserted that he had *de facto* taken over the tenancy from his uncle, Mohammad Bashir, in December 2010. (The averments for the applicant are confusing here because they refer exclusively to him, whereas the application was a joint one.) The Tribunal rejected the application. Even if it could be established that Mr Chaudhry (and his wife?) had been providing the funds to pay the rent, the simple fact was that they had not become tenants until 13 June 2011.

(32) Dickson v Ore Valley Housing Association
2017 GWD 15-246, Lands Tr

Mrs Dickson sought to buy the property that she rented, in Westfield Terrace, Cardenden, Lochgelly, Fife. The application was made jointly with her granddaughter. The landlord refused the application on the ground that the granddaughter did not satisfy the residence requirement. The tenant appealed to the Lands Tribunal, but without success. The tenant argued that the landlord should have exercised its discretion in her favour, but the Tribunal's opinion was that the discretion in such cases is not open to review. More fundamentally, a tenant has one month in which to appeal to the Tribunal (Housing (Scotland) Act 1987 s 68(4)), and the tenant had missed that deadline.

This was one of a number of cases in which the Tribunal had sympathy for the applicant, but was unable to find in her favour. When the landlord rejected the application, it had advised the tenant that she could invoke the complaints procedure (which she did, but without success), but at the same time had not explained to her that to do so would be likely to result in loss of the right to appeal to the Tribunal, because of the one-month time limit. The Tribunal commented (para 10):

> What they [the landlord] certainly ought not to have done was mislead Mrs Dickson into thinking that she could challenge their decision under their complaints procedure without any risk to her statutory right of application to this tribunal … We would have been interested in hearing argument to the effect that this advice, on which Mrs Dickson acted to her prejudice, barred the respondents from relying on s 68(4) before this tribunal.

But that argument was not advanced to the Tribunal, no doubt because the applicant, having been refused legal aid, had no legal representation. The Tribunal also noted that there might have been a question as to whether the landlord's refusal letter was in fact a valid refusal. But again this point was not argued. One final consequence of her lack of legal advice was the fact that the tenant had made the application jointly with her granddaughter. She had done this because she lacked the necessary funds. But, as the Tribunal observed, there were other means whereby her granddaughter could have assisted her with the purchase without being a joint applicant. The Tribunal's sympathy is understandable.

(33) Hopwood v West Lothian Council
2017 GWD 22-380, Lands Tr

Beecraigs is a popular country park in West Lothian. It is owned by the local authority. Mr Hopwood was the tenant of a house in the park. As well as being Mr Hopwood's landlord, the local authority was his employer. Mr Hopwood applied to buy the house, but was refused on the basis of sch 1 para 9 of the Housing (Scotland) Act 2001, which says:

> A tenancy is not a Scottish secure tenancy if the house forms part of, or is within the curtilage of, a building which –
>   (a) is held by the landlord mainly for purposes other than the provision of housing accommodation, and
>   (b) mainly consists of accommodation other than housing accommodation.

The landlord's position (which the Tribunal regarded, however, as fuzzily pled) was that the applicant's house was part of a cluster of farm buildings and that this provision was thereby engaged. But, after proof, the Tribunal disagreed. At para 39 it said:

> There is nothing about the geography of the subjects in relation to the buildings on which the respondents rely to suggest any kind of unity. Measuring the shortest distance between them, the viewing sheds are approximately 46 metres away and the animal welfare shed 38 metres, with the public road into the cul-de-sac in between ... Far from there being any kind of physical unity between them they are in three separate locations within the cul-de-sac ... and are interspersed with other buildings serving different purposes.

And at para 43:

> While we entirely understand the respondents' wish to have those houses occupied by their own employees and, in particular, employees who have knowledge and experience of the Park, it is simply not the case that the houses serve those other buildings in any necessary or reasonably useful way. Instead the viewing sheds and animal welfare shed can and do operate entirely independently of the houses. The houses are not necessary to their operation nor are they useful adjuncts of those buildings or their purposes.

(34) Barr v South Lanarkshire Council
2017 GWD 15-247, Lands Tr

Mr and Mrs Barr sought to buy the property that they rented at Meadowside, Eddlewood, Hamilton, Lanarkshire. Their application was rejected on the ground that they were ineligible, the tenancy having been transferred to them only a few weeks before they had submitted their application in July 2016. They appealed to the Lands Tribunal. The tenancy had previously been held by a cousin, with whom they had been living, with the landlord's consent, since June 2014. The cousin had later assigned the tenancy to them, again with the landlord's consent. Their main argument was that their cousin had had a right to buy and that an assignation carries with it all rights held by the assignor. (Why the cousin did not simply exercise the right to buy himself is unclear.) This ingenious argument was rejected.

One reason for the decision was that s 32 of the Housing (Scotland) Act 2001, which allows assignation if the landlord consents, speaks not of the tenancy being assigned, but of possession being assigned, and, said the Tribunal, that wording meant that common-law rules about the effect of assigning a tenancy or lease could not be invoked. The wording of the provision is as follows:

> It is a term of every Scottish secure tenancy that the tenant may assign, sublet or otherwise give up to another person possession of the house or any part of it or take in a lodger ... only with the consent in writing of the landlord...

With respect, we take the view that this should be parsed thus:

- It is a term of every Scottish secure tenancy
- that the tenant may
- assign,
- sublet or
- otherwise give up to another person possession of the house or any part of it or
- take in a lodger
- only with the consent in writing of the landlord...

In other words, what is being assigned is the tenancy. Indeed, to speak of 'assigning possession' would hardly make sense: assignation can have various objects but possession is not one of them. Moreover, if merely 'possession' were to be assigned, the assignee would not become tenant, would not be bound to pay the rent and so on. The assignor would remain tenant. That cannot be the meaning. Indeed, since what the provision is saying is that the tenant is not to do certain things without the landlord's consent, it would be odd if assigning the tenancy were not one of those things.

The Tribunal commented, at para 8, that the applicant's argument 'would mean that the previous tenant would have been denuded of his right to rely on his history of occupation of secure tenancies up to that point, so that, were he to move to another such tenancy he would be starting all over again: his earned eligibility to buy having been assigned to his successor.' As against that it might be replied that if the previous tenant chose to give up his right, that was his choice.

Only that which is transferable can be transferred. This self-evident truth is perhaps the best starting-point. After all, not all rights can be transferred. The assignation could transfer the right to buy only if it was a transferable right. And the whole tenor of the legislation indicates non-transferability. Subject to certain qualifications, the right to buy is personal to the tenant. It could not therefore be assigned to the applicant.

(35) Pettigrew v River Clyde Homes
2017 Hous LR 15, Lands Tr

A public-sector tenant, Ms Pettigrew, sought to buy the property that she rented in Glamis Place, Greenock, Renfrewshire. The landlord issued an offer to sell, but the tenant did not accept. She wished the contract to include a clause binding the landlord to produce a completion certificate in respect of sound insulation work (in the ceiling) that had been done some time previously, when the property had been owned by a different landlord. (She had successfully sued her then-landlord in 2000 to compel this to be done.) A comfort letter was available. This, however, did not satisfy the tenant.

Section 64(1) of the Housing (Scotland) Act 1987 provides that an offer to sell is to contain such conditions as are reasonable, provided that:

(a) the conditions shall have the effect of ensuring that the tenant has as full enjoyment and use of the house as owner as he has had as tenant;

(b) the conditions shall secure to the tenant such additional rights as are necessary for his reasonable enjoyment and use of the house as owner (including, without prejudice to the foregoing generality, common rights in any part of the building of which the house forms part) and shall impose on the tenant any necessary duties relative to rights so secured; and

(c) the conditions shall include such terms as are necessary to entitle the tenant to receive a good and marketable title to the house.

The applicant, who was a party litigant, focused on para (c). But the Tribunal held that the lack of a completion certificate has nothing to do with good and marketable title and accordingly the tenant's application to the Tribunal failed. This decision was surely correct. The exact boundaries of the concept of 'good and marketable title' are to some extent open to debate, but clearly the lack of a completion certificate is nothing to do with title.

As the Tribunal observed, the applicant would have had more mileage out of paras (a) and (b) of s 64(1), although the result would probably have been the same (para 25): 'Given the apparent practice of conveyancers to accept letters of comfort ... instead of completion certificates .... absent more evidence we would not have been prepared to find in the circumstances that the offer to sell was deficient for not requiring the production of a completion certificate.'

(36) Hosie v West Dunbartonshire Council
2017 GWD 23-399, Lands Tr

The right-to-buy legislation has a provision to cover the case where a person seeks to exercise the right for different properties at different times: Housing (Scotland) Act 1987 s 62(3A) and (3B). Such 'double dipping' is permissible, but if it happens the discount on the second purchase is reduced by the amount of discount on the first: thus double-dipping is allowed but not double-discounting. Presumably such cases are rare anyway.

In the present case the applicant sought to buy the property of which she was the tenant. She had previously been the co-purchaser of another public-sector property, together with her mother. In that previous purchase she had not been the co-tenant: the tenancy had been held solely by her mother. In the present case the landlord proposed reducing the discount by one-half of the discount obtained in the previous purchase. That was not acceptable to the applicant who appealed to the Lands Tribunal. Her argument was that the anti-double-discount provisions applied only where the person in question had been a tenant or co-tenant. The Tribunal found in favour of the landlord: surely a victory for common sense.

A footnote. Nowadays people tend to rely, when consulting statutory material, on the versions available through Westlaw or Lexis. These are usually accurate and up-to-date: indeed, those too young to remember the pre-internet age can hardly appreciate how valuable the modern databases are and how much labour they save. But such databases can occasionally be wrong. This was one such case: as the Tribunal noted (para 3) the Westlaw version of s 62 contained serious errors.

(37) McCallum v City of Edinburgh Council
[2017] CSIH 24, 2017 SLT 466, 2017 Hous LR 42

In August 2015 the local authority granted to Mr McCallum a tenancy of a property in Tron Square, Edinburgh. In October of the same year the tenant sought to exercise the right to buy. The local authority agreed to give him the benefit of its discretion (as to which see s 61(10)(b)(iv) of the Housing (Scotland) Act 1987) to regard him as having been in occupation for the qualifying period even though he had in fact not been: this related to the fact that he had been in the army between 1983 (up to which time he had been a council tenant) and 2005, and while in the army had lived in army accommodation. The local authority calculated the discount at £15,000 on the basis that this was a post-2002 tenancy and accordingly subject to the lower discount rate of the 'modernised' right to buy, as opposed to the more generous rate of the 'preserved' right to buy.

The applicant raised the present action to require the local authority to sell to him at the 'preserved' rate. In the Tribunal's words (para 15):

> The applicant's position was that as the respondents had conceded continuity of occupation after the coming into effect of the 2002 Order, he was entitled to purchase on the preserved terms. Section 61(2)(c) allowed for the occupancy of armed forces accommodation to contribute to the right to purchase. He contended that he had never 'given up' a tenancy which is what was required to lose the preserved rights under the 2002 Order [ie the Housing (Scotland) Act 2001 (Scottish Secure Tenancy etc) Order 2002, SSI 2002/318].

The Tribunal held that the terms of art 4 of the 2002 Order were clear and that the applicant was not entitled to discount at the 'preserved' rate: 2016 GWD 24-450 (*Conveyancing 2016* Case (34)).

The tenant appealed to the Inner House. The appeal was dismissed, the Inner House confirming the analysis of the law that had been set out by the Tribunal. Lord Drummond Young said that (para 2):

> I am conscious that the consequences of our decision might appear harsh for the appellant. Nevertheless, I consider that our decision follows inevitably from the wording and structure of the Housing (Scotland) Act 2001 (Scottish Secure Tenancy Etc) Order 2002, in particular the provisions of Article 4 of the Order, taken together with section 61 of the Housing (Scotland) Act 1987. The effect of the Order was to preserve rights in existence as at its operative date, 30 September 2002; it did not provide for the creation of new rights thereafter. The appellant did not on that date have any rights in respect of his present house, as he was still living in Army accommodation. Consequently any right that he claims in respect of his present house must be a right that came into existence after the critical date for the preservation of existing rights to buy. Thus it is inevitably subject to the modernised regime rather than the preserved regime.

Lord Malcolm and Lady Clark also expressed some sympathy for the applicant but, like Lord Drummond Young and the Tribunal, considered the legislation to be clear.

(38) M v City of Edinburgh Council
28 June 2016, Lands Tr

The applicant obtained a public-sector tenancy in August 2015, and in December 2015 applied to buy the property. He did not have the necessary length of occupation, but the Council nevertheless conceded that he had the right to buy, because he had been a Council tenant before 1983, had been in army accommodation from 1983 to 2005, and from 2005 to 2015 had been homeless. The question for the Tribunal was whether the discount should be calculated on the basis of the 'preserved' right to buy or the 'modernised' right to buy. It was held that the latter was clearly applicable.

(39) Maloney v City of Edinburgh Council
2017 GWD 22-379, Lands Tr

A public-sector tenant, Mr Maloney, sought to buy the property that he rented at Stenhouse Avenue West, Edinburgh. The landlord offered to sell, the discount being calculated on the basis of the 'modernised' right to buy. The tenant argued that he should be allowed a discount on the basis of the 'preserved' right to buy. The applicant had been a secure tenant since 1993, but in 2005 he had moved from his original property to the present property to escape violence from a local gang. When he had moved he had been assured by the landlord that, if he thereafter exercised the right to buy, his discount would be unaffected. The Tribunal dismissed the appeal, holding that the discount fell to be determined by the 'modernised' right to buy. It commented (para 17):

The law simply does not give social landlords any discretion as to allow a preserved right to buy to be carried forward into a new tenancy except in the limited circumstances set out in para (3) of Article 4 of the 2002 Order [ie the Housing (Scotland) Act 2001 (Scottish Secure Tenancy etc) Order 2002, SSI 2002/318].

It added (para 14): 'This is not the first hard case under the provisions of the 2002 Order, although it is, perhaps, the hardest.'

LEASES

(40) Whitcombe v Bank of Scotland plc
[2017] CSOH 58, 2017 Hous LR 40

This case involved the question of whether a document that purported to be a lease was in fact a lease. Unfortunately the facts are not entirely clear. A property at 107 Lathro Park, Kinross, was, at first, co-owned by Mr and Mrs Whitcombe. Later they separated and divorced, and it seems that Mrs Whitcombe disponed her half-share to a Mr Cation. Subsequently, in 2007, an agreement was, or ostensibly was, entered into between Mr Whitcombe and Mr Cation whereby the latter leased his half share to the former for a term of ten years at a rent of £1,000 per month. Later still, Bank of Scotland plc, seemingly in its capacity as heritable creditor, raised an action of reduction of the lease. The action was not defended and decree of reduction was granted, this happening in 2012.

Thereafter Mr Whitcombe raised the present action for reduction of the decree of reduction. He averred that his failure to defend the action had been on account of mental illness. Whether Mr Cation was a party either to the original action of reduction, or to the present action, is unclear. It is also unclear in what way the bank's interests were allegedly impaired by the contract.

The bank averred, among other things, that the purported lease was a forgery, but at this stage of the action the focus of the bank's case was different: that the lease, if not forged, was intended merely as a mechanism for repayment by Mr Whitcombe to Mr Cation of certain advances that the former had received from the latter, and as such, argued the bank, was incapable of being a lease. Whether that argument (if founded in fact) could be sufficient to negate the existence of a lease we will not here enter into. But, assuming that negation to be correct, the result would, presumably, not be a reductive remedy, but merely a declaratory one – ie not 'the contract was void or voidable' but 'the contract was not a contract of lease'. After all, a contract for the occupation of property in exchange for periodical payment may be a perfectly valid contract, without being a contract of lease.

It is also unclear whether the case law on whether one co-owner can lease to another was cited. (A good short account of this obscure subject can be found in Angus McAllister, *Scottish Law of Leases* (4th edn, 2013) paras 2.23 ff.) But the case as reported is so sketchy that we offer no definite views on any of these matters. Proof before answer was allowed.

(41) Iqbal v Parnez
[2017] SAC (Civ) 7, 2017 GWD 6-81

The facts of this case are unclear. It seems to have concerned a property in Wishaw, Lanarkshire, possibly (but this is merely a surmise) a shop or fast-food restaurant, owned by the pursuer, who in this action sued for unpaid rent in terms of an alleged lease.

Apparently the pursuer was an undischarged bankrupt at the time that the lease was allegedly entered into, and the defender pled that, in those circumstances, the alleged lease, even if had ever purportedly existed, was void. It was held that a lease granted by an undischarged bankrupt is not void, but merely voidable at the instance of the trustee in sequestration, and accordingly this defence fell to be rejected.

There was also a question as to whether there had in fact ever been a lease in the first place. There seems to have been nothing in writing. Proof before answer on this point was allowed.

The pursuer also had an *esto* argument based on the law of unjustified enrichment, but this was held not to have been relevantly pled. One cannot help but wonder what the position of the trustee was, since any claim for rent would, one imagines, have been vested in the trustee, and not in the pursuer. But this aspect of the matter does not appear in the judgment.

(42) Gray v MacNeil's Exr
[2017] SAC (Civ) 9, 2017 SLT (Sh Ct) 83, 2017 SCLR 666, 2017 Hous LR 47

An agreement for a 15-year lease was entered into orally between Mr Gray and the owner, Mr MacNeil. Thereafter Mr Gray sued the owner for damages for breach of contract. The defence was that leases for longer than a year must be in writing. The pursuer lost at first instance (2016 SLT (Sh Ct) 250, *Conveyancing 2016* Case (37)), but has now succeeded on appeal to the Sheriff Appeal Court. The ratio of the decision may have been that contracts for the creation of real rights can validly be entered into orally. See **Commentary** p 171.

(43) AWG Business Centres Ltd v Regus Caledonia Ltd
[2017] CSIH 22, 2017 GWD 9-131

Defects were discovered in the concrete decking of the car-parking area in a property at Riverside House, Riverside Drive, Aberdeen. The dispute was as to who was liable to pay for the repairs. There was a lease and there was a sublease. The former, ie the head lease, imposed repairing costs on the tenant; the sublease required the subtenant to reimburse the tenant, ie the tenant of the head lease. Thus either (i) the landlord was liable or (ii) the head tenant was liable but with a right of reimbursement against the subtenant. In this action to determine allocation of liability, the head tenant was the pursuer and the two defenders were, first, the subtenant and, in the second place, the landlord.

The case was heard at first instance last year: [2016] CSOH 99, 2016 GWD 22-407 (*Conveyancing 2016* Case (40)). The position of the subtenant was evidently a difficult one, but it sought to rely on an exception ('exception (c)') as to repairing liability found in the head lease. The head tenant would not be liable for 'any expenditure incurred in respect of or pertaining to the initial construction of the Building or the Service Systems or any part thereof by the Landlord'. The problem with the concrete derived from the original construction of the building. The subtenant argued, in the words of the Lord Ordinary (Lord Tyre) (para 12), that:

> It was important to give content to the phrase 'or pertaining to' in exception (c). Those words made clear that the exception required to be construed broadly and covered not only the initial construction cost but also matters which 'pertained to' the initial construction … Costs incurred to remedy latent defects in design or construction pertained to the initial construction. As the building had only recently been constructed, it may be presumed that the original parties to the head lease were alive to the possibility of the existence of latent defects, yet no provision was made for any collateral remedy for the tenant in the event that it was liable for remedial costs. In all the circumstances it would offend against commercial common sense to construe the lease as imposing such liability on the tenant.

The Lord Ordinary did not agree, saying that (para 15):

> The first defender's contention places too much weight upon the words 'or pertaining to'. These words can be given content as a reference to costs such as professional fees associated with the construction of the building but not strictly costs of construction. To interpret them as contended for by the first defender would impose a substantial and continuing liability of uncertain extent upon the landlord in respect that it could be argued that any expense, whenever incurred, arising from a design flaw or indeed from a design decision was expenditure 'pertaining to' the initial construction of the Building. That would not be consistent with a lease such as the present one which bears the hallmarks of intending to impose a full repairing and insuring obligation upon the tenant.

Moreover, he said (para 16), referring to *Arnold v Britton* [2015] AC 1619 (*Conveyancing 2015* Case (51)) (a case that is constantly being cited in the courts at present):

> It would not be consistent with the *Arnold v Britton* approach to construe the lease on the basis of what a reasonably prudent tenant might have wished to achieve, or by attempting to assess what would have been a good or bad bargain from either point of view. The proper approach is rather to identify the parties' intention by reference to what a reasonable person having all the background knowledge available to the parties would have understood them to be using the language in exception (c) to mean.

Accordingly the Lord Ordinary held against the subtenant. The subtenant reclaimed, but the Inner House has now affirmed the decision of the Lord Ordinary, agreeing with his reasoning. The court commented (paras 18–20):

The language of exception (c) must be given its natural and ordinary meaning …
Exception (c) provides that any expenditure which is incurred 'in respect of or
pertaining to the initial construction of the Building … or any part thereof by the
Landlord' shall not be recoverable from the tenant. It is important not to place too
much emphasis on the words 'pertaining to' as distinct from the whole sub-clause,
including 'in respect of'. The natural and ordinary meaning of the exception 'in
respect of or pertaining to the initial construction' is that it relates to the costs of, or
associated with, initial construction and related snagging works.

Other relevant provisions of the lease must be taken into account. It is not disputed
that the tenant is liable to repair damage to the Premises caused by a latent defect,
whether in respect of the initial construction or otherwise (clause 3.6). In respect of
the Common Parts, clause 4.5 and part V of the Schedule provide that the landlord
must repair the Common Parts, again irrespective of the cause of the damage. The
liability to pay for such repairs is then passed on to the tenant by virtue of clause
3.1.2. That clause obliges the tenant to pay the Service Expenditure, ie the expenditure
incurred by the landlord, subject to the five exceptions.

The interpretation of exception (c), as relating only to initial construction and
snagging works, is consistent with the terms of a lease providing for liability on the
tenant to repair, or to pay for repairs to, defects in respect of both the Premises and
the Common Parts, irrespective of the cause of damage. The exception should not be
read in isolation from those provisions which transfer the general liability to repair,
or to pay for the cost of repairs, from the landlord to the tenant. It is consistent with
the full repairing nature of the lease.

(44) Moor Row Ltd v DWF LLP
[2017] CSOH 63, 2017 GWD 14-213

The subject of dilapidations often comes up in the Court of Session, the sums
sued for often being large. In this case Moor Row Ltd was the mid-tenant and
DWF LLP was the subtenant of office premises at Dalmore House in Glasgow.
Both the head lease and the sublease came to an end. Moor Row Ltd sued for
£906,294.35 in respect of dilapidations, plus expenses and interest. The defender
admitted that it had been in breach of its repairing obligations, and it further
admitted that that breach also meant that the pursuer was, in turn, in breach
of its obligations to the proprietor, ie the pursuer's landlord. But it disputed
the relevancy of the action as raised. The pursuer had no averment that it had
actually paid the proprietor in respect of the dilapidations. As summarised by
the Lord Ordinary (Lady Wolffe) the argument was that (para 17):

The defender accepted it was in breach of the repairing obligations in the Lease.
It also accepted that it had put the pursuer into a like or parallel breach under the
Head Lease. However, until the pursuer actually suffered a loss as a consequence of
that breach, there was only a potential liability not an actual one. Since the pursuer
admits … that it has not itself carried out any remedial works to the premises, a
relevant case by the pursuer for damages against the defender could only arise (if
at all) from a liability presently due by the pursuer to its head landlord, Tarn. If the
pursuer fails relevantly to aver any such liability owed by it, its claim against the
defender for damages must inevitably fail.

This argument was unsuccessful, but the Lord Ordinary stressed that the pursuer would still need to prove loss, given that the lease did not have a liquidated damages clause or anything similar to such a clause. She remarked (para 84) that 'I reserve my opinion on whether proof of estimated costs would itself suffice.' So the pursuer still has some hurdles to cross.

The Lord Ordinary's judgment contains a valuable account of the authorities in this area, and also an incisive discussion of the terms of the sublease and the head lease.

(45) H & H Properties UK Ltd v Douris
[2017] SC DUN 18, 2017 GWD 12-188

Reported dilapidations cases are almost invariably in respect of commercial property, often involving claims for large sums. But comparable issues for smaller sums can arise for residential tenancies, and the present case was an example. It has no particular legal significance, but is interesting as an example of a typical small real-life dispute, involving an ordinary residential tenancy agreement plus the usual messy facts.

The property was a three-bedroom house in Donald's Court, Dundee. The landlord sued for arrears of rent (liability for which was not disputed) plus damages for various alleged breaches of the tenancy agreement. For instance the agreement had a 'no pets' clause but the tenants had kept a cat and the cat had made the lino in one room smell. Damages for this were awarded at £55. And so on. The judgment of the sheriff (S G Collins QC) inevitably took a broad-brush approach. The sums awarded were: lino replacement: £55; redecoration: £479; wall and ceiling hole-filling: £120, scorched carpet: £25; electrical: £25; replacement of internal fire doors: £483; refitting window blind: £30; cleaning: £25. The total was around £900 less than the landlord had sued for. The sheriff looked carefully at the terms of the tenancy agreement and, on the whole, tended to interpret them more in favour of the tenants than of the landlord.

(46) Dem-Master Demolition Ltd v Healthcare Environmental Services Ltd
[2017] CSOH 14, 2017 GWD 5-72

An industrial unit (Unit 3, Centrelink 5, Calderhead Road, Shotts) was leased for five years from 1 January 2010, the rent being £82,000 per annum. The tenant did not remove at 1 January 2015, on the basis that the lease was continuing by tacit relocation. The landlord then served a notice of irritancy on the ground of failure to maintain the property, and raised the present action of declarator and removing, and with pecuniary conclusions, including a conclusion for violent profits. The cost of restoring the property, averred the landlord, would be £2,081,350.74.

The lease provided, in clause 6, that:

The Tenants accept the Premises as being in such condition as shown on the attached Photographic Schedule and in all respects fit for the Tenants' purposes and shall at

their sole expense and, to the reasonable satisfaction of the Landlords, repair and
maintain and renew (and, if necessary for the purposes of maintenance and repair, to
replace and rebuild) and decorate and keep the Premises and all permitted additions
and new buildings, if any, in like condition as is evidenced on the said Photographic
Schedule.

The parties were in disagreement as to whether the property had in fact
deteriorated during the period of the lease, and moreover were in disagreement
as to the proper interpretation of the quoted provision. Both the factual question
as to whether there had been any deterioration (which the tenant denied), and the
question of interpretation, were bedevilled by the fact that neither the landlord's
nor the tenant's copy of the lease actually contained any 'photographic schedule'.
Indeed, it rather seemed that no such schedule had ever existed.

At a hearing in 2015 the Lord Ordinary (Lord Doherty) said (para 14) that
'I am not currently in a position to determine the proper construction of the
repairing provision ... That exercise cannot be conducted in a vacuum, without
knowledge of all the material circumstances surrounding the execution of the
lease.' (See [2015] CSOH 154, 2015 GWD 38-604 (*Conveyancing 2015* Case (62)).)
The case then went to proof before Lady Wolffe. The defender argued that the
property had been in poor condition at the beginning of the lease and that its
obligations under the lease were merely to maintain it in that condition, which,
it pled, had been done. By contrast (para 27):

> The pursuers' primary position was that the Photographic Schedule was conceived
> solely for the benefit of the defenders. In the absence of a Photographic Schedule, so
> the argument ran, the repair obligation ceased to be qualified by reference to that
> Schedule. Instead, the repair obligation became an unqualified one. In other words,
> it was contended that the repair obligation became 'absolute' and the defenders were
> bound to restore the Premises to a standard that corresponded with this 'absolute'
> standard.

As a secondary position, the argument for the pursuer was that the defender
had failed to maintain the property in the condition that had existed at the
beginning of the lease. The Lord Ordinary disagreed, saying at para 213:

> I do not accept that the reference to the Photographic Schedule in Clause 6 of the
> Lease operated solely to confer a benefit on the tenants. In my view, the reference to
> the Photographic Schedule in Clause 6 serves to secure a degree of certainty as to the
> actual standard to be achieved in relation to the Premises. It precludes arguments as
> to what, precisely, a notional or objective standard would dictate, and which may be
> problematic in relation to an ageing industrial building of unique architectural merit
> and of which the Premises form only a small part. From the landlords' perspective,
> during the currency of the Lease the tenants are obliged to keep the Premises in the
> state they were in at the outset (as recorded in the Photographic Schedule). From
> the tenants' perspective, they are not obliged to keep the Premises to any higher
> standard than that depicted in the Photographic Schedule. Analysed in this way,
> the stipulation of the acceptable standard of the Premises by reference to their state,
> as evidenced in the Photographic Schedule, confers benefits or protections on both

parties. Both parties benefit from the measure of certainty achieved in agreeing the standard to be applied (being the actual state of the Premises at a certain point in time) and the reduction in the scope of arguments as to what, precisely, that is (eg because it is evidenced by the Photographic Schedule).

She continued (para 220):

> In terms of Clause 6, properly construed, the standard of the Premises, as accepted and to which they were to be repaired or kept for the duration of the Lease, is assessed by reference to their actual state at the material time, as evidenced by the Photographic Schedule. Nothing in the factual matrix leads me to displace that interpretation.

The Lord Ordinary accepted the evidence for the defender that the property had been in poor condition at the beginning of the lease. The case was continued for further procedure.

Neither side sought to argue that, since there had been no schedule, clause 6 as a whole was without effect.

(47) AWG Group Ltd v HCP II Properties 101 GP Ltd
[2017] CSOH 69, 2017 Hous LR 30

AWG Group Ltd was the lessee of eight floors of an office block at Ocean Drive, Leith, Edinburgh. There was a separate lease for each floor, but all eight leases were on the same terms, so this point was not a material one. The leases were for 20 years, beginning in 2004. Each lease had a five-yearly rent review provision, and the rents were duly reviewed in 2009. The 2014 review was delayed. The landlord thereafter issued quarterly invoices for the rent at the 2009 level. At first the invoices had a line saying that the invoice was without prejudice to the right of rent review, but in later invoices that was dropped. Each invoice was paid by the tenant. The tenant thereafter raised the present action for declarator that the landlord had, by omitting the 'without prejudice' line in the later invoices, implicitly abandoned its right to invoke the 2014 rent review. The tenant had also seen a copy of a sales brochure advertising the office in which it had been stated that the next rent review was due in 2019. The argument was one of personal bar. The core of the pursuer's case was the following averment (see para 7 of the judgment of the Lord Ordinary (Lord Doherty)):

> The reasonable inference to be drawn from the removal of the without prejudice caveat from invoices for payment of rent from 7 January 2015 and from the reference in the sales brochure to the next rent review being 27 February 2019 is that the landlord had waived the right to seek a review of the rent at the 2014 Date of Review … [T]he pursuer in reliance on the invoices from 7 January 2015, paid the un-reviewed rent. In a case of rent review, those payments constitute sufficient reliance for the purposes of waiver. In any event, the pursuer conducted its affairs in certain important respects on the basis that the defender would not instigate the 2014 rent review. The pursuer proceeded on that basis because of (a) the defender's failure to take any steps to instigate the 2014 rent review (before they purported to do so on 28 April 2016) which contrasted with the approach taken to the review in 2009 which was instigated by

the then landlord by notice dated 16 December 2008; (b) the terms of the rent invoices from 7 January 2015; (c) the clear representation in the sales brochure that the next rent review would be in 2019 ...

The 'reliance' element of this argument was perhaps not a strong one, but the case did not go as far as to test it. The Lord Ordinary, after an extensive and valuable review of the authorities, concluded that the abandonment argument was unsound. No reasonable tenant would have inferred from the omission of the 'without prejudice' clause that the landlord was abandoning its right to invoke the 2014 review, and as for what the sales brochure said, the same was true, especially since the brochure was addressed not to the tenant but to prospective buyers.

(48) St Andrews Forest Lodges Ltd v Grieve
[2017] SC DUN 25, 2017 GWD 14-224

The owner of a house raised an action to remove the occupiers. They resisted the action on the basis that they had security of tenure under an assured tenancy. The owner's position was that the agreement did not constitute a lease at all, but rather a licence, and, *esto* it was not a licence, it was a mere holiday let, with the consequence, in either case, that there was no security of tenure. After hearing evidence of the rather complex facts, the sheriff found in favour of the defenders. The case is an important decision on the lease/licence distinction. See **Commentary** p 155.

(49) Brucefield Estate Trustee Ltd v Computacenter (UK) Ltd
[2017] SC LIV 38, 2017 Hous LR 66

The doctrine of tacit relocation applies both (i) where the landlord wishes the lease to end at the ish but fails to serve timeous notice, and the tenant, who wishes to stay in the property, invokes the doctrine, and (ii) the other way round, ie where the tenant wishes to leave at the ish, but fails to serve timeous notice on the landlord, who wishes the lease to continue. The present case involved the second of these.

The action concerned a lease of commercial premises at Drummond Square, Brucefield South Industrial Park, Livingston, West Lothian. The lease seems to have been a 25-year lease beginning in 1990. The contractual ish was 29 May 2015. The tenant wished to remove as at the contractual ish, but did not send to the landlord a notice to that effect. The landlord took the view that, as a result, the lease continued for another 12 months by virtue of tacit relocation. It raised the present action seeking (i) declarator of tacit relocation, and (ii) payment of rent for the extra 12-month period. The sum sued for was £72,647.44.

The position of the tenant was clearly weak, but it came up with the argument that 'actions by (or on behalf of) the landlords ... made it clear that the landlords wished the lease to come to an end, and ... these actions were sufficient to prevent the lease continuing by tacit relocation': see para 11 of the judgment of Sheriff

Douglas Kinloch. This might have been presented as a personal bar defence, but in fact was presented as an argument that the landlord had, through actings, itself implicitly served notice. What were these actings? Paragraph 13 of the judgment quotes the defender's averment:

> In or around May 2012, the Defender was granted consent by the Pursuer to sublet the Premises to Lothian Recycling JS Ltd ('Lothian'). In or around February 2015, the Pursuer's property agent, Graeme Pollock of J A Pollock Property Consultants Ltd, contacted Simon Capaldi at Knight Frank. Mr Pollock contacted Mr Capaldi in order to inquire about the covenant strength of the then present subtenant of the premises, Lothian. Mr Pollock contacted Mr Capaldi on the belief that Mr Capaldi was instructed on behalf of the defender. Mr Capaldi understood that Mr Pollock was contacting him with a view to the continued occupation of Lothian in the premises at the end of the Defender's Lease with the Pursuer. Mr Capaldi intimated this information to Kevin Graham, Head of Facilities for the Defender. There was an effective communication transfer to the Defender.

The sheriff took the view that this averment, even if it could be proved, was simply irrelevant. At paras 18–19 he said:

> It is not averred on behalf of the tenants that the landlords themselves had any knowledge of any inquiry carried out by their agent. It is not averred by the tenants, for example, that the landlords instructed their agent to contact the tenants' agent. It is not even averred that the landlords knew that the discussions were taking place. Unless it is said that the agents were given express authority to act, or that there was implied authority, or that the principals subsequently ratified the agents' actings, it is difficult if not impossible to see that such discussions could ever be seen as a notice by or on behalf of the landlords. To my mind this is fundamental, and for that reason alone, it seems to me, the actings of the landlords' agent as founded upon by the tenants could not be sufficient to constitute notice to the tenants of the landlords' intention to terminate the lease.
>
> Even if I am wrong in that view, what is averred on behalf of the tenants is that the landlords' agent contacted the tenants' agent in order to 'inquire about' the ability of the subtenants to pay the rent. Even if this action could be seen to indicate that the landlords knew of the inquiry and were considering entering into a new lease with the subtenants, an inquiry about the subtenants' ability to pay the rent could never in my view amount to the 'explicit' notice to the tenants that the lease was being brought to an end. An inquiry is just that, an inquiry. It is not a definite and unconditional intimation to the tenants that the lease was being brought to an end. And so even if, as averred, an employee of the tenants became aware of the inquiry, all that was communicated to the tenants was the same inquiry and no more.

Accordingly he granted decree in favour of the pursuer.

Although the result was a success for the pursuer, one argument that was advanced by the pursuer was not successful, namely that any notice would have had to have been in writing, and so any actings would have been without effect in any case. The pursuer pointed to a provision of the lease that said that 'any notice, request or consent under this lease shall be in writing'. The sheriff did not consider that this extended to notices to quit, and moreover took the view that, as far as common law is concerned, such notices do not have to be in writing. We will not discuss here this aspect of the case other than to say that the question of whether and when a notice to quit must be in writing is one of some difficulty.

(50) City of Edinburgh Council v X
[2017] SC EDIN 50, 2017 SLT (Sh Ct) 225, 2017 Hous LR 61

Mr and Mrs X exercised the right to buy their flat from Edinburgh Council. Settlement took place on 10 June 2015. At that time there were rent arrears of £713.22. The new owners (and former tenants) declined to pay, and the Council sued. The defenders counterclaimed. They said that there had been a serious leak in the bathroom which had become apparent on 5 June 2015 and which had caused significant damage. The counterclaim was for the cost of repair, on the basis that the leak and consequent damage were the responsibility of the landlord in terms of the tenancy agreement. After proof it was held that the pursuer was liable to the defenders in the sum of £2,300, and consequently the net sum due by the pursuer to the defenders was £2,300, minus £713.22 (the rent arrears), ie £1,586.78. The case (decided by Sheriff William Holligan) has some interesting discussion of the effect on a lease contract where the tenant buys the property from the landlord.

(51) AB v CD
[2017] SAC (Civ) 32, 2017 GWD 36-559

The legislation about private-sector residential tenancies is, as everyone knows, often ignored in practice. In this case, involving a property in Balloch, Dunbartonshire, the landlord (i) was not a registered landlord (as to which see Antisocial Behaviour etc (Scotland) Act 2004 pt 8), (ii) did not provide the appropriate tenant information pack (as to which see 30A of the Housing (Scotland) Act 1988), and (iii) did not pay the deposit into an approved tenancy deposit scheme (as to which see the Tenancy Deposit Schemes (Scotland) Regulations 2011, SSI 2011/176). When the landlord sued the tenant for rent arrears, the tenant's defence was that the landlord's failures to comply with the various legislative provisions meant that the tenancy contract was illegal and thus void.

The sheriff rejected this defence and granted decree in favour of the landlord. The tenant appealed to the Sheriff Appeal Court, but the decision at first instance has been affirmed. The fact that the landlord was in breach of the relevant statutory provisions had various consequences, but the invalidity of the contract was not among them.

One may wonder whether the tenant's argument, had it been well-founded in law, might perhaps have been, in some respects, risky. If a contract is void, not only can there be no *liabilities* under it, but no *rights* either. Hence, for example the tenant (or on this hypothesis, the 'tenant') would presumably have turned out to have been an unlawful occupier.

So the landlord won, the court pronouncing decree in the sum of £787.50, and also holding the tenant liable in expenses. But just as a victory for the tenant might not have had a pure victory, so the victory for the landlord was not all that it seemed. Indeed, it may have been pyrrhic. We quote the last words of the judgment (para 26):

> The findings of the sheriff here suggest that criminal offences may have been committed by the respondent and I have directed that the Clerk of the Sheriff Appeal Court should forward the relevant papers in the case here to the procurator fiscal in order she may make further enquiries. I also consider that the circumstances surrounding this case may be relevant to a local authority in considering the suitability of the respondent to be registered as a landlord in terms of part 8 of the 2004 Act. I have therefore also directed the Clerk of the Sheriff Appeal Court to also forward the relevant papers to West Dunbartonshire Council who have registered the respondent as a landlord and to another Council where it was submitted to me he is acting as a landlord but is unregistered in order these councils may make further enquiries.

To give full significance to these words, against the background of the sum decerned for (£787.50), we note that unregistered residential landlords may be fined up to £50,000: see Antisocial Behaviour etc (Scotland) Act 2004 s 93(7) (as amended).

(52) Oag v Oag's Exrs
2017 GWD 25-423, Land Ct

Peter Oag owned two neighbouring farms in Caithness, Brims Mains and Burn of Brims. The farms were let to his brother William and the latter's wife, Ann, who were in partnership. Following William's death, Peter raised the present action of declarator that the lease was at an end.

It was a matter of concession that if the lease was to William and Ann as individuals, then the lease was not at an end, but that if it was to them as partners, it was at an end. The case thus turned on the interpretation of the lease. The heading of the lease read thus:

> MINUTE OF LEASE between PETER OAG, Senior and Mrs Jessie Martin Oag, both residing at West Park House, Wick, (hereinafter referred to as 'the landlords') on the one part: and WILLIAM ROBERTSON OAG and MRS ANN OAG, both residing at Brims Mains, Thurso, farming in partnership under the firm name of W and A Oag at Brims Mains aforesaid (hereinafter referred to as 'the tenants') on the other part.

The remainder of the lease did not, however, characterise the tenants as partners. (Or so it appears. We have not seen a full copy.) The court took the view that the lease was to the partnership (para 31):

> What our consideration of the lease comes to, therefore, is (i) that the clearest indication as to the identity of the tenant is the description contained in the instance, (ii) that it points to the tenant being the partnership, (iii) that the rest of the deed

contains nothing necessarily contrary or inimical to that interpretation and (iv) that the tenant was, therefore, the partnership.

The question of whether a lease to a partnership comes to an end with a death or other change in the membership of the firm is by no means straightforward. It is a matter for the interpretation of the lease, but as a rule of thumb, if the lease allows assignation, then it will survive, but if it does not allow assignation, it will not. Significant cases include *Inland Revenue v Graham's Trustees* 1971 SC (HL) 1, *Jardine-Paterson v Fraser* 1974 SLT 93, *Lujo Properties Ltd v Green* 1997 SLT 225, *Moray Estates Development Co v Butler* 1999 SLT 1338, and *Carter & MacIver v MacIver* 2010 SLCR 13. But whether the law is absolutely clear may be doubted. Some of the most incisive discussion is by Lord Maxwell in *Jardine-Paterson*, but what is said there is, we would suggest, not the last word.

It is easy to go wrong in this area. Thus even Professor J M Halliday (*Conveyancing Law and Practice* vol 2 (2nd edn, 1997) para 46–53) seems to have made an error when he wrote that 'where a lease is granted in favour of a partnership the death of a partner terminates the lease', which is true only in some cases. A short but we think generally correct summary of the law is given by Paton & Cameron (G C H Campbell and J G S Paton, *The Law of Landlord and Tenant in Scotland* (1967) p 64):

> There is no necessary connection between the endurance of the partnership and of a lease forming part of its assets. If part of the term of a lease is unexpired at the dissolution of the partnership and the lease is assignable, it is a partnership asset and should be distributed as such.

For further discussion see Angus McAllister, *Scottish Law of Leases* (4th edn, 2013) paras 9.13 ff and Robert Rennie (ed), *Leases* (2015) paras 8.06 ff.

There is a distinction between (i) a lease to a partnership, as a separate legal person, and (ii) a lease to trustees for the partnership. But this distinction tends, unfortunately, to be disregarded. For instance a common style is to grant the lease *both* to the firm *and* to its partners, which, frankly, makes little sense. (On this, see the comments of Lord Maxwell in *Jardine-Paterson*.) There is a logical case for saying that if a lease is to trustees, a change in the identity of the firm is *res inter alios acta* as far as the landlord is concerned. If that is right, the distinction between (i) a lease to a partnership, as a separate legal person, and (ii) a lease to trustees for the partnership, becomes particularly significant. But we cannot pursue this large subject further here.

(53) Lewis v Hunter
2017 GWD 19-308, Land Ct

This was an application to the Land Court for declarator of irritancy of an agricultural lease, of a farm at Castleside, Ashkirk, Selkirkshire, on the basis of various alleged breaches, such as failure to keep the farm properly stocked, failure to control thistles etc. The application was unsuccessful, the applicant having failed to prove her averments.

The court observed (para 50) that a landlord is not 'entitled to "store up" breaches ... from previous years, continue to accept rent tendered ... and then rely on those now historic breaches in a notice of irritancy'. The case also contains quite extensive discussion of whether breaches have to be material in order to justify irritancy.

STANDARD SECURITIES

(54) OneSavings Bank plc v Burns
[2017] SC BAN 20, 2017 SLT (Sh Ct) 129, 2017 Hous LR 55

There was a bulk assignation of standard securities. The deed did not follow the requirement of the Conveyancing and Feudal Reform (Scotland) Act 1970 that an assignation should include the words: 'to the extent of £... being the amount now due thereunder'. Instead, the deed said: 'to the extent of all sums now due or at any time or times hereafter to become due'. The assignee sought to enforce one of the assigned securities. The defender argued that the assignation was invalid and that accordingly the pursuer had no title to sue. This defence was upheld. See **Commentary** p 120.

(55) Shear v Clipper Holding II SARL
Outer House, 26 May 2017

A standard security was assigned using the same style as in the previous case. The debtor raised this action seeking interdict against enforcement on the ground that the assignation was invalid. The Lord Ordinary (Lord Bannatyne), disagreeing with *OneSavings*, refused to grant interdict. See **Commentary** p 122.

(56) Promontoria (Henrico) Ltd v Portico Holdings
[2018] SC GRE 5, 2018 GWD 6-87

A standard security was assigned using the same style as in the two previous cases. The sheriff (Derek Hamilton) also disagreed with *OneSavings*. See **Commentary** p 124.

(57) Royal Bank of Scotland plc v Mirza
[2017] SAC (Civ) 13, 2017 SLT (Sh Ct) 105, 2017 Hous LR 45

Where a creditor seeks to enforce a standard security over residential property, certain protections apply that do not apply in non-residential cases. But does this mean (i) any residential property, or (ii) only property used as a residence by the debtor (or by the grantor of the security, for occasionally the two may differ)? When the latest legislation on this topic was passed (Home Owner and Debtor Protection (Scotland) Act 2010) it was generally thought that (i) was right. But in *Westfoot Investments Ltd v European Property Holdings Inc* 2015 SLT (Sh Ct) 201, 2015 Hous LR 57 (*Conveyancing 2015* Case (69)) the view was taken that (ii) is right. In

that case a Panama company owned a residential property in Edinburgh and
let it out. When the company defaulted on a standard security over the property
the creditor sought to enforce. The sheriff, Tom Welsh, expressed the view that
the protective legislation was not engaged. For full discussion, see *Conveyancing
2016* pp 193–97. However, this was only a first-instance decision and moreover
the view expressed was probably only *obiter*. The matter has now come up in
an appellate case.

The detailed facts of the new case are unclear, but at all events there was a
standard security over a residential property. The owner and debtor was Mr
Mirza. But he did not live there. When he defaulted on the loan the creditor
sought to enforce and the question for the court was whether the protective
legislative was applicable. In an unreported decision, the sheriff (Paul Arthurson)
followed *Westfoot*. Mr Mirza appealed. The Sheriff Appeal Court has now, in a
very short judgment, affirmed the decision (para 4):

> We find ourselves in broad agreement with the reasoning and disposal in the court
> below. The kernel of the reasoning of the sheriff in *Westfoot Investments Ltd* on this
> point is located in 2015 SLT (Sh Ct) 208, para 24 of his judgment, where he states:
> 'However, property used for residential purposes is property used as a home. But
> whose home? . . . it must be a home used either by the grantor of the standard security
> or the maker of the obligation secured.' We would put the matter in a slightly different
> way. The mischief addressed by the 2010 Act and 2010 Order [the Application by
> Creditors (Pre-action Requirements) (Scotland) Order 2010, SSI 2010/317] is to give
> greater protection to such occupiers of security subjects. However, when one has
> regard to the scope and nature of the protective regime that is enacted, it is clear
> that not every occupier has the benefit of that regime. Since s 24(1B) is the process
> by which the protective regime is initiated, it follows that one requires to construe
> the applicability of the regime having regard to those persons intended to benefit
> by it. This generates an internal consistency within this part of the Act, as amended.
> The clause 'land used to any extent for residential purposes' admits in our view of
> a rather different and antecedent question to that posed by the sheriff in *Westfoot
> Investments Ltd*. That question is simply this: 'Were the subjects, to any extent, used
> for residential purposes?' This must always be a question of fact. In our view the
> word 'residential' qualifies the purpose rather than the property referred to in the
> clause. It follows that in certain circumstances security subjects may be occupied or
> unoccupied and yet remain residential in the sense that we have described. Factual
> presence in a property may not be a determinative factor. Temporary absence can
> and should be accommodated within the definition. The examples of a resident in a
> hospital or a hospice were helpfully raised in the discussion before us.

The legislation allows not only the debtor but also any 'entitled resident' to
'apply to the court': see Conveyancing and Feudal Reform (Scotland) Act 1970
s 24C. The present case, like *Westfoot*, did not involve any 'entitled resident'. But
we read the decision as meaning that where the property is not the debtor's home,
the protective regime as a whole is excluded, so that there can be no 'entitled
residents'. For instance at para 5 the court says that 'in the circumstances of this
case, the protective regime involves the debtor alone as the party who can come
to court and resist decree being taken'.

In cases such as these, what happens to the tenant? Of course, the property can be sold subject to the tenancy, and a buyer from the heritable creditor might well be happy to purchase a pre-let property: that will depend on various factors, especially on the rental level. But if the heritable creditor wishes to sell with vacant possession, some tricky issues can arise, discussion of which would, however, take us too far from the present topic.

(58) Burnside v Promontoria (Chestnut) Ltd
[2017] CSOH 157, 2018 GWD 2-35

Mr Burnside owned a portfolio of properties, which were rented out. He owed Clydesdale Bank money which was secured against these properties. In 2012 he was due to repay this money (which at that time amounted to £2,688,325) but was unable to do so. One might have expected that the bank would have begun to enforce the securities. That did not happen. Instead an agreement was entered into, of a type which we have never encountered before. Under this agreement the bank would organise the sale of the properties. Whether it had full agency powers (eg being able to execute the dispositions) is not clear. After the sale of the last property, the debt would be no more. Thus any shortfall would be written off. What if there was a surplus, ie what if the total proceeds of sale exceeded the debt? If we have read the case correctly, the bank would take the surplus. This seems to us a strange contract.

The contract did not lay down a timescale for the sales. It did, however, say that so long as any property remained unsold the rental income would be passed on by Mr Burnside to the bank, less any sums required for maintenance.

In 2015, ie after about three years, none of the properties had been sold. Why that was so is unclear. In that year the bank assigned its rights to Promontoria (Chestnut) Ltd. The assignation covered all the bank's contractual rights against Mr Burnside, plus the standard securities themselves. Whether the assignations were registered in the Land Register (or Register of Sasines) is not mentioned, but we assume that they were.

The properties thereafter remained unsold. In 2016 Promontoria intimated to Mr Burnside that it was rescinding the contract on account of his breach of contract, the breach being that he was allegedly failing to remit the rental income. Mr Burnside responded by raising the present action. In it he sought (i) declarator that the rescission was invalid, because he had in fact not been in material breach, and that the contract therefore remained in force, and (ii) specific implement against Promontoria to compel it to market the properties. In relation to (ii) he argued that, since the contract had no timescale for the marketing and sale of the properties, it was a matter of fair implication that this would be done within a reasonable time, and whilst he did not specify what that time was, his position was that whatever it may have been, it had clearly now been exceeded.

At this stage of the litigation the issue was whether a 'within a reasonable time' clause should fairly be implied into the contract. It was held by the Lord Ordinary (Lord Clark) that such a term should be implied. The case contains extensive discussion of this point. The case now proceeds to proof before answer.

The story is a puzzling one. The contract is strange. The fact that the properties were then not sold is strange. We can offer no explanations.

Finally, one issue that was not raised in the case is perhaps of interest. In general, and subject to exceptions, rights can be assigned, but not obligations. The bank's right to sell the properties could thus be assigned. But it is not obvious that its obligation to do so could be. But it may well be that there is an answer to this in the background documentation that does not appear in the case.

(59) NRAM plc v Cordiner
[2017] SAC (Civ) 27, 2017 SLT (Sh Ct) 217, 2017 Hous LR 100

This case concerned a narrow technical point, which could very seldom arise, in the enforcement of standard securities. The pursuer wished to enforce a standard security over residential property. It obtained decree. There was some minor technical error in the decree (what the error was is not reported) and the decree was then recalled and an amended decree granted. One of the two debtors then sought recall of the (new) decree, invoking s 24D of the Conveyancing and Feudal Reform (Scotland) Act 1970. The sheriff rejected the application for recall. The debtor appealed, but without success. It was held that s 24D, whether interpreted literally or purposively, was inapplicable.

(60) J H & W Lamont of Heathfield Farm v Chattisham Ltd
[2017] CSOH 119, 2017 GWD 30-470

The owners of land with development potential entered into a contract with a development company whereby the latter, in exchange for an advance payment, acquired an option to buy the land. The owners granted to the developer a standard security, securing its obligations under the option agreement. Planning permission for development was never obtained, and the option period eventually came to an end. The owners asked for the standard security to be discharged. The developer refused, claiming that the owners had been in material breach of their obligations under the contract, and claiming, moreover, substantial damages for that alleged breach. The developer argued that the standard security must be understood as being a valid security in respect of the money due in terms of the damages claim. It was held that, whatever the position might be as to alleged breach by the owners, the standard security fell to be discharged. See **Commentary** p 136.

(61) First Time Ltd v Denmore Investments Ltd
[2017] SAC (Civ) 4, 2017 GWD 5-64

This case was mainly about whether a guarantee can be attacked as being a gratuitous alienation, an issue on which the leading case is *Jackson v Royal Bank of Scotland* 2002 SLT 1123. No final decision was reached at this stage of the litigation. The reason we mention the case here is that it involved something that has cropped up more than once in recent years: whether an obligation owed by

X to Y can be validly secured by a standard security by X to Z, with Z in some way holding the standard security for the benefit of Y. In this case Denmore Investments Ltd granted a standard security in favour of First Construction Ltd 'for itself and as security trustee for itself and First Time Ltd'. In this case the issues were not, at least at this stage of the litigation, brought into focus. For full discussion of these issues see *Conveyancing 2016* pp 144–49. (For another split between security and secured obligation see *Onesavings Bank plc v Burns*, Case (54) above.)

SOLICITORS AND SURVEYORS

(62) Soofi v Dykes
[2017] CSOH 2, 2017 GWD 2-14 affd [2017] CSIH 40, 2017 GWD 21-332

In 2008 a company called Bonafied Enterprises International Ltd ('BEI') bought a petrol station (with car wash and shop) in Alexander Street, Airdrie, the seller being a Ms Young. The price was £450,000 for the heritable property, £385,000 for the goodwill, and £15,000 for fixtures and fittings. The business did not do as well as the buyer, Bonafied (a curious anagram of 'bona fide'), had hoped. The company went into administration in 2010 and was later dissolved. In the present action the pursuer, as assignee of Bonafied, claimed damages for professional negligence against the solicitor who had acted in the purchase. The nub of the pursuer's case is set out in para 2 of the judgment of the Lord Ordinary (Lord Mulholland):

> In advance of the purchase BEI had obtained from the seller financial information relating to the trading history of the business, which financial information was used inter alia for the purpose of valuing the business including the goodwill. The pursuer avers that the defender failed to have included in the missives a provision to warrant the accuracy and completeness of the financial information provided by the seller and relied on by BEI in the purchase. The pursuer further avers that the defender failed to take any steps to advise BEI as to whether it should seek such a warranty, or obtain the informed instructions of BEI as to whether it should seek such a warranty. It is averred in the pleadings that such warranties are commonly sought and granted in transactions of this nature and had the defender displayed the skill and care to be expected of an ordinarily competent solicitor, advice would have been tendered to the purchaser that such a warranty should be sought from the seller. The defender denies negligence. The pursuer's case is twofold. The principal case is a no transaction case, namely that had such a warranty been sought the seller would not have agreed to it and as a result the purchase would not have taken place. The alternative case is that had such a warranty been provided, the purchaser would have an action against the seller for breach of warranty.

At this stage of the case the point at issue was whether the pursuer's written pleadings should be dismissed as lacking in specification. The Lord Ordinary held against the defender on this point, who reclaimed. The Inner House has now affirmed the Lord Ordinary's decision.

Much of the factual background is unclear. It is not clear, for example, what the relationship was between Mr Soofi and the company.

Since it was averred that the seller had provided financial information about the business, that this information was not accurate, and that BEI had relied on that information, one wonders whether any claim against the seller under the doctrine of misrepresentation was considered.

(63) Hood v Council of the Law Society of Scotland
[2017] CSIH 21, 2017 SC 386, 2017 SCLR 799

This case was about a complaint against a solicitor, identified as 'WR'. It is difficult to read the case without feeling some sympathy for WR, but perhaps less so for the complainer. In the event the complaint failed. It was, at the first instance, referred by the Scottish Legal Complaints Commission to the Law Society of Scotland, which rejected it. The complainer then appealed to the Scottish Solicitors' Discipline Tribunal. The Tribunal affirmed the decision of the Law Society. The complainer then appealed to the Inner House. The latter has affirmed the decision of the Tribunal. We understand that in cases of this sort expenses are not awarded against an unsuccessful complainer. Different people will have different views about the merits of that rule.

Mr and Mrs Hood were co-owners of a house in Baillieston, Glasgow. They split up. The separation was acrimonious. At one stage one of the parties seems to have raised an action for division and sale, but details of that are obscure and in any event that action seems to have had little direct bearing on what then unfolded. Eventually an informal agreement was reached whereby the property would be sold, at an upset price of £100,000. The sale was to be handled by the wife's law agent, WR. A minute of agreement between Mr and Mrs Hood, dealing with the proposed sale, was drafted but never signed. WR began to market the property on or about 23 October 2013 at a fixed price of £115,000. He had, over the previous months, kept Mr Hood's law agents informed of what was happening. But when the property went on the market, Mr Hood objected and insisted that it be taken off the market, which accordingly happened on 26 November 2013. (We take it that Mrs Hood wished the property to remain on the market, but no specific information is available on this point.) So far as appears from the report, no offers had been received by that date, let alone any missives entered into. What happened to the property thereafter is not known to us. Was it eventually sold on the basis of a new agreement? Or was the action of division and sale continued with? Did one party perhaps agree to sell her/ his share to the other (a possibility that had been discussed at an earlier stage)? Are the parties still at loggerheads? We do not know.

What we do know is that Mr Hood launched a complaint against WR. The nub of the complaint was as follows (we quote from para 2 of the Inner House judgment):

WR and the firm of WR & Co Ltd commenced marketing the Property for sale without obtaining the petitioner's consent or instructions as a joint owner of the Property and in the absence of any minute of agreement between the petitioner and his wife, the co-proprietor, concerning the arrangements for sale of the Property and division of the net proceeds of sale ... WR purported to act for the petitioner in the marketing of the Property for sale without issuing a terms of engagement letter or marketing agreement to the petitioner in a situation where that was an actual or potential conflict of interest in WR's acting for both the petitioner and his wife.

WR's position, in response, was that the correspondence in the months leading up to October 2013 meant that it was reasonable for the property to be placed on the market even though there had as yet been no minute of agreement or letter of engagement.

The Inner House said (para 19):

The tribunal's task was not to decide whether WR was correct in his legal and factual analysis of the transaction involving the sale of the petitioner and his wife's matrimonial home. It was rather to decide whether or not WR was guilty of unsatisfactory professional conduct: whether or not his conduct was 'of the standard which could reasonably be expected of a competent and reputable solicitor'. In analysing a legal transaction, a solicitor may make an error of law, or may be mistaken as to factual matters. Errors of that nature do not necessarily amount to unsatisfactory professional conduct. They may amount to professional negligence, although in some cases they may not even reach that standard. The present case concerns aspects of the law of agency: whether WR and his firm had authority to market the property. We do not think that it was necessary for either the tribunal or the respondents' sub-committee to embark on a detailed analysis of whether as a matter of law WR had authority at any particular time to proceed with marketing. What matters is whether a competent and reputable solicitor in his position would have considered that he did have sufficient authority to market the property.

Having set out that approach the court agreed with the approach of the Tribunal. On the marketing issue it said (para 22):

The tribunal decided that, on the basis of the correspondence that was available, it was reasonable for the sub-committee to take the view that authority to market the property was provided by the correspondence considered as a whole. In our opinion that conclusion is clearly justified.

The court then turned (paras 27 and 28) to:

WR's purporting to act for the petitioner in marketing the property without issuing a terms of engagement letter or marketing agreement, in a situation where there was an actual or potential conflict of interest. The discipline tribunal held that the sub-committee had taken a correct approach in making its decision on this matter. The property had been on the market for a short period before it was withdrawn from the market, and the tribunal thought that it was reasonable to hold that a single failure to issue a terms of business letter did not amount to unsatisfactory professional conduct. So far as potential conflict was concerned, the sub-committee had given adequate reasons: both parties wanted the property to be sold and therefore there was no conflict of interest ... The tribunal's reasoning ... cannot be faulted. It involved an evaluative judgment as to whether the failure to issue a terms of business letter in the particular circumstances of the case amounted to unsatisfactory professional conduct. That was a matter that fell particularly within the expertise of a professional disciplinary body, and we can see no reason to interfere with its decision.

(64) MP Burke Transport Ltd v Charles Scott & Partners LLP
[2017] CSOH 67, 2017 GWD 14-214

The pursuer wished to buy two warehouses in Paisley. A valuation report was obtained. It gave a value of £550,000. And it said:

> The property generally appeared to be in a reasonable condition commensurate with age; however we did note during the course of our inspection that there were a number of cracks located at various points of the former bonded stores together with steel structural bracing to the rear of Unit 7C. We recommend that a structural survey is undertaken to determine the full extent of the cracking and to ascertain whether this is of a structural or progressive nature.

The defender, a firm of structural engineers, was then instructed by the pursuer, and received a copy of the valuation report. It inspected the property, but its inspection did not cover the roof. Its report included the following:

> Charles Scott and Partners were commissioned by Martin Burke of MP Burke Transport to undertake a non-disruptive structural investigation of the properties at Abercorn Street, Paisley PA3 4WH. We were requested to make specific comment on the reported cracking of the external walls of the two warehouses at the above property. We understand that MP Burke Transport is in the process of acquiring the properties from Chivas Brothers Limited.

The report was detailed and identified several problems that needed to be addressed, including certain minor issues with the roof, but mentioned no structural problems with the roof. The pursuer went ahead and bought the property. It then turned out that there were serious problems with the roof, and the pursuer made a substantial claim for damages against the firm of structural engineers. The case turned mainly on what had been said in the telephone conversation between Mr Burke (of the pursuer) and Mr Hughes (of the defender) in which the structural report had been instructed. That conversation was not recorded and had taken place a considerable time before the litigation, so memories had possibly faded somewhat. One piece of recorded evidence, however, was that immediately after the conversation a confirmatory email had been sent to the defender asking it to 'carry out a structural report'.

The Lord Ordinary (Lord Tyre) came to the conclusion that, in the light of the whole circumstances of the case, the pursuer had instructed a survey that would include the roof. This, however, was not conclusive of liability: as the Lord Ordinary observed at para 19, 'nothing in this opinion should be taken as the expression of any view as to what an inspection of the roof of these premises by a reasonably competent structural engineer would or ought to have consisted of,

or what it would or ought to have disclosed. If disputed, those will be matters
for inquiry on another occasion.'

(65) Gordon v Campbell Riddell Breeze Paterson LLP
[2017] UKSC 75, 2017 SLT 1287

In negligence claims, negative prescription is often pled as a defence, and where
it is so pled there is often a question as to the proper *terminus a quo*, that is to say
the date when the prescriptive clock began to tick, the defender arguing for an
early date and the pursuer for a later date.

The pursuers owned three fields in Killearn, Stirlingshire, all let to the same
tenant under three separate leases. It seems that the pursuers were not so much
interested in the rental income as in the fact that the fields had development
potential.

They instructed their solicitors to serve notices to quit. The three notices were
served on 8 November 2004, to take effect on 10 November 2005. The tenant did
not remove, and the pursuers raised an action, in the Land Court, for removing.
In respect of two of the fields the action failed. The reason was that the notices
had been fatally defective. They had designed the tenant as 'the Firm of Messrs
A & J C Craig and John C Craig, sole proprietor of and trustee for said Firm'.
Although at one stage the fields had indeed been let to the firm of Messrs A &
J C Craig, that had been long ago, and the current tenant was John Campbell
Craig as an individual. We pause to note that it is a familiar fact that whilst there
can be a company with only one shareholder, there cannot be a partnership with
only one partner.

The owners sought damages from their law agents for professional negligence.
The action, which was raised on 17 May 2012, was defended on the merits but
also on the basis of negative prescription. The issue boiled down to whether
the five-year period had begun to run in November 2008, when the Land Court
issued its ruling, in which case the present action had been raised timeously,
or whether the period had begun to run in November 2004, when the invalid
notices were served, or perhaps in November 2005, in either of which cases the
action had been raised too late.

The Lord Ordinary (Lord Jones) held that any claim that the pursuers might
have had had been extinguished by negative prescription: see [2015] CSOH 31,
2015 GWD 12-216 (*Conveyancing 2015* Case (74)). The pursuers reclaimed, but
without success: see [2016] CSIH 16, 2016 SC 548 (*Conveyancing 2016* Case (63)). The
pursuers then appealed to the Supreme Court, but the latter has now affirmed
the decision of the courts below. The opinion was given by Lord Hodge, with
whom the other justices concurred.

We will not enter into the complexities of calculating when the prescriptive
clock begins to tick, as to which the law was radically re-interpreted by the
Supreme Court in *David T Morrison & Co Ltd (t/a Gael Home Interiors) v ICL Plastics
Ltd* [2014] UKSC 48, 2014 SC (UKSC) 222. But as Lord Hodge notes at para 25, the
Scottish Law Commission published its Report on *Prescription* (Scot Law Com
No 247) in July 2017 in which legislative reform is recommended.

(66) The Law Society of England and Wales v Schubert Murphy
[2017] EWCA Civ 1295, [2017] 4 WLR 200

Property in a London suburb, Hadley Wood, was offered for sale, and Mr Kristofi (in some sources spelt Christofi) made a successful bid at a price of £735,000. His law firm, Messrs Schubert Murphy, was a genuine law firm, but the seller's law firm, 'Acorn Solicitors', was fake. It gave every appearance, however, of being genuine, and the fraudster who ran it evidently knew what he was doing. Messrs Schubert Murphy commendably checked 'Acorn Solicitors' on the Law Society's website, and found it listed there. The transaction proceeded. Messrs Schubert Murphy handed over the money. 'Acorn Solicitors' together with the money vanished into thin air. There was extensive fallout, which we do not seek to enter into here, except to note that Mr Kristofi sued Messrs Schubert Murphy, and eventually the case was settled, by the latter's insurer, at the sum of £500,000. We do not know the basis for this figure, but we understand that Mr Kristofi did recover at least some money from certain other persons involved. The insurer then raised the present action (doing so in the name of the insured) against the Law Society of England and Wales, the basis of the action being, of course, that Messrs Schubert Murphy had relied upon false information issued by the Law Society.

At first instance the question was, in Scottish terms, one of relevancy. The High Court found the action to be relevant: see [2014] EWHC 4561 (QB), [2015] PNLR 15 (*Conveyancing 2015* Case (78)). The Law Society appealed. The Court of Appeal has now affirmed that decision. The case remains to be decided on the merits. For a fuller account of the fraud, see *Conveyancing 2015* p 172.

SPECIAL DESTINATIONS

(67) Machin's Tr v Machin
[2017] SC GLA 29, 2017 GWD 15-253

Mr and Mrs Machin bought a flat, taking title equally between them and the survivor of them. Some years later Mr Machin died and his widow became his executor. It turned out that Mr Machin had extensive debts, and his widow decided that the only way forward was for his estate to be sequestrated. The trustee in sequestration then raised the present action, seeking payment from her of one half of the value of the flat (as at the date of the death), being the half that she had inherited from her late husband by virtue of the special destination. The flat was, said the trustee, worth £53,998, and so, he said, she had to pay to him £26,999.

Mrs Machin defended the action both on the law and on the facts. It was held that her defence on the law failed, and that she was in principle liable, but as to the facts, including what valid debts of the estate there were, proof was allowed. See **Commentary** p 182.

BOUNDARIES AND POSITIVE PRESCRIPTION

(68) Munro v Keeper of the Registers of Scotland
2017 GWD 17-277, Lands Tr

In a disposition recorded in the Register of Sasines in 1982, the property (in Midlothian) was described (i) by plan and (ii) by a statement as to area. A plot, the ownership of which was disputed, was excluded from (i) though could not be said to be excluded from (ii), which stated a larger area than was encompassed within (i). It was held that the disposition did not provide a *habile* title to the disputed plot for the purposes of prescription. See **Commentary** p 179.

[Another aspect of this case is digested at p 27 above.]

(69) Lane v Irvin Mitchell Trust Corporation Ltd
29 March 2017, Dumfries Sheriff Court

This was a dispute between neighbours as to whether a boundary hedge lay within the property of the pursuers or the property of the defenders, or indeed whether the boundary lay at the mid-point. See **Commentary** p 187.

[Another aspect of this case is digested at p 11 above.]

NEIGHBOUR LAW

(70) Green v Chalmers
[2017] SAC (Civ) 8, 2017 SLT (Sh Ct) 69

The circumstances of this case cannot be better described than by Sheriff Principal I R Abercrombie QC giving the Opinion of the Sheriff Appeal Court (paras 1–3):

> This case is about the neighbours who fell out in spectacular style. The pursuers and appellants live at Gowdiehill Farmhouse, Bankfoot. The defenders and respondents farm land adjacent to the farmhouse. After proof the sheriff found that, between July 2010 and June 2014, the defenders, or one or other of them, engaged in an intentional course of harassment of the pursuers, by committing the following acts: poisoning the pursuers' dog with rat poison; killing their pot plants by spraying weed killer on them; spraying their western boundary hedge with chemicals, damaging it; carrying out significantly noisy operations using a grain dryer operated by a tractor engine into the early hours of the morning or throughout the night; causing grain dust to adversely affect the pursuers' subjects; positioning grain dryers, combine harvesters and a cattle trailer close to the pursers' boundary for no apparent reason, so that they were easily visible to and had a visual impact upon the pursuers; further deliberate spraying of weedkiller on their hedge and birch saplings in July 2011 and the spring of 2012 damaging and killing some of them; sealing the lid of the pursuers' septic tank with silicone; positioning a tractor with its raised forks, plastic tanks and a large 'bogey' trailer in a tipped position, without reason, close to the pursuers' property so that they were clearly visible from the pursuers' house;

intentionally opening, unwrapping and leaving silage bales close to the pursuers' boundary so that they would deteriorate and create a foul smell which was very noticeable in the pursuers' garden and house; driving a tractor at speed towards the second pursuer when she was weeding the hedge; positioning two harrowers for no reason close to the pursuers' boundary so that they were clearly visible from the pursuers' house; leaving a bogey filled with cattle dung close to the pursuers' boundary for 18 days causing an unpleasant smell which prevented the pursuers from sitting in their garden or opening their windows and regularly burning rubbish including plastics, causing unpleasant acrid smoke and smells to permeate the pursuers' house.

In cases such as this a possible remedy lies under the common law of nuisance. But as the defenders' conduct went beyond mere nuisance to a deliberate and sustained programme of hostility, the pursuers sued under the Protection from Harassment Act 1997. Before the sheriff they were successful to the extent of obtaining an award of £3,000 in damages. But the sheriff declined to grant interdict from further acts of harassment on various grounds, including that the previous acts were one-off and unlikely to be repeated, and the fact that the pursuers had installed CCTV which acted as a significant deterrent. The pursuers appealed, and the Sheriff Appeal Court has now allowed the appeal. As the Appeal Court pointed out (para 38), 'just because the respondents may not have repeated a specific act for several years, it does not follow that their harassment of the appellants has ceased. As is readily apparent from the findings in fact there appears to be no end to the defenders' ingenuity in finding ways to harass the pursuers'.

(71) Woolley v Akram
[2017] SC EDIN 7, 2017 SC 642, 2017 SLT (Sh Ct) 175, 2017 SCLR 647

CCTV is not in itself objectionable. But where the cameras are trained, not on one's own property but on the property of one's neighbours, it may be a different matter. That was the situation in this case. The pursuers and the defender owned, respectively, the upper and lower flats of a semi-detached house. The pursuers lived in their flat; the defender operated a guest-house business in hers. Relations between the parties were not good, and there had been complaints to the police from both sides. The breakdown in relations seems to have started in 2013 at around the time that the pursuers, Anthony and Deborah Woolley, successfully objected to the proposal of the defender, Nahid Akram, to change the guest house into a bail hostel for up to 18 people.

Following the breakdown in relations, the defender installed a CCTV system comprising four cameras and four audio boxes. The cameras recorded anyone entering the pursuers' house, as well as activities in the pursuers' rear garden. The audio boxes picked up conversations outside the pursuers' house and also, probably, some conversation inside because two of the audio boxes were installed immediately beneath the front bedroom windows. The data so collected were retained for five days, this being the maximum storage capacity of the defender's system.

In this action the pursuers claimed that the defender had been a 'data controller' since October 2013, and as such had processed personal data, namely audio and video footage of the pursuers' property and family activities in breach of various provisions of the Data Protection Act 1998. The pursuers sought damages in respect of emotional distress in terms of s 13 of the Act. In particular, the pursuers argued that the defender had breached three of the data protection principles set out in sch 1 to the Act, namely: (a) the first principle ('personal data shall be processed lawfully and fairly ...'); (b) the third principle ('personal data shall be adequate, relevant and not excessive in relation to the purpose or purposes for which they are processed'); and (c) the fifth principle ('personal data processed for any purpose or purposes shall not be kept for longer than is necessary for that purpose or purposes').

After a proof the sheriff (N A Ross) held that all three principles had been breached and that damages should be awarded. The basis that should be used for calculating damages was unclear but the sheriff was willing to accede to the method chosen by the pursuers, which was to seek an award of £10 each for every day but under deduction of the one month per year when the pursuers were away on holiday. 'I have no doubt' commented the sheriff at para 116, 'that an award of compensation to each of the pursuers is merited. They have suffered a relatively extreme breach of the Act. The effect on their daily lives has been long-running and debilitating.' This produced a total of £8,634 for each of the pursuers, and damages in that amount were awarded.

INHIBITIONS

(72) MacMillan v T Leith Developments Ltd
[2017] CSIH 23, 2017 SC 642, 2017 SLT 415, 2017 SCLR 477

Though not a conveyancing case, this decision merits brief mention here. Mr and Mrs MacMillan bought a new house in Ayr Road, Giffnock, Glasgow, from T Leith Developments Ltd, the transaction settling in July 2010. The price is not known. It quickly became apparent that there were major defects in the house. Whether there was an NHBC certificate (or similar) is not known, but perhaps there was not, since the MacMillans were left to pursue the company for compensation. They raised an action in September 2006 and immediately inhibited. In November 2010 (why the action took more than four years we do not know) they obtained decree against the company in the sum of £333,993.42 plus interest and expenses.

But obtaining decree and obtaining payment are not the same thing. In 2000 the company had granted a floating charge to Clydesdale Bank plc and in February 2011 the bank appointed a receiver. (Perhaps surprisingly the bank did not also hold a standard security.) But while the floating charge thus pre-dated the inhibition, all sums secured by the floating charge were lent by the bank after the date of the inhibition. A few months later the company went into liquidation. By this time the only assets of significance held by the company were two unsold plots of land in Ayr Road, and, needless to say, the value of these plots was considerably less than the sums owed to creditors, the chief of whom were the bank and the MacMillans.

Mr MacMillan (by this stage his wife had passed away, and he was acting partly for himself as an individual and partly as his late wife's executor) raised the present action, seeking declarator that the inhibition was 'effectually executed diligence' in terms of s 60 of the Insolvency Act 1986, with consequences for the ranking.

The main difficulty for the pursuer was that in *Lord Advocate v Royal Bank of Scotland* 1977 SC 155 the Inner House had held that an arrestment which had not been followed up by furthcoming by the time that the debtor company went into receivership was not 'effectually executed diligence' under the equivalent provisions that were already in existence prior to the Insolvency Act 1986. That decision had been heavily criticised at the time but was never overruled.

In the Outer House the Lord Ordinary (Lord Tyre) was of course bound by *Lord Advocate v Royal Bank of Scotland* but nevertheless held in favour of the pursuer. The Inner House has now also held in favour of the pursuer but has also overruled *Lord Advocate v Royal Bank of Scotland*.

INSOLVENCY

(73) Fortune's Tr v Cooper Watson Ltd
[2017] CSOH 74, 2017 GWD 15-244

Mr Fortune owned various properties, and granted a variety of deeds relating to them. Following his sequestration these were challenged by his trustee in sequestration as having been gratuitous alienations. The challenge was successful: *Fortune's Tr v Medwin Investments Ltd and Cooper Watson Ltd* [2016] CSIH 49, 2016 SC 824 (*Conveyancing 2016* Case (75)).

But one property remained to be dealt with, because it involved a line of defence not relevant to the other properties, and it was this property that was the subject of the present case. The defender argued that the property had fallen out of the sequestration by virtue of s 39A of the Bankruptcy (Scotland) Act 1985 (since replaced by s 112 of the Bankruptcy (Scotland) Act 2016) whereby, if the trustee does nothing in relation to a 'family home' for three years, then the property shall 'cease to form part of the debtor's sequestrated estate'. The question for the court was whether this property had indeed been the 'family home' of the debtor and his cohabitant at the time of the sequestration. It was held, following proof, that it had, as a matter of fact, not been the family home, so that s 39A was inapplicable, and accordingly decree reducing the disposition was pronounced.

(74) Nolan v Nolan's Tr
[2017] SAC (Civ) 25, 2017 GWD 26-428

Mr Nolan and Ms Collins, described as 'partners', were both sequestrated. Their trustee wished to sell the house that they owned and where they lived, in Bonkle

Road, Newmains, Wishaw, Lanarkshire. They declined to flit, and accordingly the trustee raised the present action of removing. Decree passed against them in the sheriff court, and they appealed to the Sheriff Appeal Court, which has affirmed the judgment of the sheriff. Their allegation of bias against the sheriff was unsuccessful, but here we are concerned with two other issues.

The first is the argument that the continued occupation of the house by Mr Nolan and Ms Collins was protected by Article 8 (privacy) of the European Convention on Human Rights. Attempts to run that argument have been made in the past, but without success, against public-sector landlords seeking to remove tenants after the end of a tenancy: see in particular *Hounslow LBC v Powell* [2011] UKSC 8, [2011] 2 AC 186 and *McKenna v South Lanarkshire Council* [2012] CSIH 78, 2013 SC 212 (*Conveyancing 2012* Case (50)). They have also been made, equally without success, against private-sector landlords seeking to remove tenants after the end of a tenancy: see in particular *McDonald v McDonald* [2016] UKSC 28, [2017] AC 273 (*Conveyancing 2016* Case (42)). Again, they have been made, equally without success, against secured lenders seeking to enforce their security after default: see eg *Horsham Properties Group Ltd v Clark* [2008] EWHC 2327, [2009] 1 WLR 1255. But as far as we can recall, the argument has until now not been tried as against a trustee in sequestration (or trustee in bankruptcy, in English law). Readers may not be surprised to learn that the Sheriff Appeal Court had no difficulty in rejecting the argument.

The other issue concerns a remark about the relationship of sequestration to a standard security, made in response to an argument by the debtors that 'the heritable creditor (the Clydesdale Bank) would be the only person to gain from the sale of their property there being insufficient value in it to satisfy any other creditor' (para 52). It is difficult to see precisely what the argument was supposed to have been, but presumably it was that where there is negative equity the trustee cannot sell. In response, the court said this (para 54):

> The property is no longer vested in their [the debtors'] bank as their heritable creditor or mortgage holder. Once the respondent was appointed as Trustee, the property vested in him. He is the owner of it. The bank, of course, still has an interest in the property that interest being the recovery of the funds borrowed from it by the appellants. However that does not prevent the respondent from seeking recovery of the appellants' home and selling it.

With respect, this is not quite right. What is right is that where there is a security such as a standard security, the general position is that *both* the secured creditor *and* the trustee have power of sale. The fact (if it was indeed a fact) that the property was in negative equity would have been irrelevant. So the court was right to dismiss this 'argument'. What is not quite right is what is said about vesting. A standard security is a subordinate real right. The principal real right, the real right of ownership, remains vested in the debtor. There are thus two real rights in the property. If the debtor is sequestrated, that, for the time being, does not alter either real right. The debtor still holds the real right of ownership and the creditor still holds the real right of security. To say that 'the property is no longer vested in their [the debtors'] bank' is not correct. The property itself never was vested in the bank. What was vested in the bank was the security and that remained vested in the bank the day after the sequestration just as it was the day before it. Moreover, it is not accurate to say that 'once the respondent was appointed as Trustee, the property vested in him. He is the owner of it'. Sequestration does vest the estate in the trustee, but the effect of that vesting, in property terms, varies according to the type of property in question. Ownership of corporeal moveable property does pass immediately, but ownership of heritable property does not. The debtor remains owner until either the trustee completes title, or the property is sold. Of course, the debtor's ownership is drained of most of its significance, for the rights and powers normally incident to ownership are taken from him. But that fact does not mean that ownership of heritable property passes to the trustee upon appointment: it does not. Of course, these points do not detract from the correctness of the court's decision, and no doubt the court was not, in any case, trying to set out a precise statement of the position in property terms. We do not wish to criticise, but rather to head off any misunderstanding that might perhaps arise from these *dicta*.

MISCELLANEOUS

(75) Argyll & Bute Council v Gordon
[2017] SAC (Civ) 6, 2017 SLT (Sh Ct) 53

This case concerned a small aspect of a large subject. The large subject is about residential care costs and the question of their recoverability by the local authority. The small aspect is an essentially procedural question.

Mrs Jean Duncan-Jones owned a house in Kilmartin, Argyll. On 3 June 2005 she went into residential care at Ardfenaig Residential Home, Ardrishaig, Lochgilphead. On 7 June 2005 she concluded missives for the gratuitous transfer of her house to friends, Mr and Mrs Gordon. To have missives where there is a donation is unusual; we do not know the reason. Title was transferred later in the year. The property was unencumbered. From the date of her admission to residential care until 10 January 2010 Mrs Duncan-Jones paid the care charges out of her own resources, the total paid in the period being £167,000. At the latter date her resources were exhausted, and from then on the costs fell on Argyll and Bute Council, this continuing until her death on 4 January 2013. The Council then claimed from Mrs and Mrs Gordon in respect of the costs of care from 10 January 2010 to 4 January 2013, founding on s 21(1) of the Health and Social Services and Social Security Adjudications Act 1983, which provides that:

> Subject to the following provisions of this section, where –
> (a) a person avails himself of Part III accommodation; and
> (b) that person knowingly and with the intention of avoiding charges for the accommodation –

> (i) has transferred any asset to which this section applies to some other person or persons not more than six months before the date on which he begins to reside in such accommodation; or
>
> (ii) transfers any such asset to some other person or persons while residing in the accommodation; and
>
> (c) either –
>
> (i) the consideration for the transfer is less than the value of the asset; or
>
> (ii) there is no consideration for the transfer,

the person or persons to whom the asset is transferred by the person availing himself of the accommodation shall be liable to pay to the local authority providing the accommodation or arranging for its provision the difference between the amount assessed as due to be paid for the accommodation by the person availing himself of it and the amount which the local authority receive from him for it.

The sum claimed from Mr and Mrs Gordon by the Council was £42,750. This was much less than the value of the Kilmartin house, even at the time of the donation in 2005: deductions were made to reach this figure, but details on this point are not available to us.

The Gordons denied liability, offering a substantive defence why s 23 was not applicable to the facts of the case. The Council argued that the sheriff court could not consider this defence, but had to grant decree automatically, and that if the Gordons wished their defence to be heard they would have to raise an action of judicial review in the Court of Session.

The sheriff held against the Council on this procedural point: see 2016 SLT (Sh Ct) 196, 2016 SCLR 192, discussed in *Conveyancing 2016* Case (78), where more detail about the case is given. But before the substantive issue in dispute between the Council and the Gordons could be heard, the Council appealed to the Sheriff Appeal Court on the procedural point. The Sheriff Appeal Court has now affirmed the decision of the court *a quo*. The matter thus now returns to the sheriff, for the substantive issue to be determined

(76) Cleghorn v Duncan
[2017] CSOH 114, 2017 SLT 1189

James Duncan was a career criminal. Following his conviction in 2007 for drug offences and for murder, a confiscation order was made under the Proceeds of Crime Act 2002 in the sum of £159,248.66, to be paid within six months. (We will not enter into the unfathomable mysteries of how the 2002 Act directs such figures to be calculated.) Over the years part of this was paid, but not all. Eventually Mr Cleghorn, CA, was appointed as 'enforcement administrator' under s 128 of the Proceeds of Crime Act 2002, and he sought the authority of the court to sell a property in Douglas Street, Blantyre, Lanarkshire, and also to remove the occupants. The property was owned by Mr Duncan, though he no longer lived there, being provided accommodation at the public expense in another part of Lanarkshire, namely Shotts. The person who lived in the property in Blantyre was his former wife, Margaret, and her granddaughter.

Mr and Mrs Duncan had divorced in 1980, but thereafter had experienced an off-and-on relationship.

In defence Mrs Duncan invoked s 98 of the 2002 Act which provides certain protections where realisation is sought of 'the family home':

> On an application being made to it … the court, after having regard to all the circumstances of the case including –
>
> (a) the needs and financial resources of the spouse or former spouse of the person concerned;
> (b) the needs and financial resources of any child of the family;
> (c) the length of the period during which the family home has been used as a residence by any of the persons referred to in paragraph (a) or (b),
>
> may refuse to grant the application or may postpone the granting of the application for such period (not exceeding 12 months) as it may consider reasonable in the circumstances or may grant the application subject to such conditions as it may prescribe.

This is loosely modelled on s 40 of the Bankruptcy (Scotland) Act 1985 (now s 113 of the Bankruptcy (Scotland) Act 2016) and, quite rightly, the court considered the case law that exists in relation to that provision.

Mrs Duncan set forth the length of time she had lived in the house, the needs of her granddaughter, her own health problems, her financial circumstances (her income appeared to be solely from state benefits), and also a claim that at least part of the money used to buy the property had come indirectly from herself. She argued (see para 23 of the judgment) that, in the light of these circumstances, the court should:

> refuse to grant the orders sought by the noter, failing which to grant the application subject to a condition that the property be disponed to the respondent for no consideration, and failing either of those outcomes to grant the application subject to a condition that the net free proceeds of sale are divided by the noter and the respondent, with the majority going to the respondent. The fourth final fallback position was that failing any of those first three outcomes the respondent would invite the court to postpone the granting of the order for 12 months.

The Lord Ordinary (Lady Wise) held (para 37) that:

> The provisions of s 98 of the 2002 Act are clearly designed to relieve hardship on spouses, ex-spouses and children who might be rendered homeless by the granting of an order to dispose of the property. The protection is of occupation, not of any proprietorial or financial interest.

Accordingly if Mrs Duncan had any claim in relation to any moneys she might have remitted to her former husband, such claim would have to be pursued separately. It could not be pled against Mr Cleghorn. This seems to us to be the right approach.

The court granted the application, but with Mrs Duncan and her granddaughter allowed a grace period of four months.

The case did not raise the question of how an 'enforcement administrator' carries out a sale, from the standpoints of (i) the conveyancer who acts for the administrator, and (ii) the conveyancer who acts for the buyer from the administrator. The 2002 Act appears to be silent, except for the disbursement of the proceeds of sale, which is covered by s 130. If one seeks the assistance of analogous situations, sequestration would perhaps not be a good case, for in sequestration there is vesting in the trustee, whereas there is no vesting in an 'enforcement administrator'. Liquidation would be, in that respect, a closer example, for there is (one or two insignificant qualifications apart) no vesting in a liquidator. But liquidation would not be a good analogy for another reason, which is that a liquidator acts by taking over the role of the board of directors. As for sales by judicial factors, they have their own rules. It might be suggested that the 'enforcement administrator' sells as agent of the criminal. But the difficulty there is that there is no contract of agency.

Perhaps the deed runs in the name of the administrator, with an appropriate (and possibly lengthy) narrative clause, and with the deed simply being signed by the administrator. Warrandice would presumably be limited. In some types of forced disposition the disponer grants fact-and-deed warrandice and binds the owner in absolute warrandice, but it is not easy to see on what basis, in cases of this sort, the owner/criminal could be thus bound. Similar remarks would apply to the missives: it is difficult to see how the missives could impose any obligations on the owner/criminal. *Prima facie* the administrator could not include any moveables in the sale.

(77) Lindsays v Campbell
[2017] SAC (Civ) 23, 2017 GWD 25-416

This was an action for the recovery of conveyancing fees, and whilst in itself is of limited interest is perhaps worth mentioning since it reached the Sheriff Appeal Court.

The defender wished to acquire a property near Bathgate in West Lothian. We have no details of the transaction, which proved abortive. Two fee notes were rendered, on 29 January 2013 and 31 March 2013. The sum sued for was £7,680. Whether this was the amount of the fee notes, or whether some had already been paid, and whether some of the amount sued for may have been outlays, is unclear. The defender was a party litigant and his pleadings were to some extent obscure but the core appeared to be: 'The sums not due to the pursuers as work not successful and cause the defender considerable loss.' The pursuers' terms of business letter , which had been agreed to by the defender, said: 'Where a transaction does not complete for whatever reason you will be liable for the costs of our chargeable time expended up to the date the transaction is aborted.' Following proof, the sheriff agreed that a contract existed and that the fees had been properly issued in respect of the pursuers' chargeable time and granted decree for the full sum sued for.

The defender appealed. The note of appeal is summarised at para 9 of the judgment of the Sheriff Appeal Court:

The note of appeal advances four propositions:

1. No warrant exists for this action.
2. The sheriff erred by applying the wrong authority.
3. The sheriff had regard to authorities advanced on behalf of the respondent which were irrelevant.
4. The fee notes had not been taxed.

These all failed. As to the last we quote para 16:

> The appellant's submission proceeded on his understanding that the account should be taxed before decree could be allowed. This argument was not advanced before the sheriff and there is no defence on quantum in the written pleadings before the court. The basis of charge is contained in the pursuers' terms of business. Absent a dispute on quantum the pursuers come under no obligation to submit their account of fees for taxation.

PART II

STATUTORY DEVELOPMENTS

STATUTORY DEVELOPMENTS

Contract (Third Party Rights) (Scotland) Act 2017 (asp 5)

This Act reforms and replaces the common-law doctrine of *jus quaesitum tertio*. The Act implements the Scottish Law Commission's *Report No 245 on Third Party Rights* (2016).

By s 1(1) of the Act a person who is not a party to a contract acquires a 'third-party right' where (i) the contract contains an undertaking for the benefit of that person and (ii) it was the parties' intention, expressly or by implication, that the person should be entitled to enforce the undertaking. Intimation to the third party is not required (s 2(4)(b)). Of the various changes to the common law, the most important is that a third-party right is revocable by the contracting parties (s 3), though not with retroactive effect (s 4). But revocation is not possible (i) after notifying the third party of the right (s 5), or (ii) where the third party has acted in reliance on the right with the result that the contracting parties are personally barred (s 6). In enforcing the right, a third party has 'any remedy for breach which a contracting party would be entitled to were the undertaking one in favour of the contracting party' (s 7); this includes damages, which was a point of contention in the previous law.

The Act came into force on 26 February 2018: see **Contract (Third Party Rights) (Scotland) Act 2017 (Commencement) Regulations 2018, SSI 2018/8**. It will have limited impact on conveyancing but will sometimes be relevant in relation to contracts such as missives of sale and leases.

Digital Economy Act 2017 (c 30) and the Electronic Communications Code

Section 4 and sch 1 of this Act insert a new sch 3A into the Communications Act 2003. This contains a much revised version of the Electronic Communications Code, replacing the previous version which was contained in sch 2 of the Telecommunications Act 1984. It is based on a report of the Law Commission of England and Wales (*Report No 336 on the Electronic Communications Code* (2013)) and was prepared with English law in mind, although there is evidence of some Scottish input. The new Code came into force on 28 December 2017: see **Digital Economy Act 2017 (Commencement No 3) Regulations 2017, SI 2017/1286**, reg 2.

Originally designed for wayleaves for telephone lines, the Electronic Communications Code now has to cope with a large and ever-changing array of devices such as fibre-optic cables, cabinets, and mobile-phone antennae and masts. Moreover, with the opening up of the telecommunications market in the 1980s, there are a number of competing players – referred to in the Code as 'operators' – offering telecommunications services at both wholesale and retail levels. 'Operators' require to be appointed as such by the industry regulator, the Office of Communications ('Ofcom'), under s 106 of the Communications Act 2003.

The purpose of the Code is to facilitate the installation and maintenance of apparatus on both private and public land, and to provide rules in relation to matters such as assignation, termination and compensation. It is a substantial piece of legislation, amounting to 108 paragraphs and 60 printed pages. At its heart is the idea of the 'Code rights'. These are listed in para 3, the most important being the rights to install and maintain 'electronic communications apparatus' (defined in para 5(1)) on, under, or over land. For the most part, the Code only applies in cases where one or more Code rights have been conferred on an operator.

As in the previous version of the Code, conferral of Code rights will normally be done on a voluntary basis by the owner or occupier of land, in exchange for payment, whether a one-off sum or a periodical payment. The Code says relatively little as to the conferral of rights and leaves it to the parties to choose the legal form. So if an owner agrees to allow an operator to install electronic equipment on his land for a period of time, this can be achieved by a lease or, if the operator owns property which could act as a benefited property, by servitude. Other possibilities are wayleave or other contract. The Code provides merely that the agreement must be in writing, signed, and must state the duration and notice period for termination (para 11), and that the person entering into the agreement must be the 'occupier of the land' (para 9 and, for the definition of 'occupier', para 105). This last requirement may create difficulties. It means that, if land is leased, the conferral of Code rights must be made by the tenant and not by the landlord. It would be open to the landlord to confer identical rights, but they would not be Code rights and hence would not be governed by the Code. If, however, the conferral is carried out by the tenant, the landlord can accede to it, with the effect of binding the landlord and the landlord's successors (para 10(4), (5)).

There is no requirement as to registration (para 14). Nonetheless, as in the previous version of the Code, an agreement to confer Code rights has real effect in the sense that it binds the granter's successors and anyone taking derivative rights from the granter or the granter's successors (para 10). So if the conferral of Code rights is made by the owner of the land, the rights bind successive owners as well as any future acquirer of a standard security or other subordinate real right. If the conferral is made by a lessee and not by the owner, the Code rights bind successive lessees but not the owner of the land (unless the owner accedes to the conferral, as already mentioned). This real effect takes place without regard to the legal form chosen by the parties, but also without prejudice to the effect of that legal form. So if an owner grants an operator a contractual wayleave, the contract is upgraded to a real right and will bind successive owners, even although the wayleave is absent from the Land Register and, it may be, invisible from an inspection of the land. The Code, in other words, provides for the creation of a new type of real right, and one which is created off-Register. Operators are required to disclose to landowners, on request, the existence of Code rights (para 39(1)).

In a departure from the previous law, it is no longer possible to restrict the assignation of an operator's Code rights, or to require payment for the assignation (para 16). This is to promote greater flexibility in the market. There is one exception: restrictions are permitted if they are part of a 'guarantee agreement', ie an agreement under which the assignor guarantees some or all of the assignee's obligations (para 16(2), (7)). For discussion, see Calum Stewart, 'Lease rights and the Digital Economy Act' (2017) 62 *Journal of the Law Society of Scotland* Aug/34.

Provision is made for the compulsory conferral of Code rights by the court, on application by an operator, in a case where the owner or occupier of land is unwilling to grant a voluntary conferral (para 20). This, however, is subject to a number of safeguards (para 21). Thus a court cannot make an order conferring rights unless both (i) 'the prejudice caused to the relevant person by the order is capable of being adequately compensated by money', and (ii) 'the public benefit likely to result from the making of the order outweighs the prejudice to the relevant person'. No order can be made where the owner or occupier intended to redevelop the land 'and could not reasonably do so if the order were made' (para 21(5)). In the event that Code rights are conferred by the court, the owner or occupier will receive as consideration the market value of the grant of the rights (paras 23(3) and 24). Jurisdiction lies both with the sheriff court (para 94) and the Lands Tribunal (**Electronic Communications Code (Jurisdiction) Regulations 2017, SI 2017/1284**). In respect of the latter, some consequential changes are made by the **Lands Tribunal for Scotland Amendment (Fees) Rules 2017, SSI 2017/426** and the **Lands Tribunal for Scotland Amendment Rules 2017, SSI 2017/427**.

Money Laundering, Terrorist Financing and Transfer of Funds (Information on the Payer) Regulations 2017, SI 2017/692

The new Money Laundering Regulations came into force on 26 June 2017, replacing the Money Laundering Regulations 2007, SI 2007/2157. They transpose Directive (EU) 2015/849 of the European Parliament and of the Council of 20 May 2015 (the Fourth Money Laundering Directive). There are numerous small changes to the previous Regulations and a small number of larger ones. Of the latter, the most important is a mandatory requirement, introduced by reg 18, for a firm-level (as opposed to a transaction-level) risk assessment. This must take account of the following risk factors in respect of the law firm (reg (18(2)): its customers; the countries or geographical areas in which it operates; its services; its transactions; and its delivery channels. Following the risk assessment, law firms are required to 'establish and maintain policies, controls and procedures to mitigate and manage effectively the risks of money laundering and terrorist financing', and these must be reviewed regularly (reg 19(1)(a), (b)). By reg 19(2) these must include (a) risk management practices; (b) internal controls (see regs 21–24); (c) customer due diligence (see regs 27–38); (d) reliance and record keeping (see regs 39 and 40); and (e) the monitoring and management of compliance with, and the internal communication of, such policies, controls and procedures. Written records of this are needed (regs 18(4) and 19(1)(c)) and will be monitored by the Law Society: see an article by Ian Messer on p 44 of the *Journal of the Law Society of Scotland* for June 2017.

There are some changes to the rules of customer due diligence ('CDD'). For example, where a client is 'beneficially owned' by someone else, the 'beneficial owner' must be identified and, if possible, verified; and if that person is a 'legal person, trust, company, foundation or similar' then 'reasonable measures' must also be taken 'to understand the ownership and control structure' of the person (reg 28(4)). The definition of 'beneficial owner' in relation to a trust is expanded to include the settlor and trustees as well as the beneficiaries and any individual who has control over the trust (reg 6). As compared to the previous law, additional information is needed in respect of companies and other bodies corporate, notably the law to which the body is subject, its articles of association or equivalent, and the full names of the board of directors or equivalent and of the senior persons responsible for the operations of the body corporate (reg 28(4)). There is a corresponding duty on clients who are trustees or bodies corporate to provide the necessary information (regs 43 and 44). It is also and separately provided that the trustees of a UK express trust (as defined in reg 42) 'must maintain accurate and up-to-date records in writing of all beneficial owners of the trust and any potential beneficiaries' (reg 44(1)).

Personal data obtained under the Regulations may only be processed for the purposes of preventing money laundering or terrorist financing (reg 41(1)). New clients must be so informed before entering into a business relationship (reg 41(4)).

Further guidance on the Regulations can be found on the appropriate pages of the Law Society's website: see bit.ly/2qoTtRU. They include a link to the detailed guidance prepared for the legal sector by the Legal Sector Affinity Group under reg 47 of the Regulations although, at the time of writing, this was still in draft form and had yet to be approved by HM Treasury. A helpful article by Amy Bell appeared on p 44 of the *Journal of the Law Society* for August 2017.

One issue which has arisen is whether solicitors who act as estate agents need to undertake due diligence (including verifying ID) on the *purchaser* of a property, in addition to their client. Non-solicitor estate agents need to do so by virtue of reg 4(3). In a statement on its website the Law Society has indicated that, in its view, solicitor estate agents are not subject to reg 4(3). This is because reg 13(2) defines estate agency work in terms of the Estate Agents Act 1979, and the 1979 Act does not apply to solicitors.

Some initial difficulty with the Regulations was caused by the fact that, although they had previously been circulated in draft, the final version was not promulgated until 22 June 2017, four days before the Regulations were due to come into force. The initial reception was unenthusiastic. According to *The Brief* daily newsletter (prepared by *The Times*) for 27 June 2017, 'lawyers predicted that it would force banks and estate agents to conduct significant amounts of additional due diligence on both buyers and sellers of residential property'.

Private Housing (Tenancies) (Scotland) Act 2016

Introduction

This Act came fully into force on 1 December 2017: see **Private Housing (Tenancies) (Scotland) Act 2016 (Commencement No 3, Amendment, Saving Provision and Revocation) Regulations 2017, SSI 2017/346**. From that day, therefore, it ceased to be possible to create short assured tenancies, and all new residential tenancies have been 'private residential tenancies' in accordance with ss 1 and 2 of the Act. Such tenancies confer security of tenure. Further details about the Act can be found in *Conveyancing 2016* pp 84–87, and also in an article by Jim Bauld which appeared in the December 2017 issue (p 18) of the *Journal of the Law Society of Scotland*. Certain forms, including the all-important notice to leave served by the landlord on the tenant under s 50 of the Act, are prescribed by the **Private Residential Tenancies (Prescribed Notices and Forms) (Scotland) Regulations 2017, SSI 2017/297**.

Model tenancy agreement

In October 2017 and following consultation, the Scottish Government issued a model tenancy agreement (www.gov.scot/Resource/0052/00526246.pdf) which parties to a private residential tenancy can use if they wish. It comprises 39 clauses of which the first 24 are mandatory being based on provisions of the Act or of other Acts, or being the 'statutory terms' which apply to all residential leases (see below). The remaining clauses can be altered, and other clauses can be added. A facility exists for completing the agreement online: see www.mygov.scot/tenancy-agreement-scotland/?_ga=2.163694525.344768396.1514920682-1972245937.1432026515.

Statutory terms

Sections 7 and 8 of the Act allow regulations to be made setting out 'statutory terms' which apply to all private residential tenancies. Regulations have now been made: see **Private Residential Tenancies (Statutory Terms) (Scotland) Regulations 2017, SSI 2017/408**. There are nine statutory terms altogether, as follows:

Rent receipts

1. Where any payment of rent is made in cash, the landlord must provide the tenant with a written receipt for the payment stating—
    (a) the date of payment;
    (b) the amount paid; and
    (c) either (as the case may be)—
        (i) the amount which remains outstanding; or
        (ii) confirmation that no further amount remains outstanding.

Rent increases

2. The rent may be increased only in accordance with Chapter 2 of Part 4 of the Act.

Subletting etc

3. The tenant may not, without the written agreement of the landlord—
    (a) sublet the let property (or any part of it);
    (b) take in a lodger;
    (c) assign the tenant's interest in the let property (or any part of it); or
    (d) otherwise part with, or give up to another person, possession of the let property (or any part of it).

Notification about other residents

4. If a person aged 16 or over (who is not a joint tenant) occupies the let property with the tenant as that person's only or principal home, the tenant must tell the landlord in writing—
    (a) that person's name; and
    (b) the person's relationship to the tenant.

5. If—
    (a) in accordance with the term specified in paragraph 4, the landlord has been told about a person occupying the let property; and
    (b) that person has ceased to occupy the let property as that person's only or principal home,
    the tenant must tell the landlord that.

Access for repairs etc

6. The tenant is to allow reasonable access to the let property for an authorised purpose where—
    (a) the tenant has been given at least 48 hours' notice; or
    (b) access is required urgently for the purpose of—
        (i) carrying out work on the let property; or
        (ii) inspecting the let property in order to determine what work of a type mentioned in paragraph 7(1)(a) (if any) to carry out.

7.—(1) The following are authorised purposes under paragraph 6—
    (a) carrying out any work on the let property which the landlord has an entitlement or obligation to carry out;
    (b) inspecting the let property—
        (i) in order to determine what work of a type mentioned in head (a) (if any) to carry out;
        (ii) in pursuance of any entitlement or obligation which the landlord has to carry out an inspection;
    (c) valuing the let property (or any part of it).
    (2) References in sub-paragraph (1) to the landlord having an entitlement or obligation to do something are to the landlord having an entitlement or obligation to do the thing by virtue of—
    (a) an enactment; or
    (b) the terms of any agreement between the landlord and the tenant.

8. The tenant is to allow reasonable use of facilities within the let property in connection with anything done or to be done under the term specified in paragraph 6.

Termination

9. The tenancy may not be brought to an end by the landlord, the tenant, nor any agreement between them except in accordance with Part 5 of the Act.

The nine statutory terms apply automatically to all private residential tenancies whether expressed or not. In practice, of course, they should be included in the lease, as indeed they are included in the model tenancy agreement. With one exception, the terms cannot be varied. The exception is for the fourth and fifth terms but, even so, variation is not allowed where the adult resident whose presence is to be notified to the landlord is a spouse, civil partner, cohabitant, close blood relative such as a parent, child or sibling, or a resident carer: see reg 3.

Provision of documentation

Before the end of the day in which the tenancy begins, the landlord must provide the tenant with a document, in either paper or electronic form, which sets out all the terms of the tenancy (s 10). That will either be the model tenancy agreement or a bespoke lease of the landlord's own devising. In the first case, the landlord must also give to the tenant the plain-English guide prepared by the Scottish Government in respect of the model tenancy agreement (www. gov.scot/Resource/0052/00526243.pdf); in the second case the tenant must be given the plain-English guide to the statutory terms (www.gov.scot/ Resource/0052/00528473.pdf): see **Private Residential Tenancies (Information for Tenants) (Scotland) Regulations 2017, SSI 2017/407**, reg 3.

Rent pressure zones

A novelty in the Act is the special provision made for 'rent pressure zones'. On application by a local authority, the Scottish Ministers can designate an area as a 'rent pressure zone' for a period of up to five years (ss 35–37 and 39). This is for areas where (s 40(3)):

   (i)   rents payable within the proposed rent pressure zone are rising by too much,
  (ii)   the rent rises within the proposed zone are causing undue hardship to tenants, and
 (iii)   the local authority within whose area the proposed zone lies is coming under increasing pressure to provide housing or subsidise the cost of housing as a consequence of the rent rises within the proposed zone.

The expression 'rising too much' is not defined.

Following the designation of an area as a 'rent pressure zone', rents are not to be increased by a percentage greater than the consumer price index rise since the last rent increase + 1 percentage point + X (being a number prescribed by the Scottish Ministers) (s 38). The Scottish Government has issued advice to local authorities as to the requirements that must be met for designation of rent pressure zones: see www.gov.scot/Publications/2017/11/4030.

Energy efficiency

Finally, and nothing to do with the 2016 Act, it may be noted that the Scottish Government has been consulting on proposals (i) to improve the energy efficiency of the worst performing private-rented housing and (ii) to amend the repairing standard to increase the condition standards expected in the private-rented sector: see the consultation (www.gov.scot/Publications/2017/04/2510) and the analysis of responses (www.gov.scot/Publications/2017/11/6863).

Establishment of Crown Estate Scotland (Interim Management)

The Crown Estate is owned by the Crown but, until recently, was managed on a UK basis by the Crown Estate Commissioners, all profits being paid to the Treasury. That changed on 1 April 2017. While ownership remains with the Crown, the power of administration has been transferred to the Scottish Ministers by virtue of s 90B of the Scotland Act 1998, a provision which was added by s 36 of the Scotland Act 2016. From now on all profits from the Crown Estate in Scotland will be paid into the Scottish Consolidated Fund, although this will be largely fiscally neutral as there is to be a baseline deduction from the Scottish Government's block grant from Westminster equal to the net profit generated by Crown Estate assets in the year before the transfer. Long-term management of the Crown Estate on behalf of the Scottish Ministers has been the subject of consultation (see *Conveyancing 2016* pp 105–06) and there is now to be legislation: a Scottish Crown Estate Bill was introduced to the Scottish Parliament on 25 January 2018. Meanwhile, to manage the Crown Estate in the short-term the **Crown Estate Scotland (Interim Management) Order 2017, SSI 2017/36** has established a body corporate known as Crown Estate Scotland (Interim Management) (in Gaelic, Oighreachd a' Chrùin Alba (Stiùireadh Eadar-amail). Further information as to its activities and its *Business Plan 2017/18* can be found on its website (www.crownestatescotland.com/).

First-tier Tribunal: Housing and Property Chamber

The First-tier Tribunal was established by the Tribunals (Scotland) Act 2014. The Tribunal is divided into five 'chambers': Mental Health, Housing and Property, Health and Education, General Regulatory, and Tax. The Housing and Property Chamber is based at 1 Atlantic Quay, 45 Robertson Street, Glasgow G2 8JB (www.housingandpropertychamber.scot/), but tribunal hearings are held in locations across Scotland.

In 2016 the Housing and Property Chamber took over the functions of the Homeowner Housing Committees and Homeowner Housing Panel (in relation to disputes with factors under the Property Factors (Scotland) Act 2011) and of the Private Rented Housing Committees and Private Rented Housing Panel (in relation to disputes in the private-rented sector, including repossessions): see *Conveyancing 2016* pp 93–94. To this existing jurisdiction the Chamber has now added, with effect from 1 December 2017, (i) the functions of the sheriff for non-criminal matters arising from regulated, Part VII and assured tenancies (Housing (Scotland) Act 2014 s 16, brought into force by art 3 of the **Housing (Scotland) Act 2014 (Commencement No 7, Amendment and Saving Provision) Order 2017, SSI 2017/330**), and (ii) applications for rent assessments, drawing up of terms, evictions and other non-criminal matters arising from the new private residential tenancy discussed above.

The rules of procedure for the Housing and Property Chamber are now found in the **First-tier Tribunal for Scotland Housing and Property Chamber Rules of Procedure 2017, SSI 2017/328**. These replaced the First-tier Tribunal for Scotland Housing and Property Chamber (Procedure) Regulations 2016, SSI 2016/339, with effect from 1 December 2017.

New rural housing bodies

Rural housing bodies are bodies which are able to create and hold rural housing burdens under s 43 of the Title Conditions (Scotland) Act 2003. A rural housing burden is a personal right of pre-emption in respect of rural land, ie land other than 'excluded land'. 'Excluded land' has the same meaning as in part 2 of the Land Reform (Scotland) Act 2003. Until 15 April 2016, 'excluded land' meant settlements of over 10,000 people but now it has almost no content following an amendment made by s 36 of the Community Empowerment (Scotland) Act 2015. A perhaps unintended consequence of that amendment is that 'rural' housing burdens can be used over virtually all land in Scotland.

The first list of rural housing bodies was prescribed by the Title Conditions (Scotland) Act 2003 (Rural Housing Bodies) Order 2004, SSI 2004/477. More names were added by the Title Conditions (Scotland) Act 2003 (Rural Housing Bodies) Amendment Order 2006, SSI 2006/108, the Title Conditions (Scotland) Act 2003 (Rural Housing Bodies) Amendment Order 2007, SSI 2007/58, the Title Conditions (Scotland) Act 2003 (Rural Housing Bodies) Amendment (No 2) Order 2007, SSI 2007/535, the Title Conditions (Scotland) Act 2003 (Rural Housing Bodies) Amendment Order 2008, SSI 2008/391, the Title Conditions (Scotland) Act 2003 (Rural Housing Bodies) Amendment Order 2013, SSI 2013/100, the Title Conditions (Scotland) Act 2003 (Rural Housing Bodies) Amendment Order 2014, SSI 2014/130, and the Title Conditions (Scotland) Act 2003 (Rural Housing Bodies) Amendment (No 2) Order 2014, SSI 2014/220. The **Title Conditions (Scotland) Act 2003 (Rural Housing Bodies) Amendment Order 2017, SSI 2017/7** now adds Kilfinan Community Forest Company, and the **Title Conditions (Scotland) Act 2003 (Rural Housing Bodies) Amendment (No 2) Order 2017, SSI 2017/301** adds Dormont Passive Homes (Scotland) Ltd.

Following these amendments, the complete list of rural housing bodies is now:

> Albyn Housing Society Limited
> Argyll Community Housing Association
> Barra and Vatersay Housing Association Limited
> Berneray Housing Association Limited
> Buidheann Taigheadais na Meadhanan Limited
> Buidheann Tigheadas Loch Aillse Agus An Eilein Sgitheanaich Limited
> Cairn Housing Association Limited
> Colonsay Community Development Company
> Comhairle nan Eilean Siar
> Community Self-Build Scotland Limited
> Craignish Community Company Limited

Dormont Passive Homes (Scotland) Ltd
Down to Earth Solutions Community Interest Company
Dumfries and Galloway Small Communities Housing Trust
Dunbritton Housing Association Limited
Ekopia Resource Exchange Limited
Fyne Homes Limited
Fyne Initiatives Limited
HIFAR Limited
Isle of Jura Development Trust
Kilfinan Community Forest Company
Lochaber Housing Association Limited
Muirneag Housing Association Limited
Mull and Iona Community Trust
North West Mull Community Woodland Company Limited
Orkney Islands Council
Pentland Housing Association Limited
Rural Stirling Housing Association Limited
Taighean Ceann a Tuath na'Hearadh Limited
The Highland Housing Alliance
The Highlands Small Communities' Housing Trust
The Isle of Eigg Heritage Trust
The Isle of Gigha Heritage Trust
The North Harris Trust
Tighean Innse Gall Limited
West Harris Trust
West Highland Housing Association Limited
West Highland Rural Solutions Limited
Yuill Community Trust CIC

PART III

OTHER MATERIAL

OTHER MATERIAL

Forestry and Land Management (Scotland) Bill

The Forestry and Land Management (Scotland) Bill was introduced to the Scottish Parliament on 10 May 2017 and completed Stage 2 on 13 December 2017. Part 2 of the Bill transfers the powers and duties of the Forestry Commissioners in Scotland to Scottish Ministers. Under part 1 Scottish Ministers have a duty to promote sustainable forest management and publish a forestry strategy. Part 4 of the Bill updates the regulatory regime for felling trees, and provides for the registration of a number of notices in the Land or Sasine Register (s 39), including notices to comply (s 35) and notices of variation (s 37).

Registers of Scotland

Digital registration

Digital registration of discharges of standard securities was introduced on 31 May 2017 and is expected to become compulsory in the course of 2018 or early 2019. Standard securities and dispositions will then follow. For details, see **Commentary** p 141.

New application form

A new and simplified form of application for registration in the Land Register was introduced on 21 March 2018: see **Commentary** p 145.

ScotLIS

ScotLIS (Scotland's Land and Information System) was launched by Registers of Scotland on 24 October 2017: see **Commentary** p 146.

End of personal presentment for the Books of Council and Session

The facility to present deeds in person for registration in the Books of Council and Session has been withdrawn. It is still possible to drop deeds off at Meadowbank House but they must be accompanied by the C&S1 application form (www.ros. gov.uk/__data/assets/pdf_file/0014/6260/cs1.pdf) in the same way as deeds sent by post. The correct postal address for deed application submissions is: CAJR, Meadowbank House, 153 London Road, Edinburgh EH8 7AU. ('CAJR' stands for the Chancery and Judicial Registers.)

Checklist: applications for registration

The Property Standardisation Group has prepared a helpful checklist for applications for registration in the Land Register. It is available at www.psglegal. co.uk/residential.php.

Rejection fees and the one-shot rule

The fee charged on rejection of an application for registration in the Land Register is £30. An FOI request by Andrew Vennard, a solicitor from Oban, has revealed that the income generated for RoS by rejections more than quadrupled between financial years 2013–14 and 2015–16. The respective figures are £199,080 and £834,080: see (2017) 62 *Journal of the Law Society of Scotland* Jan/35. Mr Vennard commented that:

> Like most conveyancing solicitors, I find it cause for concern that there has been such a huge increase in penalties, and that there is also an increasingly adversarial relationship between solicitors and RoS. The penalties are justified on the grounds that they help to cover costs, though in ROS's accounts for the year ending 31 March 2016, they reported a surplus of £7.6 million, and so contrary to what RoS often state, the penalties are not necessary to cover the costs of rejection, as there would still be a substantial surplus without them.

Meanwhile, in a letter published in the *Journal* in February 2017 (p 6) Ceri Williams from Cupar questioned whether RoS were entitled to reject an application merely on the ground of a small mistake in the address given in the application form for the applicant ('XXX Farm' instead of 'XXX Farm House'); the address on the disposition was correct. As Mr Williams points out, the only legislative requirement, found in s 22(1)(d) of the Land Registration etc (Scotland) Act 2012, is that the application be 'in the form (if any) prescribed by land register rules'. Whether a minor error in what is otherwise a perfectly completed form is enough to breach this requirement must be open to question. As it happens, the problem will disappear on 12 March 2018 when the current prescribed form is replaced by a new non-statutory form (see p 145), with the result that there ceases to be any form 'prescribed by land register rules'. We wondered, however, whether the reason for the rejection in Mr Williams's case might have been the discrepancy between the address on the form and the address on the disposition, giving rise to a doubt as to the validity of the latter. One of the mandatory application conditions under the Act is that the Keeper must be satisfied as to the validity of the deed presented for registration (ss 23(1)(a) and 26(1)(a)).

In an article published in the *Journal* for April 2017 (p 9), RoS explain their rejection policy. Assistance with applications, they emphasise, is available from the new 'Knowledge Base' pages on the RoS website (https://kb.ros.gov.uk/registration/guidance) and from 'a dedicated account management team that is an email or phone call away'. In the event of rejection, 'our account managers can supply rejection reports, which provide details behind any rejections, and guidance on avoiding future complications'.

Behind all this discussion of rejection, of course, is concern within the legal profession about the one-shot rule, ie the rule, found in s 21(3) of the 2012 Act, that the Keeper must reject an application which is defective in the sense of failing to satisfy the statutory application conditions. This is one of Donald Reid's targets in an article published on p 33 of the *Journal* for March 2017. Mr Reid begins by accepting that: 'As practitioners we have to acknowledge that our own mistakes and laziness may have prompted this grossly unfriendly provision.' He then mounts five arguments against it. (i) 'It over-punishes obvious and trivial error and typos'. (ii) 'It under-punishes culpable errors' such as a failure to sign the application form (a requirement which will disappear under the new form). (iii) 'It offers no redress (other than refund of the £30) for improper rejection.' Meanwhile the registration date has been lost. (To this we would add that an action for wrongful rejection may lie against the Keeper in delict, and also that the Keeper will sometimes make an *ex gratia* payment.) (iv) The previous system by which applications went into 'standover' but retained their registration priority allowed for 'a useful and constructive dialogue with the Keeper'. (v) The one-shot rule is customer-unfriendly, and exploits unfairly the RoS monopoly on registration. 'If there were two equally authoritative registers competing for customers, neither would dare to have a one-shot rule.' Unhappiness with the one-shot rule also features in a letter by David R Adie of Glasgow which appears in the same issue of the *Journal* (on p 6).

400 years of registration – and a poem

2017 was the 400th anniversary of the establishment of the Register of Sasines, which was the first land register in the world to be set up on a national basis, perhaps. The Registration Act 1617 remains in force today, albeit in amended form. A commemorative booklet was produced to mark the anniversary and can be downloaded from the RoS website (www.ros.gov.uk).

As part of the celebrations, RoS commissioned a poem from Scotland's Makar, Jackie Kay. Despite being of a literary inclination, we do not often include poetry in these volumes. We are, however, prepared to make an exception once every 400 years. Entitled 'Sasine', Jackie Kay's poem reads:

Then my auld freend, as the furst sign
Let's haund ower a clod o' earth
And ken that ye and I will keep our wurd
Over time's lang in-between.

Ye came tae life in a dwam, a dream,
A name here shows whaur you've been, lang syne.
To measure time, your deeds, this record –
Seizer! The auldest o' the wurld.

Auld Caledonia: front runner, streaks ahead;
So far that you kin turn and look back;
The slow, timeless stare o' the stag,
A heap o' stones, a sma' time-lag.

Plot, bothy, shack, croft, lease.
A writ stamped, counterpart, peace.
This land register – across these four centuries:
Fast furward, back; here's your old stories.

Annual Report 2016–17

The most recent annual report of Registers of Scotland, for 2016–17, discloses that RoS received 652,000 applications across all their registers, an increase of 5.1% on the previous year (p 14). This is attributed to an increase in property market activity. Land Register applications increased by 9% compared to the previous year while applications to the Register of Sasines dropped by over 25%. At the end of the year the retained profits of RoS stood at £86.5 million, giving a total figure for reserves of £90.6 million (p 58).

Keeper steps down

Sheenagh Adams stepped down from her position as Keeper of the Registers of Scotland in March 2018. Her replacement, with effect from 1 April 2018, is Jennifer Henderson.

Landlord registration

The facility to make digital applications to the Scottish Landlord Register was introduced in February 2017. Both the application form and the Register itself are available at www.landlordregistrationscotland.gov.uk/.

Statutory guidance on landlord registration was issued by the Scottish Government to local authorities on 4 September 2017: see www.gov.scot/Publications/2017/09/9045. The guidance recognises that most landlords let their houses responsibly and encourages local authorities to take more targeted action against those landlords who operate outside the law. It highlights, through case studies, how particular local authorities are using the range of powers available to them to help drive improvements in the private rented sector, thereby ensuring that only those landlords who meet the required standards are approved to be registered landlords. It also highlights the benefits of working with the police and other agencies to take action against landlords who operate outside the law.

Asset transfer requests: buying from a public body

Under part 5 of the Community Empowerment (Scotland) Act 2015, which came into force on 23 January 2017, community bodies are able to request a whole range of public bodies to sell or lease heritable property to them (s 79). These bodies, listed in sch 3 of the Act, include local authorities, the Scottish Government, the Scottish Police Authority, Scottish Natural Heritage, and Scottish Water. In considering such an 'asset transfer request', the public body is required to assess the community body's proposals against the current use or any other proposal, and must agree to the request unless there are reasonable grounds for refusal (s 82). Among the factors that it must take into account are whether agreeing to the request would promote economic development, regeneration, public health, social wellbeing or environmental wellbeing, and whether it would be likely to reduce inequalities of outcome which result from socio-economic disadvantage. For further details, see *Conveyancing 2016* pp 88–89. Guidance has been published for community bodies (www.gov.scot/Publications/2017/01/2888) and also for the public bodies to whom requests may be made (www.gov.scot/Publications/2017/01/5463).

These provisions have implications for those (other than community bodies) seeking to buy property from a local authority or other public body. This is because, during any period when an asset transfer request is under consideration, the public body 'must not sell, lease or otherwise dispose of' the property in question (s 84(2)). It may not always be easy for a potential buyer to discover the existence of a live asset transfer request. There is no single register to search, as there is with, say, community interests in land. It is true that, on receipt of an asset transfer request, public bodies must, as soon as practicable, publish a notice of the request 'on a website or by other electronic means' as well as displaying the notice 'at a public place in the vicinity of the land to which the asset transfer request relates': see the Asset Transfer Request (Procedure) (Scotland) Regulations 2016, SSI 2016/357, reg 7. Nonetheless, rather than engage in detective work, buyers may prefer to smoke out a request by means of a suitable provision in missives. The Property Standardisation Group (www.psglegal.co.uk) has added the following clause to its Offer to Sell:

7.5.6 Community Asset Transfer Requests

(a) If the Seller is a relevant authority in terms of section 78 and Schedule 3 of the Community Empowerment (Scotland) Act 2015, the Seller confirms that it has not received any asset transfer request from a community transfer body in relation to the Property.

(b) [If the Seller receives an asset transfer request from a community transfer body at any time before and including Completion, then the Purchaser will be entitled to resile from the Missives without penalty on delivery of a written notice to that effect to the Seller's solicitors.]

Paragraph (b) is in square brackets. Strictly, it is unnecessary because the prohibition on disposal does not apply if, before the asset transfer request is made, the land has already been advertised for sale or lease, or if the public body entered into negotiations or began the process to transfer the land to another person: see s 84(12). It is included in the PSG style only to cover the case 'where the purchaser is concerned that community interest in the land could affect its proposals for the property': see (2017) 62 *Journal of the Law Society of Scotland* Sept/34.

In the unlikely event that a public body ignores an asset transfer request and sells anyway, it is provided in the Act that the contract of sale is void (s 84(11)), although – in contrast to eg the legislation on the community right to buy (see Land Reform (Scotland) Act 2003 s 40(2)) – there is no corresponding provision in respect of the disposition.

If the contract is void then presumably the 'smoking out' clause would, as part of that contract, be void too. If that is right, the clause would be either (i) valid but not needed or (ii) needed but not valid. But this is not to disparage the clause. It is useful in a practical sense, and, moreover, if it is not effective contractually it will be effective delictually, in that a public body that accepted the clause would be subject to a misrepresentation claim if in fact there were a live asset transfer request.

Extract title sheets or Registers Direct?

The following note appeared on p 35 of the August 2017 issue of the *Journal of the Law Society for Scotland*:

> The Society's Property Law Committee was asked to consider whether it should be standard practice in a conveyancing transaction, including a commercial conveyancing transaction, to rely on a Registers Direct copy of the title sheet/cadastral map rather than require an official extract of the title sheet/cadastral map.
>
> The committee agreed that as the current practice in conveyancing transactions is overwhelmingly reliant on Registers Direct copy titles and, following clarification of Registers of Scotland's terms, it was quite proper to rely on a Registers Direct copy, on the basis of pragmatism and also because (i) s 106 of the Land Registration etc (Scotland) Act 2012 applies to both extracts and Registers Direct copies; and (ii) Registers of Scotland has confirmed that (barring a system issue impacting on the currency of Registers Direct, which is rare) the information in an extract is not any more current than the information on Registers Direct – both are based on the state of the Land Register as of close of business the previous working day.

To copies from Register Direct may also now be added copies from ScotLIS.

Some anxiety as to the accuracy of Registers Direct copies was expressed in a letter to the *Scottish Law Gazette*: see (2017) 85 SLG 20. But it may be that extract copies too can suffer from such afflictions.

Scottish Standard Clauses

The first annual review of edition 2 of the Scottish Standard Clauses (effective from 3 May 2016) has taken place: see the note by Ross MacKay published at (2017) 62 *Journal of the Law Society of Scotland* July/42. Three matters are the subject of comment.

No change, yet

A couple of minor changes were identified and thought to be desirable, but these were not sufficiently important to justify a new edition of the Standard Clauses.

Suspensive conditions where buyer is awaiting a loan offer or house-sale

Where an offer is in reality conditional on the buyer receiving an offer of loan or selling an existing house, the review group's view is that this should be made apparent on the face of the offer rather than being concealed from the seller. '[T]his was a matter of good practice from the perspective of a purchasing solicitor in being open and transparent, and increasingly essential from the perspective of a selling solicitor so that they can properly ascertain the nature of a bid and advise their selling clients accordingly.' The review group offers the following styles of suspensive conditions:

> *Style A: offer conditional on loan finance*
> This Offer and any contract to follow hereon is entirely conditional and suspensive upon the Purchaser obtaining a satisfactory offer of loan finance (mortgage) and the Purchaser shall be the sole judge as to what constitutes a satisfactory offer.
>
> *Style B: offer conditional on sale of existing property*
> This Offer and any contract to follow hereon is entirely conditional and suspensive upon the Purchaser's sale of their existing property.

Style B is perhaps a little terse. Which of the following counts as sale: a sale that has proceeded to settlement; concluded missives; open missives? A small point about both styles is that 'is' should be 'are'.

Electronic delivery

It is noted that many law firms continue to include in the qualified acceptance a provision to the effect that missives letters sent electronically are to be deemed to have been delivered. As the review group point out, this ceased to be necessary with the coming into force, on 1 July 2015, of s 4 of the Legal Writings (Counterparts and Delivery) (Scotland) Act 2015: see *Conveyancing 2015* pp 167–69.

Goodbye CML, hello UK Finance

From 1 July 2017, the finance and banking industry operating in the UK has been represented by a new trade association, UK Finance. This takes on activities previously carried out by the Asset Based Finance Association, the British Bankers' Association, the Council of Mortgage Lenders, Financial Fraud Action UK, Payments UK and the UK Cards Association. On 1 July 2017 the CML *Lenders' Handbook* was renamed the *UK Finance Mortgage Lenders' Handbook*. References in the *Handbook* to the Council of Mortgage Lenders and CML have been replaced by UK Finance.

Meanwhile the following amendments were made to what must now be called the *UK Finance Mortgage Lenders' Handbook for Scotland* on 19 June 2017:

- updating the *Handbook* to reflect the closure of the Register of Sasines to new standard securities;
- removing reference to obsolete Law Society guidance in relation to coal mining;
- aligning the *Handbook* instruction with England and Wales in respect of warranties for new-build properties;
- updating the *Handbook* to reflect the use of digital discharges; and

- a minor amendment due to the fact that the FASI and MASI professional qualifications are no longer offered.

Full details of these (and previous) amendments can be found at www.cml.org.uk/lenders-handbook/summary-of-amendments/.

HSBC conveyancing panel

In 2012, at a time when a number of lenders were drastically pruning their panels of law firms, HSBC announced that they were cutting their Scottish panel to a mere four firms: see *Conveyancing 2012* pp 85–86. HSBC have, however, now changed policy, both in Scotland and in other jurisdictions. In principle, any law firm regulated by the Law Society of Scotland is eligible to become an HSBC panel member. Smaller firms, however, face some limits on transaction value. Sole-principal firms can handle loans only up to £350,000; those with fewer than four principals are allowed loans of up to £2 million. Firms of four or more principals can handle larger loans provided that they have professional indemnity insurance cover of at least £5 million. More than 400 Scottish firms have now applied and been accepted on to the HSBC panel.

Registration of letting agents

Part 4 (ss 29–62) of the Housing (Scotland) Act 2014 introduced a registration system for those, including solicitors, who act as letting agents for private-sector residential tenancies. This followed, and indeed was modelled on, earlier schemes for the registration of private-sector landlords (Antisocial Behaviour etc (Scotland) Act 2004 part 8) and property factors (Property Factors (Scotland) Act 2011). The new provisions acknowledged both the size of the private-rented sector – it has doubled in the last ten years and now stands at around 13% of the housing stock – and also the problems which some agents cause. The official Policy Memorandum listed some of them (para 211): 'agents going out of business and losing all monies held on behalf of landlords and tenants; the use of poorly drafted and legally inaccurate tenancy agreements; and tenants being charged illegal premiums for accessing privately rented accommodation'. For further details, see *Conveyancing 2014* p 70.

The primary legislation is supplemented by the Letting Agent Registration (Scotland) Regulations 2016, SSI 2016/432, which came into force on 31 January 2018. These prescribe additional information to be included in the application for registration and on the register itself (regs 3 and 4). They also provide that applicants must have a qualification at level 6 or above of the Scottish Credit and Qualifications Framework which includes training on matters such as the legal obligations relating to letting agency work, the rights and responsibilities of landlords and tenants, managing repairs, and handling money (regs 5–7). There are also CPD requirements, but Scottish solicitors will not be required to do any CPD over and above the Law Society's requirements, although a proportion of the CPD must be relevant to letting agency work.

Registration is now or will shortly be possible, and must be done by not later than 30 September 2018. The Scottish Government has published a privacy impact assessment (www.gov.scot/Publications/2017/01/8389) and a guide to registration itself (www.mygov.scot/letting-agent-registration/). In addition, the Law Society's website provides answers to some frequently-asked questions: see www.lawscot.org.uk/news-and-events/news/letting-agent-regulations-faq/. There is also a brief but helpful article by Gillian Alexander of the Law Society in the November 2017 issue of the *Journal of the Law Society of Scotland* (p 47). Only those who carry out letting agency work (eg collecting rent, performing inspections and arranging repairs) need register, and registration is not required by those who are involved in residential leasing in other capacities such as in the drafting of the lease.

In addition to a requirement of registration, letting agents are also subject to a Code of Practice. This is provided for by s 46 of the Housing (Scotland) Act 2014 and the Code itself is set out in the Letting Agent Code of Practice (Scotland) Regulations 2016, SSI 2016/133. It came into force on 31 January 2018. The Law Society was active in trying to ensure that solicitors who undertake letting agency work could avoid being regulated again, and differently, in respect of matters on which, as solicitors, they were already regulated. There were some victories. Solicitors, for example, are exempt from the requirement to obtain indemnity insurance (r 32(o)). On the other hand, and despite concerns about client confidentiality, solicitors, like other letting agents, must inform the local authority if client landlords are failing to meet their legal obligations (r 31).

Amendments to Code of Practice for Factors

Around 400 property factors are registered under the Property Factors (Scotland) Act 2011, with approximately 620,000 property addresses and 2,500 land records searchable on the register. In addition to registration, the 2011 Act provided for a Code of Conduct to be prepared by the Scottish Ministers (s 13). This was implemented by the Property Factors (Code of Conduct) (Scotland) Order 2012, SSI 2012/217; the Code itself can be found at www.scotland.gov.uk/ Publications/2012/07/6791/0. Five years on, the Scottish Government has been consulting on whether amendments are required to the Code: see www.gov. scot/Publications/2017/10/5817. For that purpose a draft revised Code has been prepared. The main proposed changes are:

- amending the Code's introductory text to provide clarification as to its purpose including what is and is not covered;
- clarifying the various situations where and when homeowners should expect to be provided with a copy of a written statement of service by their property factor;
- requiring a property factor to provide information to homeowners on how it will act in circumstances where another property factor is due to or has taken over the management of common property and land owned by those

homeowners. This includes a requirement for the incoming and outgoing property factors to co-operate with each other, as required;

- requiring an incoming property factor who purchases the assets of an outgoing property factor to provide information to relevant homeowners on any implications this may have for them. This also includes a requirement for an incoming property factor to consider and respond to any complaint made to it by a homeowner which relates to an alleged breach of the Code by the previous property factor and which may lead to a continuing breach;
- requiring a property factor to provide information to homeowners on its duties under the 2011 Act particularly in relation to its property factor registered number and the notification of its factoring portfolio;
- requiring a property factor to provide information to homeowners of any relevant professional or trade bodies it belongs to including membership details;
- requiring a property factor to confirm to homeowners its duties under the Code including making a copy available or indicating where the Code is published in the public domain. This also includes requiring a property factor to indicate to relevant homeowners where all decisions relating to compliance with the Code are published in the public domain;
- requiring a property factor to provide clear information to homeowners on how they can end their factoring arrangement, if applicable, including any information it requires from homeowners;
- requiring a property factor to take reasonable steps to ensure that any third parties appointed to act on its behalf are aware of any relevant requirements of the Code;
- specifying the requirements placed on a property factor in circumstances where it must or may consider providing information to homeowners if requested;
- including a glossary of terms used in the Code to assist the reader.

Consultees are also asked their views as to the impact of the Act as a whole. Responses were invited by 15 January 2018.

Scottish Energy Performance Certificate Register

As we noted in last year's volume (*Conveyancing 2016* pp 164–69), this is an age of registration. One register we omitted to mention in our review of registers (except for a glancing reference in the context of a note on energy performance in non-domestic buildings (pp 90–91)) was the Scottish Energy Performance Certificate Register (www.scottishepcregister.org.uk/), which was set up in October 2012. As most conveyancers know little or nothing of this register, it may be of help to reproduce some background information which is included in the opening paragraphs of a Scottish Government consultation on the funding of the Register (www.gov.scot/Publications/2017/05/1274):

The Scottish EPC Register (SEPCR) is a central register of data for all the Energy Performance Certificates (EPCs) and Recommendations Reports, Section 63 [of the Climate Change (Scotland) Act 2009] Action Plans, Display Energy Certificates and Advisory Reports, Green Deal Advice Reports (GDARs) and Green Deal Plans that are produced and lodged for properties throughout Scotland. Over 1.9 million EPCs have been lodged since its inception in January 2008, with around 20,000 further lodgements taking place on a monthly basis. With the addition of Green Deal and Section 63 assessments, the register now holds in excess of 2 million assessment records … The Energy Saving Trust (EST: www.energysavingtrust.org.uk/scotland) has been appointed by the Scottish Ministers as 'the Keeper of the Register' and is responsible for the daily operation and maintenance of the register. In addition, the keeper manages the regular development work and software upgrades required for the register to maintain function in response to changes to the National Calculation Methodology (NCM) and changing requirements arising from policies that access and use the data held by the register …

[T]he creation of a central repository of energy performance data has now been of benefit to building owners and practitioners and is essential to the delivery of both EU and domestic energy efficiency and emissions reduction policies. The SEPCR now provides a rich source of data on the energy performance of our existing building stock. The Scottish Government has designated energy efficiency as a National Infrastructure Priority, the cornerstone of which will be Scotland's Energy Efficiency Programme (SEEP) – a 15 to 20 year programme. The Programme for Government commits to investing more than half a billion pounds to SEEP over the next four years, setting out a clear commitment to develop this programme with substantial annual funding. By 2035, SEEP will have transformed the energy efficiency and heating of Scotland's buildings so that, wherever technically feasible, and practical, buildings are near zero carbon. An effective and well-resourced register of energy performance data is integral to that process – helping to target improvements as well as tracking progress.

The proposal in the consultation document is that the fee for lodgement of data be increased to £2.60 for domestic EPCs (an increase of £1.45), and to £12.10 for non-domestic EPCs (an increase of £6.74). By the standards of the registers normally encountered by conveyancers, these seem small sums.

Register of 'beneficial owners' of overseas companies

Since 6 April 2016 UK companies have been required to maintain a public register of those who have significant control over the company (the 'PSC register'), 'significant control' being defined to include direct or indirect ownership of more than 25% of the shares or direct or indirect control of more than 25% of the voting rights. The relevant provisions can be found in part 21A (ss 790A–790ZG) and sch 1A of the Companies Act 2006, both of which were added by the Small Business, Enterprise and Employment Act 2015. The aim is to increase transparency, especially in the cause of detecting money laundering, tax evasion, and other forms of crime. One result of the PSC register is that, where land is owned by a UK company, it is possible, at least in theory, to find out from Companies House the 'true' owner or owners of the company.

More recently, the UK Government has indicated an intention to establish a comparable regime for overseas companies and other legal entities but only where they own or are purchasing UK land and buildings. A call for evidence was issued on 5 April 2017 by the Department for Business, Energy and Industrial Strategy, and this was accompanied by the publication of a consultation paper, *A Register of Beneficial Owners of Overseas Companies and other Legal Entities* (www.gov.uk/government/consultations/property-ownership-and-public-contracting-by-overseas-companies-and-legal-entities-beneficial-ownership-register). The consultation closed on 15 May 2017, and further developments are awaited.

The paper gives outline details of how the scheme might work (paras 43–60). Overseas companies wishing to buy land and buildings in the UK would have to register information as to 'beneficial ownership' with Companies House. The resulting registration number would be needed in order to register a title to the property in the Land Register. Entities that already own property would be given a year in which to disclose the required information or alternatively to sell their property; failure to do either would result in a prohibition on selling the property or granting a lease or standard security over it, and a note to that effect would be put on the title sheet.

What happens if an overseas company buys property before it has registered the necessary information with Companies House? The answer given in the consultation paper does not suggest a close acquaintanceship with Scots law (para 52):

> This may create a situation where completion (or settlement, in Scotland) has already taken place but the new owner cannot be registered as the legal owner because the title cannot legally be transferred to an overseas entity without an overseas registration number. In this situation the overseas entity would hold 'beneficial interest' in the property, because beneficial interest transfers on completion and settlement. This would put the seller in the position of holding the property on 'trust' for the overseas entity.

In Scotland, of course, there would be no trust, and the recalcitrant overseas company would be left unprotected. That is regarded by the paper as a desirable outcome because otherwise there is no incentive to supply the necessary information to Companies House. The suggestion made by the paper is that legislation should provide that, in the absence of a registration number, the disposition is void. (This suggestion is, however, scarcely relevant to Scotland, where registration is essential to the effect of a disposition.) The paper adds (para 53) that '[s]ellers to overseas entities might choose not to enter into a contract at all without reassurance that an overseas buyer has a valid registration number'.

The existing provisions about the 'beneficial ownership' of UK companies and the proposals about the 'beneficial ownership' of overseas companies have obvious implications for the plans to set up a Register of Controlling Interests in Land as required by s 39 of the Land Reform (Scotland) Act 2016 (as to which see p 147 below).

Land Rights and Responsibilities Statement

Part 1 (ss 1–3) of the Land Reform (Scotland) Act 2016 requires the Scottish Government to issue and keep under review a 'land rights and responsibilities statement' having regard to certain criteria such as human rights, community empowerment, diversity of land ownership, and sustainable development (s 1). In implement of the Act (s 2(2)), a draft statement was published for comment in December 2016: see www.gov.scot/Resource/0051/00511857.pdf). The 62 responses to the draft were analysed at www.gov.scot/Publications/2017/09/8363/0, and the Scottish Government's consideration of the responses was published at www. gov.scot/Publications/2017/09/6645. The final version of the Statement (www. gov.scot/Publications/2017/09/7869) was published on 28 September 2017. It comprises a Vision and six Principles:

Vision
A Scotland with a strong and dynamic relationship between its land and people, where all land contributes to a modern and successful country, and where rights and responsibilities in relation to land are fully recognised and fulfilled.

Principles
1. The overall framework of land rights, responsibilities and public policies should promote, fulfil and respect relevant human rights in relation to land, contribute to public interest and wellbeing, and balance public and private interests. The framework should support sustainable economic development, protect and enhance the environment, help achieve social justice and build a fairer society.
2. There should be a more diverse pattern of land ownership and tenure, with more opportunities for citizens to own, lease and have access to land.
3. More local communities should have the opportunity to own, lease or use buildings and land which can contribute to their community's wellbeing and future development.
4. The holders of land rights should exercise these rights in ways that take account of their responsibilities to meet high standards of land ownership, management and use. Acting as the stewards of Scotland's land resource for future generations they contribute to sustainable growth and a modern, successful country.
5. There should be improved transparency of information about the ownership, use and management of land, and this should be publicly available, clear and contain relevant detail.
6. There should be greater collaboration and community engagement in decisions about land.

The Scottish Land Commission, established in April 2017, is required, among other things, to have regard to the Scottish Land Rights and Responsibilities Statement in exercising its functions. The Statement and the Scottish Land Commission are important elements of our commitment to ensure that land reform continues to progress.

The word 'citizens' in the second 'principle' is a curious word in this context and might perhaps raise questions of discrimination law and also of compatibility with EU law.

A gloss is provided in part 3 of the document. It is noted in part 1 that, while the publication of the Land Rights and Responsibilities Statement is the responsibility of Scottish Ministers, the Scottish Land Commission, which was established in April 2017 under part 2 of the 2016 Act, will play a key role in supporting the development and realisation of the Statement's principles through the provision of expert guidance and advice. Their work will help inform the review of the Statement which Ministers are required to undertake at least every five years. Part 1 of the document further notes that '[t]he vision and principles are high-level and ambitious and, together, provide a goal to work towards. The Statement intentionally does not define how land rights and responsibilities should apply in specific or day-to-day situations.'

The housing land market in Scotland

As just mentioned, the Scottish Land Commission was established in April 2017 under part 2 of the Land Reform (Scotland) Act 2016. The first of a number of projected independent papers in the Land Commission's 'Land Lines' series was published on 6 December 2017. In *The housing land market in Scotland: a discussion paper* (https://landcommission.gov.scot/wp-content/uploads/2017/12/Land-Lines-Discussion-Paper-Housing-Land-Market-Dec-2017.pdf), Laurie Macfarlane examines how the public sector could intervene to improve the operation of the land market and increase the supply of land for new housing. He explains the background in this way:

> The failure of housing supply in Scotland to keep up with demand has been the subject of intense public discussion for several years. Many commentators are now openly talking of a 'housing crisis', and this has profound socio-economic implications in both urban and rural areas and has the potential to act as a constraint on long-term economic growth. With the price of land accounting for a substantial and growing proportion of the cost of a new home it is clear that land economics is at the heart of this crisis. In order to address this many commentators now recognise a clear need for the public sector to intervene in order to improve the operation of the land market.
>
> This paper provides an overview of how the market for housing land currently operates in Scotland, and identifies the various types of ways in which the public sector could seek to intervene in the land market in order to increase supply.

Mr Macfarlane's 'main findings' are as follows:

- House prices have risen dramatically in Scotland in recent decades, far outpacing growth in incomes. The driving force behind rising house prices has been increasing land prices. The way the land market operates depends largely on the laws, institutions and political history of particular nations, and so varies widely. In Scotland, the key characteristics are a reliance on the private sector operating on a speculative model to deliver new house building; a legal framework that allocates the uplift in the value of land resulting from planning permission to landowners rather than public authorities; a liberalised mortgage credit market;

a taxation system that is highly favourable to land and property; and a paucity of publicly available information on land values and ownership.

- This system has resulted in an under-supply of housing and escalating housing costs, which in turn has undermined living standards, exacerbated economic inequality, and stifled productivity growth and output.

- Policy options to improve the supply of land for housing include public land value capture, compulsory sale orders, a new housing land development agency, tax reform, and greater market transparency.

- Intervening in the land market would have a number of long-term economic benefits including a more productive and dynamic economy; a fairer and more inclusive society; improved living standards; and healthier public finances.

No doubt Mr Macfarlane's 'findings' will be controversial, as presumably they are intended to be.

'Engaging communities' in decisions relating to land

Section 44 of the Land Reform (Scotland) Act 2016 requires the Scottish Government to issue guidance to those who own and control land as to the need to engage local communities in respect of decisions which might affect them. No sanction is provided for ignoring the guidance other than the prospect that this will be taken into account, under s 56(4) of the Act, in the event of a community application to buy land to further sustainable development being made under part 5 of the Act. Section 44 came into force on 1 November 2016 (see Land Reform (Scotland) Act 2016 (Commencement No 2 and Transitory Provisions) Regulations 2016, SSI 2016/250) and five months later, on 24 March 2017, the Government issued a consultation paper containing draft guidance (www.gov. scot/Publications/2017/03/9042).

The paper begins by drawing attention to the *National Performance Framework* (www.gov.scot/About/Performance/scotPerforms/NPFChanges) which dates from 2007 and which governs all public services in Scotland. The NPF comprises one 'Purpose' and 16 'National Outcomes'. The Purpose is: 'To focus government and public services on creating a more successful country, with opportunities for all of Scotland to flourish, through increasing sustainable economic growth.' The consultation paper envisages that the new guidance on the need to engage communities in decisions relating to land will engage seven of the National Outcomes, namely:

- We live in a Scotland that is the most attractive place for doing business in Europe.
- We have tackled the significant inequalities in Scottish society.
- We live in well-designed sustainable places where we are able to access the amenities and services we need.
- We have strong, resilient and supportive communities where people take responsibility for their own actions and how they affect others.
- We value and enjoy our built and natural environment and protect and enhance it for future generations.

- We reduce the local and global environmental impact of our consumption and production.
- Our public services are high quality, continually improving, efficient and responsive to local people's needs.

The draft guidance is set out in chapter 3 of the consultation document. It is too long to quote in full but the most important parts are as follows:

Why should I engage with communities?

Land is a resource for the people of Scotland. Land and buildings help to shape our urban and rural communities and impact on economic, social and environmental development and wellbeing. Community engagement is the process of involving people in decisions that affect them. In relation to land, this means involving communities when decisions relating to the use and management of land and buildings impact on people who live, work and spend time in the area.

It is in the public interest that the ownership, management and use of land and buildings in Scotland contribute to the collective benefit of the people of Scotland. Land owners and land managers have a responsibility to practise good stewardship of their land and, as part of this, when their decisions impact on local communities they should give consideration to the views of these communities. Positive, co-operative working relationships between land owners and managers and communities can identify mutually beneficial solutions to local barriers to sustainable development and promote better local outcomes.

This guidance on engaging communities in decisions relating to land contains a set of good working practices for land owners and land managers when they take decisions that impact on their local community. When community engagement is carried out well it can lead to the following outcomes:

- Land owners and land managers are valued members of the community and contribute to the community's wellbeing and sustainable development.
- Land owners and land managers recognise the value of the local community's views, and see the community as a valuable partner when taking important decisions relating to land.
- There are increased opportunities for local economic, social, cultural and environmental development, bringing improved local outcomes.

Best practice principles for fair engagement

Engagement will always be specific to the context in which it is taking place. Land owners and land managers should choose the means of engagement most appropriate to them and the decision being taken. These high-level, best practice principles should guide how that engagement is carried out.

Proportionate

Engagement is proportionate to the impact that the decision may have on the community. Engagement is not an undue burden on either the land owner, land manager or community. Impact is thought about in a holistic way, including environmental, economic, social and cultural impacts. Appropriate and accessible methods of communication are used.

Collaborative

Engagement is a genuine exercise in collaboration, and consideration of community views helps to achieve mutually beneficial outcomes. Engagement is started at the earliest opportunity in the decision-making process. Community views are given due consideration. Communication is open, clear and two-directional.

On-going

On-going engagement and communication fosters positive relationships between communities and land owners and managers. Feedback is provided to the community on the final decision taken, and the reasons for it. The community is kept informed by on-going communication and updates.

When should I engage?

Community engagement should be undertaken when making a decision relating to land that will have a significant impact on the local community.

Who should I engage with?

One of the challenges to engaging with communities is identifying the correct people with whom to engage. You may be able to get help with this from community councils or similar bodies. Community councils are statutory, elected bodies whose role is to represent the views of the community. There may also be a development trust or residents' association for the area, and groups for local businesses such as a Chamber of Commerce or Business Improvement District.

While the focus of this guidance is on engaging with local communities, you may sometimes find it useful to consult bodies that represent certain groups within the local population. For example when taking a decision that could impact on, or offer opportunities for, disabled people in the local community it could be useful to contact a relevant national representative body.

It is not always necessary to engage everybody within a community, for example when taking a decision relating to a sports facility, it may be sufficient to engage those who make use of the facility.

If bodies such as community councils are unable to help, then reasonable steps can be taken to advertise more broadly, for example by advertising a public meeting on a community notice board, in a local newspaper or via social media.

Where possible, effort should be made to minimise any practical barriers which might prevent people in the community from taking part in engagement activities. This can be as simple as ensuring that meetings are organised at appropriate times, in accessible venues and ensuring that any written material is clear and easy to understand.

In addition, there is a flowchart and an attractive if complicated table indicating when 'community engagement' might be appropriate and how it might best be done.

An analysis of the responses to the consultation was published on 9 November 2017: see www.gov.scot/Publications/2017/11/8407. There were 43 responses, 40 from organisations and three from individuals. Of the 28 respondents who provided a view, 20 agreed that the draft guidance responds appropriately to the considerations of s 44 of the Act; eight respondents disagreed, largely on the grounds that they perceived the guidance to lack due consideration of human rights, tackling inequality, or furthering the achievement of sustainable development. Many respondents requested further clarity around terms such as 'communities' and 'significantly impact'. Others asked that the guidance make clear that communities can initiate engagement; that all land owners and managers are encompassed and not just those in the private sector; and that the guidance applies to urban as well as rural areas, and to buildings as well as land. There were repeated calls for greater clarity on the circumstances in which engagement should take place, and the form that this should take. Many respondents called for examples to enhance clarity.

Publication of the guidance in its final form is now awaited, and will presumably happen in the first half of 2018.

Estimate of community-owned land

The Scottish Government has a target of there being one million acres of land in community ownership in Scotland by 2020. This is now to be tracked by a series of annual publications, the first of which was issued on 8 December 2017: see *Estimate of Community Owned Land in Scotland* (www.gov.scot/ Publications/2017/12/1288). This explains that (para 2.1):

> The target of one million acres of land being in community ownership was set with the intention that it would focus minds to spread the benefits experienced by communities already owning land much more widely. The Scottish Government acknowledge that it is an ambitious target, but see it as not only important in its own terms, but as a driver to step up and encourage a greater appetite for and interest in community ownership and remain committed to maintaining this momentum to increase the area of land in community ownership.

There is still some way to go. Since 1990, there has been more than a fivefold increase in the area of land in community ownership, from 112,158 acres to 562,223 acres, which is 2.9% of the total land area of Scotland. Most was acquired in the form of whole estates, predominantly crofting estates, and forestry or woodland. Altogether there are 492 land parcels/assets in community ownership owned by 403 community groups.

Paragraph 2.2 gives information as to definitions. 'Ownership' means ownership in the strict sense, so that leased property, for example, is excluded. 'Community' is defined on a geographical basis, whether by postcode units or a prescribed area. To qualify as a 'community body', a body is required to have the following six characteristics: (i) have a clear definition of the geographical community to which the body relates; (ii) a membership which is open to any member of that community; (iii) be locally-led and controlled; (iv) have as its main purpose the furthering of sustainable development in the local area; (v) be non-profit distributing; and (vi) have evidence to demonstrate a sufficient level of support/community buy-in.

Common good property

In provisions not yet in force, the Community Empowerment (Scotland) Act 2015 requires every local authority to compile a 'Common Good Register', ie a register of all property which is held as part of the common good. This must then be made available for public inspection free of charge, including on a website (s 102). In addition, before taking any decision to dispose of or change the use of common good property, a local authority must publish details of its proposal, notify community councils and any community body with an interest in the property, and consider representations (s 104).

During the course of 2017 the Scottish Government undertook a public consultation on statutory guidance for local authorities as to how to fulfil these requirements: see www.gov.scot/Publications/2017/06/7704. An analysis of the responses to the consultation was published on 24 November 2017 (www.gov. scot/Publications/2017/11/9276). The consultation asked for views on (i) proposed timescales for consulting on the production of the Common Good Register, and (ii) the method and scope of consultation on plans to change the use or dispose of common good property.

In relation to the latter, local authorities are required by the Act to publish details of any proposed disposal or change of use of common good property. The consultation document emphasised that the proposal should include enough detail to enable members of the public to identify and locate the property. For this purpose, the local authority should use the same information about the property as was included in the Common Good Register. In relation to cash funds, 'change of use' would not cover every payment to different people, or moving investments about, but would include, for example, changing the rules about what type of things could be funded. As a minimum, local authorities should publish the details of the proposal on their own website and should ensure that this is publicised widely. If the request relates to a building or area of land, a public notice should be placed on the building or land, or on an object close to it. However, said the consultation document, it is more important that the notice is put up where interested people will see it than that it is on or adjacent to the land in question. It could, for example, be displayed in a village shop, on a community noticeboard or an information point in a car park – wherever local events and notices are normally advertised.

The responses to the consultation focused in particular on timescales. The consultation document proposed that the public should have a minimum of 20 working days to make representations in relation to a proposed disposal or change of use. Many respondents argued that timescales should be longer in order to allow time to be aware of the chance to respond, time to digest, research and consult others, and also in order to take account of potentially infrequent community organisation meetings and holiday periods.

Seaweed Cultivation Policy Statement 2017

In last year's volume we mentioned a Strategic Environmental Assessment of wild-seaweed harvesting which had been carried out by Marine Scotland and was largely negative in character: see *Conveyancing 2016* pp 106–07. The Scottish Government has now issued a policy statement on the cultivation of seaweed, ie on farmed (as opposed to wild) seaweed: see www.gov.scot/Publications/2017/03/1340. This begins by noting that the west coast of Scotland has suitable inlets and sea lochs for seaweed cultivation, with many already used for aquaculture production, and that there may also be potential for seaweed growing in other areas.

The policy statement covers commercial seaweed cultivation either grown on its own or as part of an 'Integrated Multi Trophic Aquaculture' ('IMTA') system. The latter involves the co-culture of species for environmental and economic benefit. In IMTA systems, species which are fed or farmed (for example Atlantic salmon) are grown alongside species whose culture results in nutrient (or energy) extraction (for example sea urchins, mussels or seaweeds). The aims are for greater efficiency in resource use such as feedstuffs, space, and labour, with a consequent reduction in negative environmental impacts.

The policy statement comprises seven policies:

- *Policy 1*: In principle, the SG is supportive of small-medium farm seaweed cultivation, subject to regulatory consideration; the General Policies set out in Chapter 4 of Scotland's National Marine Plan; and any other relevant policies within that Plan. Applications for such seaweed farms should demonstrate that mitigation measures have been considered to prevent adverse environmental impacts, and set out how these will be delivered.
- *Policy 2*: Only species native to the area where seaweed cultivation will take place should be cultivated, to minimise the risk from non-native species.
- *Policy 3*: Where seaweed is grown for human consumption, cultivators should site farms away from sewage outfalls and other potential sources of pollution.
- *Policy 4*: Equipment used in seaweed cultivation should be fit for purpose to withstand damage from adverse weather conditions.
- *Policy 5*: Other marine users and activities should be considered in the siting of farms.
- *Policy 6*: Small-medium size farming is unlikely to be spatially limited, and may be located anywhere in Scotland, subject to agreement and appropriate local conditions.
- *Policy 7*: The SG is supportive of IMTA.

Post-legislative scrutiny of the High Hedges (Scotland) Act 2013

The High Hedges (Scotland) Act 2013 is aimed at protecting owners of residential property against the high hedges of their neighbours. On payment of a fee, the aggrieved owner applies to the local authority, requesting the authority to issue a 'high hedge notice' requiring the neighbour to reduce the size of the offending hedge. The local authority may or may not agree to do this, and if it does there is a right of appeal to the Scottish Ministers. Quite a number of appeals have been decided or are pending, suggesting that high hedge notices are being quite widely used. Reasoned decisions on the appeals can be found by inserting the case reference 'HHA' into the search engine at www.dpea.scotland.gov.uk/casesearch.aspx?T=1. More on the High Hedges Act can be found in *Conveyancing 2013* pp 163–67 and *Conveyancing 2014* pp 87–88.

The Local Government and Communities Committee (Comataidh Riaghaltas Ionadail is Coimhearsnachdan) of the Scottish Parliament has been conducting a post-legislative scrutiny of the 2013 Act. The results were published on 10 September 2017 (https://sp-bpr-en-prod-cdnep.azureedge.net/published/LGC/2017/9/10/Post-legislative-scrutiny-of-the-High-Hedges--Scotland--Act-2013/7th%20Report,%202017.pdf). The Committee received 64 responses, mainly from individuals involved in disputes with their neighbours over high hedges. In its report, the Committee notes a clear difference of opinion as to what qualifies as a 'hedge' and concludes that this is hindering the effective operation of the Act (para 67). Another concern is the apparent reluctance on the part of some local authorities to use their enforcement powers in respect of high hedge notices (paras 87–97). The Committee's overall conclusion is as follows (paras 98–100):

> The Committee believes that the High Hedges (Scotland) Act 2013 has been beneficial for some of those affected by high hedges. However further work is needed to ensure its effectiveness. The Committee is concerned that the Act is not currently operating in the spirit that was intended and that, despite having this Act, some people are still unable to enjoy their homes as a result of nuisance high hedges. Consequently, we encourage the Scottish Government and local authorities to consider and take on board our recommendations on how the provisions of the Act – in practice – can be made to work better to the benefit of all.

Scottish Vacant and Derelict Land Survey 2016

The Scottish Government conducts an annual survey of vacant and derelict land based on returns from local authorities. 'Vacant' land is land which is unused for the purposes for which it is held and is viewed as an appropriate site for development; the land must either have had prior development on it or preparatory work must have taken place in anticipation of future development. 'Derelict' land (and buildings) is land which has been so damaged by development that it is incapable of development for beneficial use without rehabilitation. The annual surveys may be watched with greater attention following the introduction of a community right to buy abandoned, neglected or detrimental land by s 74 of the Community Empowerment (Scotland) Act 2015.

Key findings from the 2016 survey (published on 25 April 2017: www.gov.scot/Publications/2017/04/3409) include (pp 7–9):

- The total amount of derelict and urban vacant land in Scotland has decreased by 253 hectares (2%) in the latest year, from 12,688 hectares in 2015 to 12,435 hectares in 2016.

- The decrease of 253 hectares (2%) between 2015 and 2016 is explained by 321 hectares that were brought back into use and 142 hectares that were naturalised (93 hectares of which is for a former surface coal site in East Ayrshire). This balances against 165 hectares of new derelict and vacant land reported by local authorities, along with a net increase of 45 hectares due to changes in existing sites.
- The most common new use for derelict and urban vacant land was residential, with 62% (199 hectares) of the land that was brought back into use since the previous survey reclaimed for this purpose.
- Of the 165 hectares of new derelict and urban vacant land reported by local authorities, the most common previous land uses were related to manufacturing or other general industrial uses, which accounted for 75 hectares or 45% of new land reported.
- The total amount of derelict and urban vacant land has decreased in each year between 2010 and 2016 (annual decreases ranging from 0.2% to 3%), except for 2014 when there was an increase of 2,090 hectares (19%) compared to 2013, largely due to over 2,200 hectares of former surface coal mine sites in East Ayrshire that had become derelict following the liquidation of Scottish Coal and ATH Resources in 2013.
- These annual changes have combined to show a cumulative increase of 1,064 hectares (9%) in the total amount of derelict and urban vacant land recorded since 2010, from 11,372 hectares in 2010 to 12,435 hectares in 2016. However when excluding derelict mineral sites there has been a cumulative decrease of 741 hectares (8%) in the total amount of derelict and urban vacant land since 2010.
- Of the 12,435 hectares of derelict and urban vacant land recorded in the 2016 survey, 2,156 hectares (17%) were classified as urban vacant and 10,279 hectares (83%) were classified as derelict.
- The local authority with the largest amount of recorded derelict and urban vacant land is East Ayrshire, containing 2,457 hectares (20% of the Scotland total). Highland has the second largest amount with 1,342 hectares (11%), North Ayrshire is third with 1,330 hectares (11%), followed by North Lanarkshire with 1,222 hectares (10%) then Glasgow City with 1,111 hectares (9%).
- For those sites where the previous use is known, 36% of derelict land recorded in 2016 had been previously used for mineral activity (3,606 hectares), 19% for defence (1,906 hectares), and a further 19% for manufacturing (1,859 hectares). The most common previous use for urban vacant land, where previous use is known, was agriculture (18%, or 328 hectares) and the second most common previous use was residential development (17%, or 318 hectares).
- 3,189 hectares (28%) of derelict and urban vacant land in 2016 was reported to be developable in the short term, with an expectation of development within five years. A total of 2,918 hectares (26%) of derelict and urban vacant land is seen by local authorities as being uneconomic to develop and/or is viewed as suitable to reclaim for a 'soft' end use (i.e. non-built use).
- Of the 321 hectares of derelict or urban vacant land reused in 2016, a total of 90 hectares (28%) involved some form of public funding, either a full or partial contribution.
- Since its inception in 2005/06, the Scottish Government's Vacant and Derelict Land Fund has contributed (either fully or partially) to the reuse of 367 hectares (in total) of previously derelict and urban vacant land across Dundee City, Glasgow City, Highland, North Lanarkshire, South Lanarkshire and more recently Fife.

Scottish House Condition Survey 2016

Key findings from this informative annual study (published on 5 December 2017: www.gov.scot/Publications/2017/12/5401) include the following:

- In 2016, 39% of Scottish homes were rated as EPC band C or better and half had an energy efficiency rating of 66 or higher (SAP 2012). This is similar to 2015 but an increase from 35% in 2014, the first year in which data based on SAP 2012 is available.
- The share of the most energy-efficient dwellings (rated C or better) increased from 24% in 2010 to 43% in 2016. In the same period, the proportion of properties in the lowest EPC bands (E, F or G) has almost halved, reducing from 27% to 14%.
- The level of disrepair reduced by 5 percentage points in the last year. In 2016, 68% of all dwellings had some degree of disrepair, however minor it may be, down from 73% in 2015. Disrepair to critical elements stood at 48% while 28% of dwellings had some instances of urgent disrepair and 6% had some extensive disrepair.
- Levels of damp and condensation remained similar to 2015. Around 9 out of 10 (89%) properties were free from any damp or condensation.
- Compliance with the tolerable standard in 2016 also remained similar to 2015: 2% (or 39,000) of all dwellings fell below the tolerable standard. This represents an improvement of 2 percentage points since 2012.
- Across the stock as a whole, Scottish Housing Quality Standard (SHQS) compliance remained at 2015 levels. In 2016, 45% of Scottish homes failed to meet the SHQS.
- The SHQS failure rate in the social sector was 38%, not allowing for abeyances and exemptions. This has fallen from 60% in 2010. 26% of properties did not meet the Energy Efficient criterion.
- Overcrowding levels in Scotland remain unchanged: 3% of all households (67,000) were living in overcrowded accommodation in 2016.

Housing Statistics 2016–17

The annual survey of housing discloses the fourth consecutive annual increase in completion of new-build homes, this now being the highest level since before the recession in 2009–10. Council house sales rose by 68% to 3,510, reflecting a final scramble prior to the abolition of the right to buy on 1 August 2016. This scramble is equally reflected in the large amount of litigation on right to buy before the Lands Tribunal (see p 28 above). Full details of the housing statistics can be found in *Housing Statistics for Scotland 2017: Key Trends Summary* (www.gov.scot/Publications/2017/09/4158).

Housing Supply (Private and Public Sector)
- *New housing supply*: New housing supply (new build, refurbishment and conversions) increased by 571 homes (3%) between 2015–16 and 2016–17, from 17,968 to 18,539 units. Housing association new builds increased by 428 homes (18%) and local authority new builds increased by 5 homes, whilst private-led new builds decreased by 182 homes (1%). Refurbishments (rehabilitations) increased by 142 homes (31%) and conversions increased by 178 homes (26%).

- *New house building*: In 2016–17, 17,078 new build homes were completed in Scotland, an increase of 251 homes (1%) on the 16,827 completions in the previous year, the fourth consecutive annual increase and the highest annual number of completions since 2009–10. During the same time-period the number of homes started rose by 626 homes (4%) from 17,765 to 18,391, the fourth consecutive annual increase and the highest annual number of starts since 2008–09.

- *Affordable housing*: In 2016–17, there were 7,336 units completed through all Affordable Housing Supply Programme (AHSP) activity, an increase of 818 units (13%) on the previous year. Approvals increased by 2,331 units (29%) in the latest year to reach 10,276 in 2016–17, and starts increased by 1,626 units (21%) to reach 9,308. This activity represents the first year in the target period to build 50,000 affordable homes, including 30,000 for social rent, over 5 years.

Local Authority Housing

- *Local authority housing stock*: At 31st March 2017, there were 314,816 local authority dwellings in Scotland, a decrease of 1,737 units (1%) from the previous year.

- *Sales of local authority dwellings*: Sales of public authority dwellings (including local authorities with total stock transfers) rose by 68% in 2016–17, to 3,510. This is the fourth consecutive annual increase after years of declining numbers of sales. The increases are likely to be due to the announcement in 2013 that right to buy was to be ended for all tenants, following which the scheme closed to all new applicants in July 2016.

- *Vacant stock*: Local authorities reported 6,164 units of vacant stock at 31st March 2017, slightly lower than the 6,181 vacant units in the previous year. Around a third (38%) of the vacant stock at end March 2017 was normal letting stock, which equates to 1% of normal letting stock that was vacant.

- *Lettings:* During 2016–17 there were 25,788 permanent lettings made, a decrease of 2% compared to 26,258 lettings in the previous year. There were 10,436 lets to homeless households in 2016–17, which equates to 40% of all permanent lets by local authorities.

- *Evictions:* Eviction actions against local authority tenants resulted in 1,421 evictions or abandoned dwellings in 2016–17 (927 evictions, 494 abandoned dwellings). This is up by 9%, or 121 actions of evictions or abandonments, on the 1,300 in the previous year.

- *Housing lists:* Household applications held on local authority or common housing register lists decreased by 3% or 4,970 households to 162,152 at March 2017, the ninth consecutive annual decrease.

Local Authority Housing Assistance and Licensing

- *Scheme of assistance:* There were 10,483 scheme of assistance grants paid to householders in 2016–17, 270 grants (3%) fewer than in 2015–16. Spend on scheme of assistance grants totalled £31.8 million, which is similar to 2015–16. The majority of grants in 2016–17 were for disabled adaptions, 5,967 grants totalling £22.8 million.

- *Houses in multiple occupation:* In 2016–17, 9,668 applications were received in respect of the mandatory licensing scheme for houses in multiple occupation (including new applications and applications for renewal). At 31st March 2017 there were 15,289 licences in force, representing a decrease of 2% over the previous year.

Paying in digital currency

A flat in the south side of Glasgow is said to be the first property in Scotland to have been acquired by payment in a digital currency: see eg *The Herald* for 20 August 2017. The price was 10 million Scotcoin (https://scotcoinproject.com/) which is the equivalent of £60,000.

Fraud

A valuable text about fraud, published jointly by the Law Society of England and Wales and HM Land Registry, appeared on 8 September 2017. It is called *Property and Title Fraud*, and can be found at www.lawsociety.org.uk/Policy-campaigns/Articles/property-and-title-fraud-advice-note. Almost all of it is as applicable to Scotland as it is to England and Wales.

Books

Kenneth S Gerber, *Land and Property Development in Scotland* (W Green 2017; ISBN 9780414059795)

George L Gretton and Andrew J M Steven, *Property, Trusts and Succession*, 3rd edn (Bloomsbury Professional 2017; ISBN 9781526500564)

Donna McKenzie Skene, *Bankruptcy* (W Green 2017; ISBN 9780414059450)

Kenneth G C Reid and George L Gretton, *Conveyancing 2016* (Avizandum Publishing Ltd 2017; ISBN 9781904968818)

Kenneth G C Reid and George L Gretton, *Land Registration* (Avizandum Publishing Ltd 2017; ISBN 9781904968702)

Andrew J M Steven, Ross G Anderson and John MacLeod (eds), *Nothing so Practical as a Good Theory: Festschrift for George Gretton* (Avizandum Publishing Ltd 2017; ISBN 9781904968870)

Articles

Matthew Andrews, 'The quiet evolution of the mortgage' (2017) 148 *Greens Property Law Bulletin* 4

Zibya Bashir, 'Assigned standard securities' (2017) 62 *Journal of the Law Society of Scotland* Sept/35

Jim Bauld, 'Private tenancies: rebalancing or just upheaval?' (2017) 62 *Journal of the Law Society of Scotland* Dec/18 (considering the Private Housing (Tenancies) (Scotland) Act 2016)

Amy Bell, 'AML: risk and the new rules' (2017) 62 *Journal of the Law Society of Scotland* Aug/44 (discussing the Money Laundering, Terrorist Financing and Transfer of Funds (Information on the Payer) Regulations 2017)

Stewart Brymer, '400th anniversary of the Register of Sasines' (2017) 149 *Greens Property Law Bulletin* 2

Stewart Brymer, 'Cyber fraud in modern conveyancing transactions' (2017) 151 *Greens Property Law Bulletin* 3

Stewart Brymer, 'E-conveyancing: challenges and solutions' (2017) 150 *Greens Property Law Bulletin* 5

Stewart Brymer, 'The case for a residential property charter' (2017) 148 *Greens Property Law Bulletin* 1

Stewart Brymer and Robert Rennie, 'Missives: can we conclude more quickly?' (2017) 62 *Journal of the Law Society of Scotland* May/34

Debra Clapham, 'Standard missives: an unachievable dream?' (2017) 62 *Journal of the Law Society of Scotland* Oct/32 and Nov/32

Malcolm Combe, 'Access exclusions under the Land Reform (Scotland) Act 2003: when does a building stop being a building?' 2017 SLT (News) 163

Malcolm Combe, 'Access to land: responsible landowner conduct under the Land Reform (Scotland) Act 2003' 2017 SLT (News) 201

Malcolm Combe, 'Fine to park here?' (2017) 62 *Journal of the Law Society of Scotland* June/26 (discussing *ParkingEye Ltd v Beavis* [2015] UKSC 67, [2016] AC 1172 and *Vehicle Control Services Ltd v Mackie* [2017] SC DUN 24, 2017 SLT (Sh Ct) 111)

Malcolm Combe, 'Human rights and limited partnership tenancies, again' 2017 SLT (News) 79

Malcolm Combe, 'Land law responses to the sharing economy: short-term lets and title conditions' 2017 *Juridical Review* 219

Malcolm Combe, 'The Indycamp: demonstrating access to land and access to justice' (2017) 21 *Edinburgh Law Review* 228

Pamela Coulthard, 'The Assessment of Energy Performance of Non-domestic Buildings (Scotland) Regulations 2016' (2017) 146 *Greens Property Law Bulletin* 5

Douglas J Cusine, 'Access for photography' 2017 SLT (News) 21 (considering s 1 of the Land Reform (Scotland) Act 2003)

Douglas J Cusine, 'Access to gardens' 2017 SLT (News) 25

Iain Doran, 'VAT for property lawyers' (2017) 146 *Greens Property Law Bulletin* 1, 147 *Greens Property Law Bulletin* 6, 148 *Greens Property Law Journal* 6, 150 *Greens Property Law Bulletin* 2

Lindsay Dougall, 'STOP! Is a (Scottish) sign enough' (2017) 146 *Greens Property Law Bulletin* 3 (considering whether a signpost instructing the public not to use an area prevents the acquisition of a servitude by prescription)

Matthew Farrell, 'Dilapidations: the pitfalls' (2017) 62 *Journal of the Law Society of Scotland* Dec/44

Andrew Gilchrist, 'Scotland's Land Information Service' (2017) 151 *Greens Property Law Bulletin* 6

Andrew Gilchrist, 'Voluntary registration – making your Land Register complete' (2017) 149 *Greens Property Law Bulletin* 6

Laura Hay, 'Late rent reviews in commercial leases' (2017) 149 *Greens Property Law Bulletin* 4 (considering *AWG Group Ltd v HCP II Properties 101 GP Ltd* [2017] CSOH 69, 2017 Hous LR 30)

Laura Hay, 'The forgotten schedule of condition' (2017) 147 *Greens Property Law Bulletin* 3 (considering *Dem-Master Demolition Ltd v Healthcare Environmental Services Ltd* [2017] CSOH 14, 2017 GWD 5-72)

Gordon Junor, 'Demolition order(s) demolished' (2017) 84 *Scottish Law Gazette* 63 (considering *Ewing v Inverclyde Council* 2016 Hous LR 121)

Gordon Junor, '*Hussain v Glasgow City Council* [2017] CSOH 1, 2017 SLT 231' 2017 SLT (News) 61

John Kerrigan, 'Survivorship destinations – yet more developments' 2017 SLT (News) 125 (considering *Machin's Tr v Machin* [2017] SC GLA 29, 2017 GWD 15-253)

Tim Macdonald, 'Modern limited duration tenancies – a new long-term letting vehicle in Scotland' (2017) 151 *Greens Property Law Bulletin* 5

Reema Mannah, 'Transitions in tenure: evolving perceptions of property' (2017) 146 *Greens Property Law Bulletin* 7

Ian Messer, 'AML: Regulations bring new focus' (2017) 62 *Journal of the Law Society of Scotland* May/41

Ian Messer, 'AML: sizing up the risk' (2017) 62 *Journal of the Law Society of Scotland* June/44

Peter Nicholson and Jaime Hill, 'Altis: platform party' (2017) 62 *Journal of the Law Society of Scotland* March/22 (reviewing the first year of Altis)

Matthew Nicol, 'Rent deposits – filling in the gaps' (2017) 62 *Journal of the Law Society of Scotland*, online edition: bit.ly/2n99Dmo (considering *Russell-Smith v Uchegbu* [2016] SC EDIN 64, 2016 GWD 31-553, *Conveyancing 2016* Case (49))

Donald Reid, 'The 2012 Act: a bold step forward?' (2017) 62 *Journal of the Law Society of Scotland* March/33

Donald B Reid, 'The case for resisting a residential property charter' (2017) 149 *Greens Property Law Bulletin* 5

J Keith Robertson, 'Ticking timebombs at the Land Register' (2017) 85 *Scottish Law Gazette* 28; also at (2017) 62 *Journal of the Law Society of Scotland*, online edition: bit.ly/2xPgZLr

Frances Rooney, 'Registration rejections – more than formalities' (2017) 62 *Journal of the Law Society of Scotland* Dec/34 (considering aspects of the law of execution of deeds)

David Sellar, 'When does the English liquidation regime govern land in Scotland?' 2017 SLT (News) 195

Michael Sheridan, 'Land registration problems – the cadastral map' (2017) 85 *Scottish Law Gazette* 1

Mitchell Skilling, 'The fifth element: should exclusive possession be considered an essential requirement for the constitution of a contract of lease in Scots Law? (2017) 7 *Aberdeen Student Law Review* 1

Andrew J M Steven, 'Scottish property law 2017' 2017 *Juridical Review* 21

Calum Stewart, 'Lease rights and the Digital Economy Act' (2017) 62 *Journal of the Law Society of Scotland* Aug/34

Ashley Swanson, 'Practitioners or salesmen' (2017) 62 *Journal of the Law Society of Scotland* July/34 (discussing the importance of proper examination of title)

Ken Swinton, 'Assigning heritable securities' (2017) 85 *Scottish Law Gazette* 23 (considering *Onesavings Bank plc v Burns* 2017 SLT (Sh Ct) 129)

Ken Swinton, 'Gratuitous alienations and the CML Handbook' (2017) 85 *Scottish Law Gazette* 14

Ken Swinton, 'Three and four party heritable securities: now available in 3D!' (2017) 84 *Scottish Law Gazette* 60 (considering *3D Garages Ltd v Prolatis Co Ltd* 2017 SLT (Sh Ct) 9)

Ken Swinton, 'Vulnerable elderly clients, gifts and wills – professional precautions' (2017) 85 *Scottish Law Gazette* 34

Pamela Todd, 'Crown Estate minerals – devolution' (2017) 147 *Greens Property Law Bulletin* 2

Robin M White, 'Parking's not fine' 2017 SLT (News) 151 (considering *Vehicle Control Services Ltd v Mackie* [2017] SC DUN 24, 2017 SLT (Sh Ct) 111)

⊰ PART IV ⊱
COMMENTARY

COMMENTARY

MISSIVES OF SALE: TIME TO ENFORCE

Two difficulties

Like all contracts, missives of sale have a limited lifespan. Delay, therefore, can sometimes be fatal to the prospects of enforcement.

Usually, the difficulty as to time comes from the doctrine of supersession. At common law, delivery of the disposition brought the missives to an end except in respect of collateral matters. Older readers will recall without pleasure *Winston v Patrick*,[1] a case from 1980 in which this rule was emphatically established, and the attempts subsequently made to get round the rule. In the end the accepted solution was to have a clause in both missives and disposition providing that the disposition did *not* supersede the missives until the expiry of a fixed period of time after settlement, a period which was normally two years. This was the so-called 'non-supersession clause' – the clause which kept missives alive.

The law was changed by legislation. In terms of s 2 of the Contract (Scotland) Act 1997, 'where a deed is executed in implement ... of a contract, an unimplemented, or otherwise unfulfilled, term of the contract shall not be taken to be superseded by virtue only of that execution or of the delivery and acceptance of the deed'. In other words, a rule of 'the disposition supersedes the missives' was replaced by a rule of 'the disposition does *not* supersede the missives'. But this rule too was judged unsatisfactory by conveyancers. Having missives last indefinitely was thought to be just as bad as having them die almost at once. So the non-supersession clause was replaced by a supersession clause – by a clause which brought missives to an end after a stipulated period of time. As before, the period was normally two years. The end result, therefore, was no real change. After enactment of the 1997 Act, just as before, missives generally lasted for two years after settlement, so that a party seeking to enforce the contract had to act with reasonable despatch. Inevitably, not everyone remembered to do so. That remains the law and the practice today.

Not all missives, however, have supersession clauses, especially missives in respect of commercial property; and even where a supersession clause is used, one or more provisions may be excluded from its ambit. So for example clause 18 of the Scottish Standard Clauses, which deals with the seller's obligation

---

1 1980 SC 246.

to produce a good and marketable title and a validly executed disposition, is excluded from the two-year supersession provision found in clause 24 and which applies to the rest of the contract. But this brings us to a second difficulty facing enforcers. Even without a supersession clause, missives provisions do not last for ever. In due course they will be extinguished by negative prescription. Furthermore, prescription is a mandatory rule of law and cannot be contracted out of.[1] A provision that missives are to last for ten years would be of no effect in respect of obligations which, under the rules of prescription, are extinguished after five.

The standard period of prescription for contractual obligations is five years,[2] but the five-year prescription does not apply to obligations 'relating to land'[3] which, as a result, prescribe only after 20 years.[4] That is a big difference in duration. Now, missives of sale are a mixture of obligations which relate to land, in the required statutory sense, and obligations which do not. Some obligations, therefore, prescribe after 20 years and some after five. But which are which? What, in other words, is the meaning and scope of the exception for obligations 'relating to land'? That was the question raised in *JAL Fish Ltd Small Self-Administered Pension Scheme, Trustees v Robertson Construction Eastern Ltd*.[5]

The facts

On 2 May 2008 missives were concluded for the sale of commercial premises at 34, 36 and 47 South Esplanade West, Torry, Aberdeen, at a price of £475,000. Clause 8.1 of the offer provided that:

> In exchange for payment of the Purchase Price, there will be delivered (a) a validly executed Disposition of the Subjects in favour of the Purchaser ... and (b) the duly executed Overage Agreement (in duplicate to allow the parties hereto to retain one copy each).

A draft overage (or clawback) agreement was included in the schedule to the missives. It provided for further payment to be made to the sellers in the event that the buyer obtained certain types of development consent.

In fact, no overage agreement was ever finalised or signed, and the transaction settled on the basis of payment of the price only. Settlement was on 9 May 2008. Just a little more than five years later, on 7 August 2013, the buyer applied for planning permission for development of the property as offices. The seller's claim for payment under the overage agreement was rejected by the buyer on

---

1 Prescription and Limitation (Scotland) Act 1973 s 13. For discussion, see David Johnston, *Prescription and Limitation* (2nd edn, 2012) para 4.05.
2 PL(S)A 1973 s 6, sch 1 para 1(g).
3 PL(S)A 1973 sch 1 para 1(2)(e).
4 An obligation (or correlative right) which does not fall within s 6 and the five-year prescription falls within s 7 and the 20-year prescription except where the obligation is one of the imprescriptible obligations listed in sch 3.
5 [2017] CSOH 70, 2017 SLT 577.

the basis that no such agreement had ever been signed. Three years later, in October 2016, the seller raised the present action, seeking specific implement of the obligation in clause 8.1 to execute and deliver an overage agreement, which failing damages of £1,025,000.

But was clause 8.1 still enforceable, more than eight years after settlement? In most cases the answer would have been an emphatic 'no' because of the existence of a two-year supersession clause. But far from containing a supersession clause, the present missives contained a *non*-supersession clause:

> The terms and conditions of this offer and all that may follow hereon will remain in full force and effect and binding on both parties, in so far as not implemented, notwithstanding entry having been taken, delivery of the Disposition hereinbefore mentioned and payment of the Purchase Price.

The intention and effect were for missives to remain in force and enforceable. That disposed of the first of the two difficulties mentioned above. But the second difficulty remained. Contractual obligations normally prescribe after five years. The only relevant exception in a case such as the present was for obligations 'relating to land'. The question to be determined, therefore, was whether clause 8.1 was such an obligation. If so, it remained enforceable. If not, the buyer could keep all profits deriving from the grant of planning consent.

An obligation 'relating to land'?

It is not intuitively clear what is meant by an obligation 'relating to land'. But there has been a certain amount of case law, and there is a full and helpful discussion in David Johnston's book on *Prescription and Limitation*.[1] As it turned out, facts similar to those presently at issue had been litigated before. In *Smith v Stuart*,[2] the defender gave a written undertaking in favour of the pursuer, his sister, to enter into a formal minute of agreement in terms of which the pursuer would be entitled to a share of the development value of the defender's land in certain stipulated circumstances. When no minute of agreement was forthcoming the pursuer raised an action of implement. As more than five years had passed since the original undertaking was made, the pursuer's case depended on the question of whether the undertaking was an obligation 'relating to land'. It was held that it was not. Since this was a decision of the Inner House it was binding on the Lord Ordinary (Lord Doherty) in *JAL Fish Ltd*.

What, then, was the *ratio* of *Smith v Stuart*? Lord Doherty found it to comprise the following four propositions.[3] (i) Obligation 'relating to land' is to be given its natural and ordinary meaning. (ii) It is apt to cover a wide range of obligations. (iii) It is not limited to real rights in land. (iv) But land must be the main object of the obligation.[4]

---

1 David Johnston, *Prescription and Limitation* (2nd edn, 2012) paras 6.54–6.62.
2 [2010] CSIH 29, 2010 SC 490, discussed in *Conveyancing 2010* pp 182–84.
3 Paragraph 17.
4 This final point derives from the first significant case on the topic, *Barratt Scotland Ltd v Keith* 1993 SC 142.

As thus stated, these propositions are unexceptional. Only proposition (iii), while certainly deriving from *Smith v Stuart*, is perhaps a little misleading. Obligations 'relating to land', it is true, are not limited to real rights in land; but more than that, they cannot apply to real rights at all. They are necessarily confined to personal rights. The reason lies in the structure and internal logic of the Prescription Act. Obligations 'relating to land' are an exception to the five-year prescription set out in s 6 of the Act. Section 6, however, applies only to 'obligations' and, by s 15(2), to any rights correlative to those obligations. A real right, being a right in a thing, lacks correlative obligations. Hence real rights cannot prescribe under s 6. The Act instead makes a special provision for real rights, in s 8; this applies the 20-year prescription to rights 'relating to property, whether heritable or moveable'. Real rights, therefore, where they prescribe at all – and rights of ownership and long lease do not prescribe[1] – prescribe after 20 years.

The right correlative to the obligation in clause 8.1 to deliver an executed agreement was certainly a personal right. But could it be said, as proposition (iv) required, that its main object was land? The answer, said Lord Doherty, was no. That was plainly the position in relation to the primary obligation, which was merely an obligation to deliver a document. But even if regard was had to the obligations which the document was to contain, it could not be said that their main object was land. On the contrary, their only object was to require payment of a sum of money. That was the view taken in *Smith v Stuart*. It must equally be the decision in the present case. The seller's action, therefore, must fail.

Two observations

Having regard to *Smith v Stuart*, the decision in *JAL Fish Ltd* comes as no surprise. In the end, its significance may turn out to lie, less in the decision itself, than in two observations offered by Lord Doherty by way of *obiter dicta*.

The first concerns counterpart obligations. One obligation in a contract is often the counterpart of another. This can be seen from clause 8.1 itself where the buyer's obligation to pay the price had as its counterpart the seller's obligation to deliver a disposition. In an earlier decision of the Outer House, *Glasgow City Council v Morrison Developments Ltd*,[2] the court appeared to accept that (i) where obligation A is a counterpart of obligation B, and (ii) obligation B is an obligation 'relating to land', then (iii) obligation A too is an obligation 'relating to land'. This view seems to have derived from s 15(2) of the Prescription Act, which provides that any reference in the Act to an obligation is to be read as including any right correlative to that obligation. It would mean, in the context of clause 8.1, that since the obligation to deliver a disposition is an obligation 'relating to land',[3] so then must be the counterpart obligation, to pay the price.

---

1 Prescription and Limitation (Scotland) Act 1973 sch 3 paras (a) and (b).
2 2003 SLT 263.
3 See *Barratt Scotland Ltd v Keith* 1993 SC 142.

The trouble is, as Lord Doherty points out, that s 15(2) is dealing with correlative rights and obligations and not with counterpart obligations. It says no more than that, where X has an obligation to Y, then, for the purposes of prescription, that obligation includes Y's correlative right, under the *same* obligation, against X. Section 15(2) says nothing about the relationship between two *different* obligations owed by different parties. Indeed to link them up – to say that because obligation B relates to land then so must a counterpart obligation A – is, as Lord Doherty says, a *non sequitur*.[1] Lord Doherty's own analysis of the matter is much more compelling:[2]

> The bilateral nature of the parties' obligations, and the extent to which there were counter prestations, are matters to which the court ought to have regard when characterising the nature of the obligation and whether it relates to land. However, in my opinion it is important to remember that ultimately the focus should be on the nature and main object of the particular obligation in issue, not on the nature and main object of any counterpart obligation. It does not necessarily follow from the fact that a counterpart obligation is an obligation relating to land that the obligation itself must also possess that character.

Assuming that to be correct, what effect does this have on one of the central obligations in missives, the obligation to pay the price? This has as its counterpart an obligation which plainly relates to land, namely the obligation to deliver the disposition. But can the obligation to pay the price be said to relate to land? The logic of Lord Doherty's analysis is to say that it does not. If that is correct, it will prescribe after five years. On this view, it could in theory happen that a seller is bound to grant a disposition while, due to a prolonged delay in settlement, the buyer is no longer bound to pay the price. That result seems odd if not indeed unacceptable.

The second observation can be disposed of more briefly. The full text of the exception for obligations 'relating to land' is this:

> except as provided in paragraph 1(a) to (ae) of this Schedule, to any obligation relating to land (including an obligation to recognise a servitude and any obligation of the Keeper of the Registers of Scotland to pay compensation by virtue of section 77 or 94 of the Land Registration etc (Scotland) Act 2012 (asp 5));

In trying to tease out the meaning of obligation 'relating to land', it might be supposed that assistance could be derived from the savings mentioned at the start of the provision. For if certain obligations are expressly excluded from the class of obligations 'relating to land', it could be argued that, but for the exclusion, they would be such obligations. That, certainly, has been the view taken hitherto.[3] The obligations listed in the savings (ie those in para 1(a)–(ae)) are obligations to make payments, but payments which have some connection with land such as

---

1 Paragraph 23.
2 Paragraph 23.
3 See eg Johnston, *Prescription and Limitation* para 6.56, but compare para 6.60 where doubt is expressed as to whether a tenant's obligation to pay rent is truly an obligation 'relating to land'.

rent under a lease or compensation payable by the Keeper in respect of losses suffered in consequence of an inaccuracy on the Land Register. Lord Doherty's view, however, is more cautious, perhaps indeed too cautious:[1]

> I have some reservations as the extent to which the suggested approach may be a reliable aid to the construction of the expression at issue. First, in my opinion the words of exception in para 2(e) are a saving. It is well recognised that savings may be regarded as unreliable guides to the provisions to which they are attached. Very often a saving is unnecessary but is put in *ex abundante cautela* (Bennion on *Statutory Interpretation* (6th edn) s 243). In *Ealing London Borough Council v Race Relations Board* Lord Simon of Glaisdale observed (at [1972] AC, p 363D–E): '... I think that considerable caution is needed in construing a general statutory provision by reference to its statutory exceptions. "Saving clauses" are often included by way of reassurance, for avoidance of doubt or from abundance of caution.' Second, while it is true to say that the saving would have been unnecessary if no obligations within each of para 1(a)–(ac) were capable of being obligations relating to land, it does not follow from the presence of the saving that every obligation falling within each of those categories must be an obligation relating to land.

Direct and indirect obligations

Suppose that the missives in *JAL Fish Ltd* had contained a direct obligation to pay sums by way of clawback rather than adopting the indirect structure of taking the buyer bound to enter into such an obligation. In that case time bar would not have operated. The prescriptive clock begins to run on the date when the obligation in question first becomes enforceable.[2] In the indirect structure used in *JAL Fish Ltd*, the obligation, being an obligation to deliver a document, became enforceable immediately on settlement of the transaction. By contrast, a direct obligation to pay on receipt of planning consent would not have become enforceable until planning consent was granted, an event which occurred only three years before the current action was raised. This striking difference in result should be borne in mind when drafting provisions of this kind.

ASSIGNING STANDARD SECURITIES: A QUESTION OF STYLE

Introduction

Fussiness in statutory style

The Conveyancing and Feudal Reform (Scotland) Act 1970 was, most people would agree, a great improvement on the previous law. But nothing in this world is perfect and the 1970 Act, for all its merits, is open to certain criticisms. One such criticism is that it is fussy and over-prescriptive. The styles in the schedules can be difficult or even impossible to follow faithfully. The Scottish Law Commission is

---

1 Paragraph 26.
2 Prescription and Limitation (Scotland) Act 1973 s 6(1) ('... an obligation to which this section applies has subsisted for a continuous period of five years ...').

embarking on a review of the law of heritable security, and it may be hoped that the eventual result will be a certain degree of defussification (we just made this word up) of the legislation. This is not to say that styles are bad in themselves. On the contrary, statutory styles are good. But there is a distinction between a statutory style that says 'you must do it this way, however awkward it may be in the actual facts of your case, and if you don't, you proceed at your peril, and should consider future alternative career options, like stacking shelves at the supermarket' and a statutory style that says 'if you do it this way then it will work, so you can chill out, but you can do it in a different way if you like, provided that the basics are present'. The latter is a 'safe-harbour' provision, a 'this is sufficient' provision. The former is a 'this is necessary' provision, and is fine and good if limited to the basics. The problems arise if a statutory style is a 'this is necessary' style but then goes into detail that is really not necessary. The 1970 Act sometimes makes this mistake. Of course, there will always be room for disagreement, in particular cases, as to just how prescriptive/permissive a statutory style should be.

It is against this background that we should view a decision from 2017 which has caused some consternation, a case holding that failure to follow the fussy prescribed form of assignation results in invalidity. But before we come on to that case,[1] and two subsequent cases which decided the exact opposite,[2] we first offer a little commercial background, and then will go through what the 1970 Act says about how standard securities can be assigned.

Commercial background

The sale of secured (and indeed unsecured) loans is nothing new. It can be done by actual assignation, so that the debtor has a new creditor to deal with. Or it can be done without actual assignation, the original creditor remaining the legal creditor in the loan, so that the legal relationship with the debtor remains unchanged, but with the original creditor acting merely on behalf of the buyer, so that, for instance, all payments by the debtor are promptly remitted to the buyer. Often what happens is a sort of combination. There is a transfer contract, which is backed up by a declaration that the transferor will henceforth hold as trustee for the transferee, with the further backup of a deed of assignation which, however, will only be activated (by registration) if the transferee later thinks it appropriate. The deal could relate to a single secured loan, or to a large number (dozens, or hundreds, or thousands) ie a bulk transfer.

The statutory rules about the assignation of standard securities

Section 14 of the Conveyancing and Feudal Reform (Scotland) Act 1970 says that 'any standard security duly registered or recorded may be transferred, in whole or in part, by the creditor by an assignation in conformity with Form A

---

1 *OneSavings Bank plc v Burns* [2017] SC BAN 20, 2017 SLT (Sh Ct) 129, 2017 Hous LR 55.
2 *Shear v Clipper Holding II SARL*, Court of Session Outer House, 26 May 2017, unreported; *Promontoria (Henrico) Ltd v Portico Holdings* [2018] SC GRE 5, 2018 GWD 6-87.

or B of Schedule 4 to this Act'. Form B of schedule 4 is about assignations that are endorsed on the original deed. These are in practice seldom used (in fact, we suspect that they are never used), so we shall ignore them and concentrate on Form A.[1] The statutory style of assignation runs thus:

> I, AB (*designation*), in consideration of £   hereby assign to CD (*designation*) a standard security for £   (*or* a maximum sum of £   , to the extent of £   being the amount now due thereunder; *in other cases describe as indicated in Note 2 to this Schedule*) by EF in my favour (or in favour of GH) registered in the Land Register of Scotland on   over title number   (*or*[2] recorded in the Register for   on   ) (*adding if necessary*, but only to the extent of £   of principal); With interest from   .

Note 2 is as follows:

> In an assignation, discharge or deed of restriction, (1) a standard security in respect of an uncertain amount may be described by specifying shortly the nature of the debt or obligation (e.g., all sums due or to become due) for which the security was granted, adding in the case of an assignation, *to the extent of £   being the amount now due thereunder* and (2) a standard security in respect of a personal obligation constituted in an instrument or instruments other than the standard security itself may be described by specifying shortly the nature of the debt or obligation and referring to the other instrument or instruments by which it is constituted in such manner as will be sufficient identification thereof.

The last snippet of the 1970 Act that needs to be quoted is s 53(1), which says:

> It shall be sufficient compliance with any provisions in this Act which require any deed … to be in conformity with a Form or Note … that that deed … conforms as closely as may be …

The cases

OneSavings Bank plc v Burns[3]

In 2007 Mr and Mrs Burns granted a standard security over their property, the Old School, Bogton Row, Forglen, near Turriff,[4] in favour of GMAC-RFC Ltd. Their title was in the Register of Sasines and the standard security was accordingly recorded there.[5] The following year GMAC-RFC Ltd assigned the security to J P Morgan Chase Bank National Association. In 2012 the latter assigned the security to OneSavings Bank plc. Both of these assignations were recorded in the Register

---

1 Having two forms is a good example of the Act's fussiness.
2 If the security is in the GRS, that is inserted here instead of the Land Register reference. Occasionally a standard security is assigned that was recorded in the GRS but the property is now in the Land Register. In that case we think that the correct reference is to the GRS recording, though the Land Register title number should be added.
3 [2017] SC BAN 20, 2017 SLT (Sh Ct) 129, 2017 Hous LR 55.
4 Turriff lies in Aberdeenshire, but Forglen is in Banffshire.
5 Under current law, registration in the Land Register would be required, but this was in 2007.

of Sasines. Both were one element in a bulk assignation, ie an assignation of a whole portfolio of standard securities. OneSavings raised the present action to enforce the security over the property in Forglen.

The defenders argued that enforcement would not be 'reasonable' but that is not the aspect of their case with which we are concerned here. In addition, they pled that the assignations were invalid and that accordingly the pursuer lacked title to sue. This was a big claim since the assignations were done in the way that most assignations are nowadays done. The attack on the validity of the assignations had two prongs, the first being that bulk assignations of standard securities are incompetent, and the second being that the styles used – and both assignations were in the same form – were disconform to the statutory requirements, and thus invalid.

As to the first prong, counsel for the defenders argued that:[1]

> The statutory provisions did not envisage an assignation of multiple standard securities by way of a single deed … He maintained that, inter alia, form A and the notes to schedule 4 of the 1970 Act did, in fact, indicate a contrary intention by requiring the drafter of the deed to specify various matters particular to the standard security in question. This suggested clearly that single assignations of single securities were envisaged.

This was evidently a bold argument, and unsurprisingly it did not find favour with the sheriff (Philip Mann) who said:[2]

> Quite apart from the terms of s 6(c) of the Interpretation Act 1978, there is nothing in s 14(1) of the 1970 Act which restricts 'an assignation', by which a standard security may be transferred, to a deed which deals solely with that standard security. The relevant deed merely has to be 'an assignation'. It is true that Form A in schedule 4 to the 1970 Act is cast in the form of a deed dealing with a single standard security but the purpose of Form A is to prescribe those details in respect of a standard security which must be included in the deed. The purpose of the form, in my view, is not to make it mandatory that the deed be concerned with a single standard security. In any event, s 53(1) of the 1970 Act allows the deed to conform as closely as may be. The assignations in this case gave effect to transactions involving multiple standard securities. It is abundantly clear that they were capable of being framed in such a way as to include all the mandatory details in respect of each standard security, including the standard security relevant to this case, even though they may not have done so.

The second prong was the sharper prong. It was this: 'the assignations did not include the words which were required to be added by Note 2(1) in schedule 4 to the 1970 Act, namely the words "to the extent of £   being the amount now due thereunder"'.[3] What the bulk assignation said was that the cedent assigned to the assignee:[4]

---

1 Paragraph 14.
2 Paragraph 22.
3 Paragraph 5.
4 Paragraph 13.

the Standard Securities granted by the respective parties whose names are specified in Column 2 of the Schedule annexed and signed as relative hereto in favour of [GMAC-RFC Ltd] for all sums due, to the extent of all sums now due or at any time or times hereafter to become due under the respective Standard Securities, the creditor's interest in which is currently vested in the Transferor, the said Standard Securities being recorded in the Register for the County specified in the relative entry in Column 4 of the said Schedule on the date specified in the relative entry in Column 5 of the said Schedule.

Thus instead of the statutory words 'to the extent of £   being the amount now due thereunder' the words actually were 'to the extent of all sums now due or at any time or times hereafter to become due'. Was this fatal?

The sheriff noted that when a similar problem had occurred in *Sanderson's Trs v Ambion Scotland Ltd*,[1] the court had been prepared to overlook it. But the circumstances of *Sanderson's Trs*, thought the sheriff, were very special, so that the case did not lay down any general rule. The sheriff went on:[2]

> I can identify no circumstances in this case which make it inappropriate or unnecessary to include the words which were omitted … I do not see any justification for departing from the mandatory terms of an assignation on that account. I accept Mr Stalker's[3] suggestion that it would have been a very easy matter to include an additional column in the schedule to each assignation to specify the amount outstanding in respect of each standard security as at the date of the assignation.

So the assignations were held to be invalid. To be precise, what was held was that the assignations *of the standard securities* were invalid. When a standard security is assigned, what is assigned is normally both (i) the debt and (ii) the security for the debt. The sheriff saw no reason why the assignations of the debts were not valid.[4] Thus the pursuer was the creditor of the defenders – but not the secured creditor. The security was still held by the original creditor: the debt and the security for the debt had parted company.

The significance of the decision was such that it was generally expected that there would be an appeal. But in fact the decision was not appealed.

Shear v Clipper Holding II SARL[5]

OneSavings was decided in March 2017. Just a few weeks later it was invoked in an Outer House case, *Shear v Clipper Holding II SARL*. The background

---

1 1994 SLT 645.
2 Paragraphs 27 and 28.
3 Adrian Stalker was counsel for the defenders.
4 At para 35 the sheriff noted: 'The defenders had received advice from solicitors that they had no obligation to pay anything to the pursuers because the standard security had not been properly assigned to them. On that account they had stopped making payments to the pursuers towards the mortgage account. In my view that advice was erroneous.'
5 Court of Session Outer House, 26 May 2017, unreported. It is curious how often standard securities are assigned to foreign companies, such as J P Morgan Chase Bank National Association in the previous case. 'SARL' stands for *société à responsabilité limitée*, corresponding to a private limited company in the UK. It indicates that the company was incorporated either in France or in one of the many countries where French is the language of law.

facts were much the same. Mr Shear granted a standard security to a bank, 'AIB',[1] that later assigned it to the defender. Mr Shear then raised the present action seeking to interdict the defender against enforcing, his argument being that the assignation was invalid. Thus procedurally the case differs from *OneSavings*, but the legal issues seem to have been the same, except that in *Shear* the pursuer does not seem to have claimed that bulk assignations are incompetent. This phase of the case was concerned with the pursuer's application for interim interdict. His application was unsuccessful. That does not mean that he lost his case: the hearing was on whether *interim* interdict should be granted.

Regrettably, the decision has not been reported, even on the Scottish Courts website.[2] Decisions on interim interdicts are seldom reported. Nothing else has been heard about this action, so it is possible that the pursuer, having lost at the interim interdict stage, decided to give up. We merely speculate.

The Lord Ordinary, Lord Bannatyne, was referred to the decision in *OneSavings*. He disagreed with it, quite emphatically. We quote at some length to give a flavour of his remarks. 'The approach of the pursuer is wholly misconceived.'[3] Nowadays, he said, courts have a 'flexible' attitude to statutory requirements.[4] He cited at this point an English case, *Newbold v Coal Authority*,[5] and a Montserrat case in the Privy Council, *Central Tenders Board v White*.[6] He said that there was no averment as to how the omission of the statutory words could have prejudiced the pursuer: 'Absolutely nothing was put forward on behalf of the pursuer that he was affected in any way, far less materially affected, by their omission.'[7] Moreover 'the pursuer is doing nothing more than to rely on a technicality to delay payment'.[8] He continued: 'To take the approach urged upon me by the pursuer would be to frustrate the purpose of the legislation.'[9] 'The assignation' he said, 'is crystal clear.'[10] Moreover, 'it is not an argument which can be advanced when considering the issue of validity with respect to the pursuer, who is, of course, not a party to the assignation'. Parliament must be assumed to have intended a sensible result and … if failure to comply with this part of the note led to invalidity a sensible result would be wholly frustrated.[11]

Finally, however, the Lord Ordinary took the same view of *Sanderson's Trs v Ambion Scotland Ltd* as Sheriff Mann, namely that its facts were so special that it could not serve as a precedent.

---

1 Presumably Allied Irish Banks plc.
2 A copy can be found at www.addleshawgoddard.com/globalassets/insights/litigation/shear-v-clipper.pdf.
3 Paragraph 2.
4 Paragraph 2.
5 [2013] EWCA Civ 584, [2014] 1 WLR 1288.
6 [2015] UKPC 39, [2015] BLR 727.
7 Paragraph 3.
8 Paragraph 3.
9 Paragraph 4.
10 Paragraph 7.
11 Paragraph 7.

Promontoria (Henrico) Ltd v Portico Holdings[1]

The facts of Promontoria (Henrico) Ltd were essentially the same. Portico Holdings, a partnership, was a property developer. With its partners, Mr and Mrs Arthur, it granted 34 standard securities to Clydesdale Bank plc. These securities were later assigned to Promontoria (Henrico) Ltd. The assignations were in the form already mentioned – that is to say, with no mention of the sums due. That company then raised an action to enforce the securities.[2] The defence was as above: that the standard securities had not been validly assigned and that, accordingly, there was no title to sue. Both *OneSavings* and *Shear* were cited to the court. The sheriff (Derek Hamilton) preferred the latter. His judgment follows its reasoning, and does not add much to it.

Why?

Why do banks disregard the statutory style? We do not know. There could be several reasons. The amount might be in dispute with the borrower.[3] Or the security might secure contingent as well as actual sums. In some types of contract, such as shared equity mortgages, establishing the amount due at any particular time would require a complex process. More generally, 'in the case of larger scale bulk assignations there are considerable practical challenges in assembling the necessary data to quote the sums due at the precise date of assignation'.[4] And the parties will always have the worry that stating an inaccurate figure might have negative consequences.

One way of dealing with the problem would be, not to subtract words from the statutory style, but to add them. For instance, the words used could be: 'to the extent of £   or thereby being the amount now believed (but not warranted) to be due thereunder'. This would have the merit of being nearer the statutory style.

Evaluation

The law seems to us unclear, though with the current score being 2–1 it seems reasonably likely that the *OneSavings* decision will not prevail. Yet the decision in *Shear* is not beyond criticism.

The cases cited in *Shear* seem of only limited relevance. They are not conveyancing cases. They are not even private-law cases.

In *Shear* much is said about the argument of the pursuer being a mere technicality, intended to delay the day of reckoning. This does not seem a strong ground of decision, and indeed *Shear* has, perhaps, too much of rhetoric. Debtors

1 [2018] SC GRE 5, 2018 GWD 6-87.
2 The action was against two defenders: (i) the partnership and (ii) Mrs Arthur 'as partner and trustee for' that partnership. But it seems that the partnership had been dissolved by the death of Mr Arthur. So did the first defender exist? And was the second defender a 'partner of and trustee for' it? These issues seem not to have been raised and we offer no views on them.
3 Which was in fact the situation in *Promontoria (Henrico) Ltd*.
4 We quote from the useful briefing note on the Shepherd & Wedderburn website: https://shepwedd.com/sites/default/files/OSB_v_Burns_overview_0.pdf.

are entitled to plead technicalities, and often do so, sometimes successfully. The same is true of other areas of law. Examples are so numerous that it would take a book to cite them.

Again, *Shear* was wrong to say that, even if the assignation was invalid, the debtor had no locus to object to it. If the assignation was invalid, the defender was not the holder of the security. If it was not the holder of the security it had no right or title to enforce it.

Shear also has the argument that the omission of the statutory words did not prejudice Mr Shear. Again, that seems a doubtful argument. The question is not one of prejudice. The question is whether the security was in fact validly assigned. If it was not validly assigned, the putative assignee could not enforce it, and that would be true regardless of any question of prejudice. The issue was not 'prejudice' but 'validity.' The 'no prejudice' argument could have been used round the table when the Parliamentary draftsmen were putting together the Bill that became the 1970 Act. It might have persuaded them. But that is history. The fact is that the legislation, good or bad, is what it is.

Ken Swinton, in a valuable article,[1] has pointed to the word 'may' in Note 2 in schedule 4, and takes the view that 'it is clearly permissive'.[2] This point seems not to have been picked up in any of the cases. He contrasts this with the legislative provisions that were invoked in the *Beneficial Bank* cases[3] which said that certain wording 'shall' be used. This argument is a powerful one. Yet we think that it falls short of being conclusive. If the statutory words are merely optional, why are they there at all? After all, parties are free to *add* words to a deed. That is a general principle, and in fact s 53 of the 1970 Act makes that specifically clear. If the schedule means 'you can add these words if you feel like it' then it is wasting its breath, because that would have been true anyway. The wording, it may be argued, is not permissive because permission is not needed.[4] We do not conclude that here 'may' means 'must', but we do conclude that at least a reasonable case could be made for saying that here 'may' means 'must'.

Another pointer in that direction is that the statutory words apply not only to all-sums standard securities, but also to assignations of standard securities for a maximum amount, and in the latter case, unlike in the former, the words are in the style itself and not in a note prefaced by the word 'may'. Significantly, the words do not apply to assignations of standard securities for a fixed amount. Of course, in the last case the assignation would be free to mention the amount still outstanding. For instance, if a standard security is assigned for a fixed loan of £100,000, and after two years it is assigned when £40,000 has been paid off, the assignation would be free to state that the amount now secured is £60,000.

---

1 'Assigning Heritable Securities' (2017) 85 *Scottish Law Gazette* 23.
2 At p 25.
3 *Bennett v Beneficial Bank* 1995 SLT 1105; *Beneficial Bank v McConnachie* 1996 SC 119.
4 Might this be a 'safe harbour' provision of the type mentioned at the start of this section? We think not. A safe harbour approach would (i) set out the basics that are needed and then (ii) say 'if you do it this way then it is guaranteed that the basics have indeed been covered'. It is the distinction between necessary conditions and sufficient conditions. (i) sets out the necessary conditions, but (ii) says 'this will be sufficient'. We do not see sch 4 as taking that approach.

But the statutory styles do not call for it in that case. Why not? There must be some point of difference.

That difference lies in the fact that, on the conventional view at least,[1] if a security for all sums (or for all sums up to a stated maximum) is assigned, that has a 'freezing' effect, in the sense that in the hands of the assignee it can secure only the sum owed to the assignor (plus interest etc) at the time of assignation. For example, suppose that the Bank of Pictavia plc lends £100,000 to Mary and is granted by her an all-sums standard security. Two years later, when the balance is £60,000, it assigns to the Bank of Dalriada plc. If thereafter the latter lends Mary further sums, those further sums would not – on the standard view – be secured by that standard security.[2] So here we have a reason for the statutory wording, including why it applies to assignations of all-sums standard securities but not to assignations of fixed-sums standard securities. It is not mere fusspottery.

There is some suggestion in *Promontoria (Henrico) Ltd* that if there is a freezing effect, this results from the statement itself, so that if the assignation is silent as to the amount, then there is no freezing. That suggestion is incorrect. If an assignation of an all-sums standard security has a freezing effect, which is the conventional view, that effect follows from the fact of the assignation itself, and the wording of the assignation is wholly irrelevant.

So was *OneSavings* decided correctly? We are uncertain.

Fallout

If *OneSavings* was not correctly decided, and that is probably, at the time of writing, the way to bet, then it has no consequences. But if it was correctly decided, what then? Much could be said, but we will be brief.

Most standard securities are never sold,[3] and most standard securities are never enforced, the debtor paying off the debt. So the scale of the problem, in the sense of sales by assignee banks, would be fairly small.

If, however, there is a sale by an assignee bank, the buyer should be reasonably safe. In the first place, the bank implicitly warrants that it has power of sale, so that there would be a comeback if the buyer's title were to be challenged. But even more importantly, in almost all cases where property is sold under a standard security the creditor will have obtained decree, and in the action leading to the decree the debtor either will have pled 'no title to sue' and failed (as in *Promontoria (Henrico) Ltd*) or (much more probably) will have not raised the point at all. In either case it is difficult to see how the debtor could, after the sale has, following the decree, gone ahead, raise the point in court. It would be too

---

1 See generally G L Gretton, 'Assignations of all-sums standard securities' 1994 SLT (News) 207. The conventional view has been questioned by Ross Anderson, 'Assignations of All Sums Securities', in Frankie McCarthy, James Chalmers and Stephen Bogle (eds), *Essays in Conveyancing and Property Law in Honour of Professor Robert Rennie* (2015) 73. If the conventional view is correct, the words, used in all the cases, 'to the extent of all sums now due or at any time or times hereafter to become due' look odd.

2 And likewise, if the Bank of Dalriada had already, pre-assignation, been a creditor of Mary, that pre-assignation debt would not become secured.

3 And many of those that are sold are never actually assigned, as noted above.

late, or, in traditional language, any such plea, at *that* stage, would be met with the answer (i) 'proponed and repelled' or (ii) 'competent and omitted.'

A further point is that even if *OneSavings* is right, the debt is still owed, and the assignee is the new holder of that debt. So the debtor is not off the hook. And just as the debt still exists, so the standard security still exists. It would still be held by the original creditor, and could be enforced, with or without a corrective assignation to the current creditor.

Assuming that the debtor carries on paying, the payments will be going to the right party, because even on the *OneSavings* view the debt is validly assigned even if the security is not.

As and when a discharge is granted, however, it will be granted by the wrong party, assuming *OneSavings* to be correct. But that is unlikely to matter much, for the debt will have been validly paid off, so the security will be dead anyway. Even without a discharge, it would be unenforceable.

We understand that since *OneSavings* some assignee banks, instead of seeking to enforce a standard security directly, have been placing the debtor in sequestration or liquidation, and leaving the enforcement to the trustee or liquidator, the question of the effectiveness of the assignation thus becoming an issue between bank and trustee/liquidator.

Caution!

One final reflection. Even if *OneSavings* is wrong, which it may well be, there is a sense in which it would be risky to ignore it. Statutory provisions are statutory provisions and 'but they are poorly drafted!' may not always be a winning plea in court. Difficult though it often is to comply with the styles in the 1970 Act, and, indeed, sometimes impossible, the cautious drafter will keep a careful eye on the statutory provisions and will keep, in the words of the Act itself,[1] 'as closely as may be' to their requirements.

TENEMENTS AND OTHER DEVELOPMENTS

Going it alone for repairs

Collective action v individual action

Almost always, tenement repairs are a matter of collective action. The owners meet together or otherwise get in touch. A decision is reached as to what repairs are needed. Estimates are obtained and a choice made between them. On completion of the work the cost is shared. All of this is, or should be,[2] done in accordance with applicable rules covering matters such as meetings, notices, majorities, and liabilities. In modern developments, and in some older tenements too, these rules are found in the titles. Where they are not, the position is

---

1 Section 53.
2 For a case where it was not, see *Garvie v Wallace* 2013 GWD 38-734, discussed in *Conveyancing 2013* pp 156–63.

regulated by rule 2 of the Tenement Management Scheme ('TMS'), which provides that 'scheme decisions' can be made simply and informally by the owners of the majority of the flats.[1]

But what of individual action? Could an owner simply bypass the management arrangements, consult no one at all, carry out whatever repairs took his fancy, and then look to the other flat-owners for a contribution towards the cost? This may look like a purely theoretical question, because it is hard to see why anyone, however headstrong and impatient, would wish to proceed in this manner. Yet there will be cases where this is an attractive way, or even the only way, of doing things. One such case is where an owner has tried but failed to get agreement through the decision-making procedure in the titles or the TMS. In a converted villa, for example, the owner of the upper flat may be faced with both a leaking roof and an unco-operative downstairs neighbour.[2] Another case concerns social housing where, despite some of the flats in a block having been sold under the right-to-buy legislation, the local authority continues to see to the repairs and then to look to the owner-occupiers for a contribution. A third possibility is where, in attempting to use the prescribed decision-making procedure, the owner fails to comply in full with its requirements so that a doubt arises as to the validity of the decision in respect of repairs. The new case of *Donaldson v Pleace*[3] appears to be an example of the last of these.

Repairs in respect of shelter and support

The tenement at 14–18 Bow Street, Stirling is a stone building comprising a café on the ground floor and three upper flats, one on each floor. The pursuers in *Donaldson v Pleace* were the owners of the flat on the first floor; the defender was the owner of the café. The background to the litigation was as follows. The roof of the building leaked. There was also water ingress though one of the outside walls. The pursuers arranged for repairs to be done. It appears that they first consulted the owners of the other two flats. They did not, however, consult the defender because, at the stage of instructing the work, they did not realise that the café bore a share of the cost of repairs.[4] Now, too, late, the pursuers realised their mistake. The share attributable to the café[5] was 25.9%. The pursuers raised an action for payment to recover this amount.

This, then, has the appearance of a blundered attempt at a common repair. Instead of seeking the approval of all three owners in the tenement, the pursuers had contacted only two.[6] As the resulting decision was open to challenge, the

---

1 The Tenement Management Scheme is set out in sch 1 of the Tenements (Scotland) Act 2004.
2 As in *Humphreys v Crabbe* [2016] CSIH 82, 2017 SCLR 699, discussed in *Conveyancing 2016* pp 172 ff. In that case the owner of the upper flat carried out repairs to the roof, of which she was sole owner, having failed to gain the agreement of the proprietor of the lower flat, and then looked to the proprietor of the lower flat for a share of the costs of the repairs under s 10 of the Tenements (Scotland) Act 2004.
3 22 September 2017, Stirling Sheriff Court, unreported. This was a decision of Sheriff A Wyllie Robertson.
4 Paragraph 9.
5 Whether under the titles or r 4 of the TMS is not clear.
6 We infer this to be the case although the position is not explained in the sheriff's judgment.

pursuers sought some other basis for finding the defender liable. In other words they treated what appears to have begun life as a collective repair as if it had been all along a repair at the instance of only one of the owners.

It is worth pausing to consider whether some means might have existed for correcting the defective decision. The answer may well have been yes. In terms of the TMS, the validity of a decision is unaffected by minor procedural irregularity.[1] And even if the irregularity in the present case was too serious to fall within this rule it would have been open to the owners to make a fresh decision homologating the repair which had already been carried out.[2]

Be that as it may, however, the pursuers chose to find some other ground for liability on the part of the defender. Their argument may seem surprising at first sight because the provisions they invoked are not well-known. Yet there can be no doubt that the argument was sound.[3] It proceeded in a number of distinct stages. (i) The repair was necessary for the purposes of 'shelter', ie in order to make the building wind and watertight. (ii) According to s 8(1) of the Tenements (Scotland) Act 2004, restating the common-law doctrine of common interest,[4] the owner of any part of a tenement building that provides shelter (or support) for the building must maintain that part so as to secure the shelter (or support) in question. (iii) Where the part is owned in common, any one of the owners may carry out the repair.[5] (iv) Under the titles to 14–18 Bow Street, both the roof and the outside walls were the common property of all of the owners in the tenement; hence the pursuers were entitled to carry out the repair. (v) By s 10 of the Act, where an owner carries out a repair under s 8 (ie in respect of shelter or support), liability for the cost is apportioned as if the repair had followed on from a valid decision taken by the owners. (vi) If such a decision had been taken, the defender would have been liable for 25.9% of the cost. (vii) Hence the pursuers, having carried out the repair under s 8, were entitled to be reimbursed by the defender under s 10.

The purpose of these provisions of the Act is to help ensure that, whatever repairs are or are not undertaken in respect of a tenement, repairs going to the integrity of the building should always take place and should be the common responsibility of all the owners.[6] A particular concern is for tenements where the core parts of the building are in separate ownership, under the default rules of tenement law, rather than being owned in common under the titles in the manner of the tenement in Bow Street. In such cases there is a danger that the other owners might block a scheme decision to repair, say, the roof, in the knowledge that the top-floor proprietor, as the roof's owner and the person most affected by a leak, would have to repair it anyway. Section 10 ensures that any such repair is a shared responsibility and not a repair at the owner's sole expense.[7] But s 10

---

1 TMS r 6.
2 TMS r 3(1)(h).
3 See eg W M Gordon and S Wortley, *Scottish Land Law* vol I (3rd edn, 2009) paras 15-122–15-129.
4 Which itself was abolished by s 7 of the Tenements (Scotland) Act 2004.
5 Tenements (Scotland) Act 2004 s 8(4).
6 Scottish Law Commission, *Report No 162 on the Law of the Tenement* (1998) para 5.46.
7 *Report No 162* para 7.7.

is wider than that, as *Donaldson v Pleace* demonstrates, and is equally applicable where the parts in question are common property.

The defender did not dispute the pursuers' basic argument. But he sought to show that it did not apply to him. Step (iii) of the pursuers' argument, which was based on s 8(4) of the Act, required the pursuers to own the relevant parts of the building 'in common'. But, said, the defender, the pursuers did no such thing. There was a difference between 'common property' and the 'common parts' of a tenement. The pursuers, who were husband and wife, owned their own flat as common property. In contrast, the 'common parts' of a tenement were 'not owned by any individual title owner' but rather were 'parts in which each owner has a *pro indiviso* right'.[1] Section 8(4) therefore could not apply.

This argument is certainly not lacking in enterprise and ingenuity. It seems to have been based on an intuition that the common parts in a tenement are different from common ownership in the context of individual flats, not least because the common parts pass automatically, as a pertinent, with a conveyance of the flat.[2] But the argument is plainly wrong. It is wholly unsupported by authority. It would leave the common parts owned by no one. And it seeks to make a distinction which does not exist between *pro indiviso* rights and rights of common ownership. The argument was dismissed without difficulty by the sheriff. The defender was liable for a share of the repairs.

Other cases

Repairs to preserve shelter and support are not the only cases where individual owners can go it alone. Another example is emergency repairs, although few repairs will satisfy the statutory definition, which is work which cannot wait for a scheme decision but which must be carried out right away in the interests of health or safety or to prevent damage to any part of the tenement.[3]

The truth, however, is that the shelter and support provisions are only a particular example of a more general rule. That rule is that owners are entitled to repair their own property.[4] If the property is solely owned, as in the case of a tenement flat, the rule is absolute. If the property is owned in common, as in the case of the common parts, the rule is qualified and unilateral repair is allowed in two circumstances only. One, a rule of the common law, is where the repair is a 'necessary' one.[5] The other is the rule under s 8(4) which we have already met: in a tenement, unilateral repair of common property is permitted where the property contributes to shelter and support. To this second rule there is an important qualification. A unilateral repair cannot be carried out 'if it would not be reasonable to do so, having regard to all the circumstances (and

---

1 Paragraph 13.
2 Paragraph 15. Here we build a bit on the defender's argument. What the defender actually argued was that a share in the common parts cannot be disponed separately but only in association with a conveyance of a flat. This, however, is not the case.
3 TMS r 7.
4 Scottish Law Commission, *Report No 162* para 5.50.
5 K G C Reid, *The Law of Property in Scotland* (1996) para 25. This right was deliberately left undisturbed by the 2004 Act: see *Report No 162* para 10.30.

including, in particular, the age of the tenement building, its condition, and the likely cost of any maintenance)'.[1] So if a building is on the point of falling down, a co-owner acting alone cannot incur enormous cost in order to secure its survival.

Thus far we have discussed the question of whether repairs can be carried out. But a right to carry out repairs does not always imply a right to recover a share of the cost from the other owners. Sometimes it does but sometimes it does not. In fact, the recovery of the cost is allowed in two circumstances only. One, the subject of the litigation in *Donaldson v Pleace*, is where the repair goes to shelter or support – as many repairs must of course do.[2] The other is where the titles contain a real burden requiring a contribution to the repair in question.[3] In any other case, the go-it-alone owner must bear the cost himself and so is most unlikely to embark on the repairs in the first place.[4]

Evaluation

These various instances where an owner can go it alone have, perhaps, a slightly random feel about them. Each, however, has its own strong justification. Owners should be allowed to maintain their property. Repairs which go to the very fabric of a building should be enabled and encouraged. In all of this there might seem a danger of rights being abused. An owner, unwilling to engage with his neighbours, might proceed with repairs by himself and then look to his neighbours for a contribution. Experience, however, does not suggest that this is a problem.[5] Only the rich or the foolish would needlessly instruct a repair without consultation, pay for it themselves, and then hope to make recovery from neighbours who might be unwilling to pay and may challenge the legal and factual basis of the repair. The problem with tenements is not that too many repairs are carried out but too few. It is reasonable that an owner who wishes to bear the financial risk of carrying out a repair should be allowed to go ahead and do so.

Park, if you dare

Contract

When Carly Mackie moved back to her parents' house in September 2013 she brought her car with her. With hindsight, that might have been a mistake. Her parents lived in the Waterfront District of Dundee in a new-build development

---

1 Tenements (Scotland) Act 2004 s 8(2).
2 Tenements (Scotland) Act 2004 s 10.
3 Scottish Law Commission, *Report No 162* para 5.47.
4 Section 16 of the Tenements (Scotland) Act 2004 disapplies for tenements the rule of the common law whereby responsibility for the cost of a necessary repair to common property is shared by all the co-owners. This was to prevent a single co-owner from circumventing the provisions for collective decision-making in the titles or the TMS: see *Report No 162* para 10.30. The mere fact that property is held in common is not sufficient justification for such circumvention.
5 Nor did long experience of the law prior to the 2004 Act where individual owners were also entitled, in certain circumstances, to go it alone with repairs.

in West Victoria Dock Road known as 'River Court'. Parking in the development was at a premium. Some houses, such as her parents', had integral garages. Some had dedicated parking spaces. Otherwise parking took place on communal parking areas. The development was factored by an organisation called Factor4You.

In order to stop members of the public from using the development for parking – a significant problem, it appears – the factors arranged for a company, Vehicle Control Services Ltd ('VCS'), to provide a 'parking management solution'. The solution was as follows. Each owner within the development was issued with a parking permit (or permits) which were free of charge and could be used for any car. When a car was parked, a permit had to be displayed. In this way VCS could determine which cars were authorised and which were not. Those parking without a permit, even residents, were liable to a charge of £100 a day, reduced to £60 if paid within 14 days. This was made clear from notices, eight in all, which were displayed prominently around the entrance points to the property.

Ms Mackie parked her car but did not display a permit because she did not have one.[1] Every day she received a new parking ticket; every day she ignored it. In her view, the parking scheme was unlawful, and the charges were unenforceable. Eventually, VCS put that view to the test by raising an action for payment against her. By this time Ms Mackie had collected 245 tickets and so the sum sued for was £24,500.[2]

As a result of several cases over the last few years,[3] including a decision of the Supreme Court in an English appeal,[4] the law on private parking schemes is much clearer than it once was.[5] The legal analysis turns on the law of contract. The notices at the entrance to private car parks form an offer to park on certain terms. By parking a car the offer is deemed to have been accepted. The person parking the vehicle is then bound by the terms of the contract as set out on the notices. Invariably this involves the payment of a charge, either immediately or after parking for more than a certain period of time. A person who has incurred a charge is bound, as a matter of contract law, to pay it.

The details of the contract vary from scheme to scheme but essentially there are two ways in which parking notices operate. One is to say: 'Come and park, and if you do it will cost you £X per day' or 'Come and park for X hours for free but if you stay for longer it will cost you £Y per day'. The other is to say: 'Don't

---

1 The reasons are not wholly clear. 'Her father could have sought a permit for her to use but did not do so' (para 10 of the sheriff's 'facts proven or admitted or agreed.') Later: 'She [the defender] was offered a permit by the factors (at a reasonable charge I think) but she refused on principle' (para 5 of the sheriff's note).

2 *Vehicle Control Services Ltd v Mackie* [2017] SC DUN 24, 2017 SLT (Sh Ct) 111. This was a decision of Sheriff G A Way. For commentary, see Robin M White, 'Parking's not fine' 2017 SLT (News) 151; Malcolm Combe, 'Fine to park here?' (2017) 62 *Journal of the Law Society of Scotland* June/26.

3 Indeed there was another case in 2017, *Indigo Park Services UK Ltd v Watson* 2017 GWD 40-610, involving a parking scheme operating at Ninewells Hospital in Dundee.

4 *ParkingEye Ltd v Beavis* [2015] UKSC 67, [2016] AC 1172.

5 In England and Wales there has also been a certain amount of statutory regulation: see Protection of Freedoms Act 2012 s 56, sch 4.

come and park, but if you do it will cost you £X per day.' Either approach – both the invitational and the prohibitory – is, it seems, legally effective.[1] The notices put up by VCS were, however, a rather confusing mixture of the two. In Robin White's words, 'they displayed something of a mish-mash of information'.[2] They began with a prohibition: 'Private Property' and 'No Parking'. Next there was an invitation: 'By parking on this land you are entering into a contract with [VCS]. Do not park on this land unless you understand and fully agree to the contractual terms and conditions stated on this sign.' Then there were words which, by using the language of breach, seemed to indicate that the invitation had been withdrawn: 'If you breach the terms and conditions you agree to pay the Parking Charges stated below.' Finally, there was a statement of the level of charges.

With the contractual analysis so firmly established, the main danger for private parking schemes is greed. If they ask for too much, the amount claimed by way of a charge may be unenforceable either as an unfair term under the Consumer Rights Act 2015 or, where the prohibitory model is used so that the charge is in respect of a notional breach, as a penalty clause. Following the decision of the Supreme Court in *ParkingEye Ltd v Beavis*,[3] neither seems much of a risk. For example, in relation to penalty clauses, Lord Hodge said that 'the correct test for a penalty is whether the sum or remedy stipulated for a breach of contract is exorbitant or unconscionable when regard is had to the innocent party's interest in the performance of the contract'.[4] Viewed from this perspective, the daily charge of £100 exacted by VCS would seem acceptable.[5]

At one level, therefore, Ms Mackie's case was a straightforward application of the contractual analysis. She saw the notices. She parked. She received a ticket. She parked again the next day. By parking she was, as the notices said, 'entering into a contract'. Now she must pay the agreed charge. Decree was accordingly granted against her.

Property

But there is another way of looking at things which was set out, in part, in the defence offered on behalf of Ms Mackie:[6]

> The defender focused on the question of authority to contract. The main thrust of submissions was that the factors could have no better power and authority to contract with the pursuers [VCS] than the owners themselves. In the defender's submission,

---

1 Doubt might possibly have surrounded the prohibitory model but its validity as a contractual arrangement was upheld by Sheriff Principal Iain Macphail QC in *University of Edinburgh v Onifade* 2005 SLT (Sh Ct) 63 despite wording which referred to liability for a 'fine'.
2 White, 'Parking's not fine' 155. We take the terms of the notice from White's article, which offers an insightful analysis of different types of parking scheme and of the cases that have considered them.
3 [2015] UKSC 67, [2016] AC 1172.
4 *ParkingEye* para 255.
5 It is worth adding that a Members' Bill is to be introduced to the Scottish Parliament by Murdo Fraser MSP seeking to regulate parking charges by private companies: see www.parliament.scot/parliamentarybusiness/Bills/106912.aspx.
6 Paragraph 11.

the powers of the owners relate to maintenance, repair and preservation. Nowhere is there power to levy financial penalties ... The defender's agent concedes that there is a power [in the deed of conditions] that authorises the doing of 'any other matter which the convenors of the meeting shall consider desirable for the benefit of the parking proprietors or any part thereof'. The defender, however, submits that this would require proof of a motion or resolution of the proprietors and no evidence of this was advanced. In brief then the factor had no power or authority to contract with the pursuers and therefore the pursuers had no mandate. The pursuers' contract being invalid they, in turn, could not enter into any contract to offer or indeed restrict parking on the property. The defender was not in breach of contract as there was no contract in the first place. She should be assoilzied with expenses in her favour as taxed.

For a full understanding of this view it is necessary to go back to first principles and to look, not just at contract law, but at the law of property. The communal parking areas, it seems, were the common property of all the house-owners in the development.[1] Under the rules of common property, each *pro indiviso* owner is allowed to use every part of the property. More than that, each owner can authorise someone else, such as a member of the owner's family, to share in the exercise of those rights of use.[2] Ms Mackie was characterised by the sheriff as being 'the same as any other interloper'.[3] But that is hardly correct. She was, so to speak, an insider rather than an outsider. She was the daughter of and living with the tenant of one of the houses in the development.[4] The tenant, her father, was standing in for the owner for the duration of the lease and, like the owner, was entitled to share possession with his daughter. In the same way, therefore, as Ms Mackie was entitled to live in her father's house so also, as a matter of common law, she was entitled to park her car on the common areas.

That, then, is the starting-point. Now of course co-owners can come to an agreement as to how the property is to be used. They can allow certain uses and disallow others. They can even surrender their use rights altogether or, as in the case of a parking scheme, agree to exercise them only on a certain basis. But there are only two ways in which this can be done. One is by contract. The other is by real burdens. In relation to the first of these, there is uncertainty as to whether any agreement as to use must be unanimous or whether a majority of co-owners can bind the others.[5] In relation to the second, community burdens can be imposed in a deed of conditions. The non-exhaustive list of community burdens set out in s 26(1) of the Title Conditions (Scotland) Act 2003 includes 'the procedures to be followed by the owners in making decisions about matters affecting the community' and also 'the matters on which such decisions

---

1 Paragraph 3 ('owned jointly by all').
2 Though this is subject to the 'no excessive use' principle. For the whole issue, see K G C Reid, *The Law of Property in Scotland* (1996) para 24.
3 Paragraph 5.
4 Rather oddly, the sheriff uses English-law terminology in talking of the 'demise of the landlord's interests': see finding-in-fact 2. Nothing in this case turns on the fact that the house was leased rather than owned.
5 Reid, *Property* paras 23 and 24.

are made'. So long as the burdens are 'for the benefit of the community', a requirement of s 3(3), there is considerable flexibility as to content. If, therefore, a deed of conditions chooses to provide for the introduction of a parking scheme, such as the one in the present case, there seems no reason to doubt the validity of the burdens.

How, then, were matters arranged in the River Court development in Dundee? In terms of the deed of conditions, the factors were entitled to exercise the rights of the house-owners. The question therefore was, as Ms Mackie pointed out, whether the house-owners would have been entitled to enter into a parking scheme with VCS. Had they, in other words, agreed to surrender the unqualified rights which they otherwise would have had to park in the communal areas? The answer does not appear clearly from the sheriff's judgment. There seems to have been no question of a contract among the owners. And while there were certainly real burdens, it is uncertain whether these could be read as allowing the introduction of a parking scheme.[1] Perhaps they could. If so, VCS was entitled to its money from Ms Mackie. Indeed, as a matter of future drafting, it would now seem sensible to make express provision for parking schemes in the deeds of conditions of developments where the introduction of such a scheme might be seen to be desirable. But if the deed of conditions did not cover the point, the owners – and hence the factors – had no authority to enter into contractual relations with VCS. What then?

The result would not, we think, prevent Ms Mackie and others from entering into contractual relations by parking their cars. The notices would still constitute an offer which Ms Mackie and others accepted by parking. But the resulting contract might be one which VCS would be unable to perform; for if VCS was not authorised to operate a parking scheme in the first place, then they had no authority to allow Ms Mackie and others to park their cars. And being thus in breach of their own contractual obligations, VCS would be unable to require Ms Mackie to perform her obligations by making payment of the agreed charge.

There is, however, a counter-argument which may require the analysis just given to be qualified. VCS was not operating its parking scheme in secret. On the contrary, the house-owners in the development were participants, willingly or unwillingly, in the whole enterprise. They accepted the free parking permits. They displayed them in their cars. They allowed the notices to remain in place and did nothing to challenge VCS. Even, therefore, if the scheme was not authorised by the deed of conditions, it may separately have been authorised by a contract with each of the owners. A question would still arise, however, as to the terms of such a contract. To what, precisely, would the owners be taken to have agreed? Presumably they could be taken to have agreed to the scheme to the extent that it imposed charges on 'interlopers'. But whether such an agreement would have extended to giving up their own rights to park – the rights to which their very ownership of the parking areas gave rise – is another matter entirely.

---

1 We have not seen the deed of conditions and so cannot provide a view of our own.

WHAT DOES A STANDARD SECURITY SECURE?

Standard securities and non-monetary obligations

A standard security typically secures a monetary obligation – a loan. But could it secure a non-monetary obligation? Section 9(8) of the Conveyancing and Feudal Reform (Scotland) Act 1970 says that:

> 'debt' means any obligation due, or which will or may become due, to repay or pay money, including any such obligation arising from a transaction or part of a transaction in the course of any trade, business or profession, and any obligation to pay an annuity or *ad factum praestandum*, but does not include an obligation to pay any rent or other periodical sum payable in respect of land, and 'creditor' and 'debtor', in relation to a standard security, shall be construed accordingly.

So the answer to the question whether a standard security secures a non-monetary obligation (an obligation *ad factum praestandum*) is: yes. Yes, but …

The trouble is that the 1970 Act, having made that basic point clear, then falls silent.[1] The various provisions of the Act proceed on the assumption that the debt is a monetary debt. The difficulty is most acute in the provisions of the Act about enforcement. For example, s 27(1) says:

> The money which is received by the creditor in a standard security, arising from any sale by him of the security subjects, shall be held by him in trust to be applied by him in accordance with the following order of priority –
>
> (a) first, in payment of all expenses properly incurred by him in connection with the sale, or any attempted sale;
>
> (b) secondly, in payment of the whole amount due under any prior security to which the sale is not made subject;
>
> (c) thirdly, in payment of the whole amount due under the standard security, and in payment, in due proportion, of the whole amount due under a security, if any, ranking pari passu with his own security, which has been duly registered or recorded;
>
> (d) fourthly, in payment of any amounts due under any securities with a ranking postponed to that of his own security, according to their ranking,
>
> and any residue of the money so received shall be paid to the person entitled to the security subjects at the time of sale, or to any person authorised to give receipts for the proceeds of the sale thereof.

This all makes good sense assuming that the obligation secured is monetary, but it does not make such good sense if the obligation is non-monetary. Money generated by a sale will pay off a monetary obligation. It cannot pay off a non-monetary obligation.[2] Given the silence of the Act, is there some clue in the

---

1 A very minor exception is in sch 5, Form A, where the term used is 'non-monetary obligation'. The use of different terms (ie *'ad factum praestandum'* in s 9 and 'non-monetary' in sch 5) suggests a lack of joined-up thinking.

2 At this point, to avoid any possible confusion, it may be as well to point out the distinction between (i) a standard security for a non-monetary obligation and (ii) non-monetary breach of a standard security. The latter happens in respect of ordinary standard securities, securing monetary obligations: see Mark Higgins, *The Enforcement of Heritable Securities* (2nd edn, 2016) ch 2.

background to the Act or in the contemporary discussion of the legislation? The answer, unfortunately, is negative.

The 1966 report that led to the 1970 Act does not mention the possibility of a standard security for non-monetary obligations.[1] The authoritative commentary on the 1970 Act was by Professor Halliday, but whilst he mentions that a standard security can be for a non-monetary obligation, he does so only in passing and does not discuss the issue.[2]

If the only type of standard security that can be enforced is one that secures a monetary obligation, it would follow that a standard security for an obligation *ad factum praestandum* cannot be enforced. And an unenforceable standard security would be pointless: a control switch on a machine that is disconnected. A standard security for a non-monetary obligation must, therefore, be enforceable *somehow*. Given that enforcement generates money and the money is payable to the secured creditor (subject to any prior-ranking claims), the conclusion would seem to be that what the enforcing creditor obtains, through the sale, is monetary compensation – damages – for default on the non-monetary obligation.[3] In short, the view to which one is driven is that a standard security for a non-monetary obligation is in fact a standard security for the sum contingently due by way of damages for breach of that obligation.

But it would be idle to suggest that this conclusion removes all difficulties. One such difficulty is that, if this is the law, then the '*ad factum praestandum*' provision in s 9 of the 1970 Act was unnecessary since there could be no objection to a standard security drafted as one in security of damages due for breach of a primary obligation. Another difficulty is that a damages claim needs quantification, whereas the enforcement provisions of the 1970 Act presuppose that the sum due is already quantifiable.[4] Despite these problems, however, we think that a standard security for an obligation *ad factum praestandum* must be understood as a standard security that secures the damages due for breach. No other view seems possible. If it did not secure such damages, then it would be without effect.

Just as there has been more or less no academic discussion of this issue, so there has, it seems, been no case law – until now. Unfortunately, however, the

---

1 *Conveyancing Legislation and Practice* (1966, Cmnd 3118), commonly called the Halliday Report. The only pre-1970 discussion we have noted is by John Burns, in his *Conveyancing Practice According to the Law of Scotland* where he wrote: 'Securities *ad factum praestandum* ... are, it is thought, within the definition of "security" in the 1868 Act [Titles to Land Consolidation (Scotland) Act 1868, s 3], but even that might be doubtful. Further, the sales clauses in the Act are not appropriate': see p 444 of the 3rd edn (1926), the last by Burns himself. The same passage can be found in the 4th edition (1957, edited by F MacRitchie) at p 451. Burns did not take the point further. One must suspect that the draftsman of the 1970 Act had not read this passage, for despite its brevity, the warning about the problem of sale is clear.

2 J M Halliday, *The Conveyancing and Feudal Reform (Scotland) Act 1970* (2nd edn, 1977) para 6–05. The same is true of J M Halliday, *Conveyancing Law and Practice* (2nd edn, 1997, ed I J S Talman) para 51–02.

3 See G L Gretton, 'The Concept of Security', in D J Cusine (ed), *A Scots Conveyancing Miscellany: Essays in Honour of Professor J M Halliday* (1987) 126; D J Cusine and R Rennie, *Standard Securities* (2nd edn, 2002) p 28.

4 But a creditor could always, following breach of a non-monetary obligation, sue and obtain decree quantifying the damages, and then enforce the security.

case is of limited assistance, for the case was argued on the basis of contract law and not on the basis of the law of heritable security.

J H & W Lamont of Heathfield Farm v Chattisham Ltd

Standard securities for non-monetary obligations do occur in practice, chiefly in relation to commercial transactions. *J H & W Lamont of Heathfield Farm v Chattisham Ltd*[1] is an example. In 2010 the owners of 73 acres with development potential entered into a contract with a development company whereby the latter acquired an option to buy the land. The price paid for this option was £135,000. The option period was ten years, but with the proviso that on a certain eventuality either party would be entitled to resile before the end of the ten-year period. 'The Option Agreement is an extremely detailed agreement extending (together with its appendices) to 35 pages', noted the Lord Ordinary (Lady Wolffe),[2] but despite this remarkable length[3] it did not deal with the matters that came to be litigated.

'As security for implementation of [the owners'] obligations under this Agreement, [the developer] shall be entitled to require and [the owners] shall be obliged to provide' a standard security, said the contract.[4] A standard security was duly granted and registered, and was 'in security of performance of all obligations undertaken by us [the owners] to [the developer] in terms of the Option'.[5] The contract further provided, in clause 11.3:[6]

> Upon the earlier to occur of (a) the expiry of the Option Period and (b) the termination of this Agreement, [the developer] shall deliver to [the owners] a discharge duly executed in a Self Evidencing Manner of the [standard security].

This clause was the battleground of the case.

Planning permission for development was never obtained, and the option period came to an end, not by the expiry of the ten-year period but earlier, by the owners exercising their right to resile. The owners then invoked the clause just quoted and asked for the standard security to be discharged. The developer refused, claiming that the owners had been in material breach of their obligations under the contract. In the action that followed the developer sought extensive damages for that alleged breach by means of a counterclaim.[7] The basis for that counterclaim is not entirely clear, but at least part of it was that the owners were, said the developer, in breach of their contractual obligation to assist in

---

1 [2017] CSOH 119, 2017 GWD 30-470.
2 Paragraph 5.
3 We have not seen the contract. Fragments are quoted in the judgment.
4 Paragraph 5.
5 Paragraph 9.
6 Paragraph 5.
7 At para 3 of the judgment two sums are mentioned: 'about £5,000,000' and 'in excess of £500,000'. It seems that the lower claim was a 'wasted expenditure' claim: see para 11. We surmise that the higher claim was based on the amount of profit that the developer would, allegedly, have obtained had the development gone ahead.

the obtaining of planning permission.[1] At this stage of the litigation no final decision was made on the counterclaim; the decision was solely as to whether the owners and pursuers should be granted the order they sought that the standard security be discharged.

The action by the pursuers did not take the form of declarator that the security was in fact discharged *rebus ipsis et factis*, but rather it was a demand for specific implement of the obligation to deliver a discharge. This approach made sense tactically, for it was clause 11.3 (above) that was the tool that the pursuers needed. They had a better chance of winning through specific implement than through declarator.

In defence the developer laid emphasis on the counterclaim. If there was a valid claim for damages, said the developer, a discharge could be refused. There were two strands to this argument. In the first place there was the doctrine of mutuality: the pursuers were refusing to perform (by paying damages) and so the defender was entitled to refuse to perform (by discharging the security). In Latin, this is the *exceptio non adimpleti contractus*, or, in plain language, 'if you won't do your bit, I shan't do mine, so there!' This first strand of the argument involved no particular claim about the ongoing effect of the security. As far as this branch of the argument was concerned, the security might have had no more than nuisance value. It was, so to speak, a negative argument.

The second strand of the defender's argument was, by contrast, positive. It was that the standard security was now a security for the damages due in respect of the pursuer's alleged breach. There was, said the defender, an implied term to that effect. The standard security secured the whole obligations under the contract. Those obligations included not only the contingent obligation to dispone (in the event that the option was exercised) but also other obligations including the obligation to co-operate in the obtaining of planning permission. The standard security was thus 'for implement of [the owners'] obligations ... These obligations embrace both their primary obligations and their secondary obligations to make reparation for loss caused by breach of their primary obligations.'[2] The breach of a primary obligation here referred to was not breach of the obligation to dispone, for the developer had never exercised the option, but alleged breach of the duty to co-operate in the obtaining of planning permission.

The pursuers rejected both strands of the defender's argument. As to the first, clause 11.3 was, they said, plain: the defender was now bound to grant a discharge. As to the second, the security did not secure damages for any alleged breach.

The Lord Ordinary agreed with the owners and pursuers on both points. As to the first, she considered that clause 11.3 was clear, and fell to be implemented regardless of any damages claim that there might be. And as to the second, she

---

1 See para 34, which quotes the contract as saying that the owners were to 'provide all necessary assistance'.
2 Paragraph 10.

agreed that the standard security was not worded in a way that could extend to damages. She said:[1]

> The Standard Security secured the exercise of an option that was never exercised and, following the due termination of the Option Agreement, can now never be exercised. There is no subsisting contractual obligation under the Option Agreement for the Standard Security to secure ... [T]he defender's interpretation is inconsistent with the clear language and the commercial purpose of the Option Agreement. In short, I accept Mr Thomson's[2] submission that this is, indeed, the correct construction of the Option Agreement; that that meaning is clear; and that these clauses were habile to exclude and did exclude any remedy arising as a matter of common law of the kind founded upon by the defender.

So the owners won. But as we have mentioned, the counterclaim remains outstanding. And if the counterclaim is successful,[3] one wonders how much real value the discharge of the security will give to the owners. If the counterclaim is successful, and if it is of such a size that the owners are unable to pay it, then insolvency would loom, and the presence or absence of the security would, presumably, be of little significance. Conversely, if the counterclaim fails, or succeeds only to the extent of a sum that the owners are able to meet, nothing would then, on any view, be secured by the security anyway.

Reflections

The case prompts two reflections. The first is about drafting. Those who draft contracts which provide that there will be a standard security for a non-monetary obligation, such as an option, need to choose their words carefully. One way to do that would be to provide expressly that the security is to secure not only the non-monetary obligation itself but also damages for breach. Even that may not always be enough. If a contract contains a clear provision, such as clause 11.3 (quoted above), the holder of the security may be at risk. Thus in the *Lamont* case, even if the developer had persuaded the court as to the second strand of its argument, it still might have lost on the basis of the clear language of clause 11.3. A 'discharge' clause (11.3 in the actual case) could, of course, be modified by adding something like: 'But this is subject to the developer's right to retain and enforce the security in respect of any damages that may be due for breach of the terms of this agreement.' One might go further and wonder whether a discharge clause is needed anyway. Once the granter of a heritable security has performed the secured obligation, the creditor must, as a matter of law, grant a discharge.[4]

The other reflection is not about drafting but about the law itself. The case does not, with respect, clarify matters. Earlier we suggested that a standard security

---

1 Paragraph 51.
2 David Thomson was counsel for the pursuer.
3 The pursuers sought dismissal of the counterclaim, but were not successful. The counterclaim thus remains to be judged.
4 Conveyancing and Feudal Reform (Scotland) Act 1970 sch 3, standard condition 11(5). There is also the possibility of declarator.

for a non-monetary obligation is a security for the damages that will be due in the event of the breach of that obligation. If that is right, and we think that it is, the view taken in the case, that the security secured the primary obligation (the obligation to dispone if the option was exercised, and the obligation to co-operate in obtaining planning permission) but not the substitutionary obligation to pay damages, was not correct. This is not to say that the ultimate decision was wrong: there is clearly a case for saying that, whatever the law of standard securities may be, clause 11.3 imposed an unambiguous and strict obligation on the developer, and if that obligation drained the standard security of any value, so much the worse for the developer.

There are suggestions in the case that the purpose of the security was 'to preclude the pursuers from disposing of the subjects'.[1] In a sense this is no doubt correct. The existence on a title of an undischarged standard security makes the property more difficult to sell, since it is an implied term of a contract of sale of heritable property that there shall be no undischarged securities.[2] But property can as a matter of law be disponed subject to an outstanding security, and that does sometimes happen for one reason or another. So 'preclude' is not true in a legal sense and not wholly true in a practical sense. Moreover, if a standard security cannot be enforced, then it is without any legal effect. Indeed, if the position taken by the pursuers was correct, namely that the standard security did not secure damages for breach, the security was, it would seem, unenforceable and probably a nullity from the very beginning.

So where does the law now stand on standard securities for non-monetary obligations? The answer is: not much further forward. The trouble with the *Lamont* case is that its primary focus is contract law and it does not really turn its attention to the law of heritable security. For example, the key term *ad factum praestandum* is not mentioned.

The Scottish Law Commission is embarking on a project to review the law. Perhaps the provision that a standard security can secure an obligation *ad factum praestandum* should simply be done away with. As mentioned earlier, the objective can be attained quite simply by drafting a standard security in terms that secure any damages due.

LAND REGISTRATION

Digital registration

Background

Towards the end of 2016 Registers of Scotland published a consultation document, *Digital Transformation: Next Steps*,[3] which sets out an ambitious

---

1 This idea crops up more than once. The quotation is from para 17 of the judgment, quoting counsel for the pursuers.
2 G L Gretton and K G C Reid, *Conveyancing* (4th edn, 2011) para 6–03.
3 Registers of Scotland, *Digital Transformation: Next Steps* (2016; www.gov.scot/Publications /2015/11/9619).

programme of e-registration in respect of discharges, standard securities and dispositions. The new system was to replace ARTL and would, it was promised, be much sleeker and faster. Furthermore, unlike ARTL, it would be compulsory.[1] Responses to the consultation were invited by 22 February 2017. 44 responses were received, including from the Law Society of Scotland, the Council of Mortgage Lenders, the Church of Scotland, Scottish Water and from 14 firms of solicitors.[2] In general the responses were positive and supportive, although a number counselled against rushing things, emphasising the importance of a strong and stable system.

Legislative basis

The switch to digital registration requires legislation. But when the necessary statutory instrument[3] was laid before the Scottish Parliament, it was rejected by the Economy, Jobs and Fair Work Committee, on 21 November 2017, by a majority of 5:4.[4] The objection was not to the provisions on digital registration as such, but to an additional provision concerning applications in respect of *a non domino* dispositions. Such applications must be notified to the owner of the land or, failing identification of the owner, to the Queen's and Lord Treasurer's Remembrancer, and this must be done at least 60 days before the application is submitted. The provision to which objection was taken would have allowed this period to be reduced with the written agreement of the owner or QLTR.[5] The amendment was hardly an important one, especially in view of the tiny number of *a non domino* applications – only 17 so far[6] – which have proved able to negotiate the discouraging new procedure introduced by ss 43–45 of the Land Registration etc (Scotland) Act 2012. Nevertheless, the amendment was rejected, and with it the entire statutory instrument. This was partly on the ground of lack of consultation and partly because of a fear that a reduced period for *a non domino* applications might prove to

---

1 For discussion, see *Conveyancing 2016* pp 152–56.
2 An analysis of all the responses was published in May 2017, and 36 of the responses have been made available in their entirety: see www.ros.gov.uk/about-us/what-we-do/our-business/consultations/digital-transformation-next-steps.
3 A draft Registers of Scotland (Digital Registration etc) Regulations 2017.
4 The four SNP MSPs were outvoted by the five MSPs from other parties. The charge was led by Andy Wightman, the land reformer and Green Party MSP.
5 Draft reg 8, amending reg 18 of the Land Register Rules etc (Scotland) Regulations 2014, SSI 2014/150. A second draft SSI, the Land Registration etc (Scotland) Act 2012 (Amendment) Order 2017, accompanied the first and was likewise rejected. It would have amended s 45(5) of the Land Registration etc (Scotland) Act 2012 in order to shorten the period in which the owner or QLTR can object to the application from 60 days to seven days if the owner/QLTR has consented in advance. A further provision would have put on a statutory basis the Keeper's practice of accepting a deed which fails to mention the relevant title number in circumstances where the title number is neither publicised in the Register nor notified by the Keeper to the granter of the deed. This mainly affects discharges granted at the time of first registration: see K G C Reid and G L Gretton, *Land Registration* (2017) para 8.8. Following its rejection, this second SSI has been dropped, at least for the moment.
6 Scottish Parliament, *Official Report: Economy, Jobs and Fair Work Committee*, 21 November 2017, col 32 (Chris Kerr of Registers of Scotland).

be too short for other interested parties, who had not been notified, to raise objections.[1]

A replacement statutory instrument, shorn of the offending provision, was laid before the Scottish Parliament and approved, and came into force on 12 March 2018. This statutory instrument, the Registers of Scotland (Digital Registration, etc) Regulations 2018,[2] makes a series of amendments to earlier statutory instruments, including the Land Register Rules.[3]

The most important single change is the repeal and replacement of rule 7 of the Land Register Rules.[4] The new version of rule 7 allows the Keeper to require that applications in respect of specified deed-types must, after a specified date, be 'sent in electronic form using a computer system under section 99 of the Act'. The deed too must be in electronic form, and authenticated by an electronic signature,[5] which can either be made using the RoS smartcard (which was issued for the purposes of ARTL) or the Law Society smartcard.[6] On the method of registration there is to be no choice for conveyancers: once the nominated date arrives in respect of a particular deed-type, the digital registration system must be used and paper applications will no longer be possible.

To this rule there are a small number of exceptions, modelled on the exceptions to digital advance notices.[7] Thus digital registration need not be used if:[8]

(a) the computer system notifies the applicant who attempts to use it that it is unavailable for a period of 48 hours or longer;

(b) the applicant has no computer facilities with access to the internet; or

(c) the Keeper is otherwise satisfied that exceptional circumstances make it impractical to do so.

---

1 *Official Report: Economy, Jobs and Fair Work Committee*, 21 November 2017, cols 27–38. See in particular the comment of Andy Wightman MSP (at col 31): 'There is no guarantee that either the applicant or the Keeper will have full knowledge of the potential parties who may have a claim to the land. One of the reasons for having a 60-day period – albeit that that comes on the back of a year's uncontested possession – is to allow other voices to come out of the woodwork.'

2 SSI 2018/72.

3 The statutory instruments affected are the Register of Sasines (Application Procedure) Rules 2004, SSI 2004/318, the Electronic Documents (Scotland) Regulations 2014, SSI 2014/83, the Land Register Rules etc (Scotland) Regulations 2014, SSI 2014/150, and the Land Register of Scotland (Automated Registration) etc Regulations 2014, SSI 2014/347.

4 Registers of Scotland (Digital Registration, etc) Regulations 2018 reg 6.

5 Land Register Rules 2014 r 7(4).

6 Electronic Documents (Scotland) Regulations 2014 reg 6(1). That is a change: until an amendment made to reg 6 with effect from 22 July 2016, only the RoS smartcard could be used.

7 Perhaps one should rather say the other way around because the existing exceptions in respect of applications for advance notices, contained in r 3(1) of the Land Register Rules 2014, are amended by the Registers of Scotland (Digital Registration, etc) (Scotland) Regulations 2018 reg 2 to bring them into line with the exceptions as now formulated in respect of digital registration.

8 Land Register Rules 2014 r 7(2). There may be a technical difficulty, both here and in previous regulations, about the word 'applicant'. Whilst in most cases applications are made through law firms, the applicant is not the firm but the client. Whilst all law firms have internet access, some clients (applicants) do not.

Exception (a) brings a smile to the lips at the thought of a computer system which is 'unavailable' but nonetheless able to notify applicants of this fact.[1] Exception (b) may encourage solicitors' firms to abandon their computer equipment and revert to paper, and perhaps to quill pens as well. As for exception (c), rule 7 goes on to say that it will be met in the case of applications by members of the public made without the help of a solicitor or other legal adviser.

Some other changes made by the 2018 Regulations may be mentioned briefly. Those firms of solicitors currently authorised to use ARTL are automatically authorised to use the new digital registration system.[2] Where a disposition triggers first registration, it will be permissible, indeed necessary, to supplement the electronic application with paper deeds such as burdens and split-off deeds. These will have to be sent in hard copy, and must, under the new Regulations, arrive at the Registers within 14 days.[3] Finally, where a disposition which requires dual registration, because it creates real burdens or servitudes, is registered in the Land Register in digital form, it may likewise be registered in digital form in the Register of Sasines.[4] This is the only example of digital registration permitted in the Sasine Register.

Progress on the ground

Meanwhile matters on the ground – if that is an acceptable metaphor for a digital process – have been moving more slowly than seemed likely a year ago. Digital registration of discharges of standard securities began on 31 May 2017 and is being used in around 15% of cases, mainly involving residential property. Currently voluntary, digital registration of discharges is set to become compulsory in the course of 2018 or early 2019. Under the 2018 Regulations, the Keeper must give at least six months' notice before digital registration is compulsory in respect of any deed-type, and in practice is likely to give more notice than this.[5] In outline, the system for digital discharges works as follows.[6] The borrower's solicitor sends an electronic request to the lender for a discharge. The lender executes the discharge and submits it directly to RoS, without returning it to the solicitor. RoS then give notice of the removal of the standard security to the borrower's solicitor and, if need be, to others such as the solicitor acting for a purchaser.

Digital discharges will be followed by digital standard securities and then by digital dispositions. Unlike with ARTL, it is intended that digital registration should apply to all types of disposition, including first registrations and split-off

---

1 These things can of course happen. As most readers will recall, the RoS systems were mysteriously unavailable on 19 July 2017.
2 Registers of Scotland (Digital Registration, etc) (Scotland) Regulations 2018 reg 12.
3 Land Register Rules 2014 r 13A. Strictly, this is an 'amendment' of the original, digital application – something which is only allowed sparingly under s 34(1)(b) of the Land Registration etc (Scotland) Act 2012.
4 Electronic Documents (Scotland) Regulations 2014 reg 6(2). See also Land Registers (Scotland) Act 1868 s 6A; Register of Sasines (Application Procedure) Rules 2014 r 4(2).
5 Land Register Rules 2014 r 7(5).
6 Registers of Scotland, *Digital Transformation: Next Steps* (2016) para 1.5.

dispositions. All of this is expected by RoS to happen within the next two or three years. 2020 is mentioned in the latest published statement by RoS as the target date by which 'the vast majority of deeds will be submitted and processed digitally'.[1]

The future of ARTL

ARTL has no future.[2] As the new digital registration system is phased in, so ARTL will be phased out. For the moment it remains possible to use ARTL for dispositions, standard securities, assignations of leases, and the other deeds listed in the relevant Regulations,[3] but the list of deeds will soon be shortened.

New application form

The existing application form for registration in the Land Register was remodelled and replaced with effect from 21 March 2018. The new form is shorter and simpler. It recasts the awkward phrasing in some questions in the previous version, notably the questions on servitudes and real burdens. It excises the question on links in title, which no one could really understand. And, in an unexpected move at least as far as paper-based transactions are concerned, it dispenses with the need for a signature. This is set to reduce the rate of rejections because unsigned forms have always been one of the most common grounds for rejecting an application. It also brings to an end the traditional rule, dating from 1858 and the introduction of warrants of registration, that registration requires a written and signed request by or on behalf of the grantee of the deed. The same form is to be used for digital as for paper-based applications.

Unlike its predecessor, the new form lacks a legislative basis.[4] The idea is to make the form easy to alter as and when this is deemed necessary by RoS. But it also means that, strictly, the form is not compulsory and that registration could be achieved without it.[5] No one is likely to try that, we imagine. What may turn out to be more significant, however, is that there will be no longer be a legislative basis for rejecting applications on the ground of an error made in completing the form.[6]

---

1 (2017) 62 *Journal of the Law Society of Scotland* Nov/9.
2 A cynic indeed would say that ARTL also has no past.
3 Land Register of Scotland (Automated Registration) etc Regulations 2014 reg 2(1), (2). These Regulations are amended by the Registers of Scotland (Digital Registration, etc) (Scotland) Regulations 2018 reg 5 to replace all references to 'ARTL' with 'digital registration'. Like the new system which is now being introduced, the old ARTL system is thus classified under the Regulations as a type of digital registration system.
4 The requirement to use the previous application form came from r 7 of the Land Register Rules 2014. Rule 7 is removed (and replaced) by reg 6 of the 2018 Regulations.
5 Land Registration etc (Scotland) Act 2012 s 22(1)(d) includes among the general application conditions, which must be complied with for an application to be accepted, a condition that 'the application is in the form (if any) prescribed by land register rules'. With the change there will no longer be such a form.
6 See also p 84 above. An application can only be rejected if it fails to satisfy one of the statutory application conditions: see Land Registration etc (Scotland) Act 2012 s 21(3). Successful completion of the new application form is not among them.

All-digital advance notices

It was always the intention that applications for advance notices on the Land Register should be made electronically, but this intention could not be fully realised until RoS had the technology to accept in digital form the plans which will usually accompany applications in respect of split-off deeds. So hitherto the position has been that a digital application is (and must be) used for standard advance notices and that a paper application is used for advance notices in respect of a split-off deed. That is about to change. The necessary technology is now in place at RoS and the necessary changes to the Land Register Rules have been made by the Registers of Scotland (Digital Registration, etc) (Scotland) Regulations 2018.[1] Hence, from a date yet to be announced but almost certain to be in 2018, all applications for advance notices will require to be in electronic form, including applications in respect of split-off deeds.[2] This, however, is subject to the same minor exceptions (eg for applications by members of the public without legal assistance) that were mentioned above in connection with the digital registration of deeds.[3]

ScotLIS

Amidst much fanfare, ScotLIS (Scotland's Land and Information System) was launched by Registers of Scotland on 24 October 2017.[4] It is available to legal and other professionals, and also in a slightly different format to members of the public. Some very basic information is free but for the rest there is a pay-wall. ScotLIS is underpinned by Land Register data and searched via different layers on the cadastral map. As well as allowing access to the Land Register it will, in time, combine with other public-sector datasets. These may include, for example, school catchment areas, mining reports, flood risks and crime statistics. That, however, is for the future. For the present, ScotLIS is an alternative method of accessing the Land Register to Registers Direct, which it is expected eventually to replace.

KIR and completion of the Land Register

The setting of 2024 for completion of the Land Register has its critics, as we will see. Be that as it may, the pace of Keeper-induced registration ('KIR') increased significantly in the course of 2017 although the total number of registrations, some 50,000, fell short of initial expectations.[5] The intention is that all of the so-called 'research areas' should have been covered by 2020, resulting

---

1 Land Register Rules 2014 r 3, as amended by the Registers of Scotland (Digital Registration, etc) (Scotland) Regulations 2018 reg 2.
2 There is to be some phasing-in. At first digital applications for split-offs will be voluntary and will only become compulsory after the Keeper gives notice of at least six months: see Land Register Rules 2014 r 3(3)–(5).
3 Land Register Rules 2014 r 3(1).
4 See https://scotlis.ros.gov.uk/; also (2017) 62 *Journal of the Law Society of Scotland* Nov/9.
5 For more on KIR, see *Conveyancing 2016* pp 158–64.

in between 500,000 and 600,000 first registrations. KIR titles are starting to be encountered in ordinary conveyancing practice. In 2017 there were more than 500 dealings with KIR titles, most of which appear to have been untroubled. But as owners are no longer notified that KIR has occurred,[1] there may be some delay before the parties to a transaction discover that the title has migrated from the Sasine to the Land Register. In some cases this has led to the discharge of the standard security being presented for registration in the former instead of in the latter. A list of postcodes in which KIR is active can be found on the RoS website.[2]

As of March 2017, 62% of property titles (around 1.69 million) and 30% of the land mass (2.38 million hectares) were on the Land Register. The respective figures for March 2016 were 60% and 28.4%.[3] This is a steady increase but one which leaves a great deal of work to do if completion is to be achieved by 2024.

The Register of Sasines may be closed before 2024. In other words, no deeds of any type would thereafter be recordable in that register. 2021 is a date that we have heard suggested. This would affect mainly advance notices on first registration, and some other arrangements would need to be made for those.

Register of Controlling Interests in Land

The Land Register discloses who owns. But knowing an owner's name takes one only so far, especially where the land in question is owned by a company or other entity in an offshore jurisdiction, or by a trust. In cases such as this, the person or persons who ultimately benefit from the property, and the person or persons who ultimately make the decisions as to what happens to it, may be hard or impossible to discover. The situation was thought, at any rate by a majority of MSPs, to be unsatisfactory, and accordingly the Land Reform (Scotland) Act 2016 provides for the establishment of a public register of 'persons who have controlling interests in owners and tenants of land'.[4] The Act itself has no details and the scope and practical workings of the register have been left to secondary legislation.

None so far has been passed, but in September 2016 the Scottish Government consulted on the subject.[5] This consultation paper was itself fairly light on details, so that it is still unclear what the final shape of the scheme might be. It is unlikely, however, that buyers would have to search the new register in relation to the seller. The concern for conveyancers acting for a buyer will rather be to check

---

1 For robust criticism of the absence of notification, see J Keith Robertson, 'Ticking timebombs at the Land Register' (2017) 85 *Scottish Law Gazette* 28; also at (2016) 62 *Journal of the Law Society of Scotland*, online edition: bit.ly/2xPgZLr. It may be questioned whether the current RoS policy in this regard is compatible with the spirit, or perhaps even with the letter, of s 41 of the Land Registration etc (Scotland) Act 2012.
2 www.ros.gov.uk/about-us/land-register-completion/keeper-induced-registration.
3 Registers of Scotland, *Annual Report 2016–17* (2017) 16.
4 Land Reform (Scotland) Act 2016 s 39(1).
5 *Improving transparency in land ownership in Scotland: a consultation on controlling interests in land* (2016; www.gov.scot/Publications/2016/09/6681). For discussion, see Frances Rooney, 'Controlling interests: problem questions' (2016) 61 *Journal of the Law Society of Scotland* Oct/34.

that registration takes place in the new register, in cases where such registration is necessary.

The consultation paper discussed the scope of the new register, as well as some of the mechanisms that might need to be adopted to ensure compliance with registration. How should 'controlling interest' be defined? Should all land be potentially registrable or only some? What about land not yet on the Land Register? Should the duty of disclosure be upon the 'person with controlling interest'? Should it be on the buyer? Should it be on the buyer's law firm? Or some combination? Should there be civil penalties for non-compliance, or criminal penalties, or both? Should disclosure (or certification that there is nothing to disclose)[1] be a condition of registration in the Land Register? What happens if a change of control occurs at a time when there is no conveyancing transaction?

The consultation closed on 5 December 2016 and an analysis of the responses was published on 28 June 2017.[2] There were 58 responses in all, 33 from organisations and 25 from individuals. In summary:[3]

> There was much support for the principle of making information about persons with controlling interests in owners and tenants of land available, this being perceived as fitting for a modern democracy and in line with practice elsewhere. Maintaining proportion and containing costs emerged as key themes. Other themes included the need to avoid burdensome procedures which may deter inward investment in Scotland; avoiding duplication in data collection between the existing databases including the Sasine and Land Registers; and ensuring a balance is struck between making information accessible whilst adhering to data protection requirements. A repeated comment relating to definitions of 'controlling interest' and 'persons with controlling interests in land owners and tenants' was that definitions will be easier to determine once the overall purpose of the proposals becomes clearer. Another common view was that Scotland should harmonise new definitions with relevant existing definitions used in other jurisdictions and contexts.

On more specific matters, the majority view favoured all land being covered by the scheme. A civil penalty was preferred to a criminal penalty, but compliance should also be a condition for acceptance of an application for registration in the Land Register. There was concern that any measures which were introduced could be avoided by those determined to do so. Circumstances in which avoidance was most likely to arise were suggested to be:[4]

- If the definition of 'controlling interest' and the scope of the regulations are not made sufficiently clear;

---

1 Presumably (though this depends on how the legislation develops) in most cases there will be nothing to disclose. If Mr and Mrs McGlumphry buy a house, it seems likely that there will be nothing to disclose, though it is likely that there would need to be certification to that effect.
2 *Improving Transparency in Land Ownership in Scotland: Consultation Analysis* (2017: www.gov.scot/Publications/2018/05/7210).
3 Paragraphs 1.5–1.7.
4 Paragraph 4.24.

- Where there are complex structures of companies or trusts registered in other jurisdictions; foreign entities; or off-shore companies; and
- If penalties are not enough to act as deterrents; where enforcement is not rigorous.

There was concern too about issues of privacy although, on the whole, disclosure was regarded as strongly in the public interest. Those who were thought particularly at risk from disclosure, and who might therefore need special protection, were people in witness protection schemes; those at risk of violence and intimidation; those with physical or mental-health problems where this could be revealed in information about legal capacity; and public figures who do not wish details of their private residence to be known.[1]

As it happens, this is not the only initiative concerned with the 'beneficial ownership' of companies and trusts. Since 6 April 2016 UK companies have been required to maintain a public register of those who have significant control over the company (the 'PSC register'), 'significant control' being defined to include direct or indirect ownership of more than 25% of the shares or direct or indirect control of more than 25% of the voting rights.[2] The aim is to increase transparency, especially for the purpose of detecting money laundering, tax evasion, and other forms of crime. The UK Government has recently been consulting on extending this scheme to overseas companies which own land in the UK, a matter which was considered earlier in this volume.[3] In addition, trustees of UK and certain non-UK trusts have, since 26 June 2017, been under a duty to maintain up-to-date records in writing of 'all the beneficial owners of the trust' although, by contrast with the PSC register, these are not publicly available.[4] All these initiatives will be of assistance to the Scottish Government in seeking to publicise controlling interests in land.

In respect of the Register of Controlling Interests in Land, the next stage is for the Scottish Government to produce draft regulations for the creation of the new register accompanied by an explanatory document. Both are requirements set by the Land Reform Act.[5] Given the difficulties involved, this is not a task to be envied or, it seems from the Scottish Government's silence, to be hurried.

'No registration without mapping'

Cadastralism

In a witty and insightful passage in a recent article, Donald Reid has drawn attention to what he calls the 'new religion of Cadastralism':[6]

---

1 Paragraph 5.24.
2 The relevant provisions can be found in part 21A (ss 790A–790ZG) and sch 1A of the Companies Act 2006, both of which were added by the Small Business, Enterprise and Employment Act 2015.
3 See p 93 above.
4 Money Laundering, Terrorist Financing and Transfer of Funds (Information on the Payer) Regulations 2017, SI 2017/692, reg 44. This duty applies to the trustees of any 'relevant trust' as defined in reg 42. For other aspects of these Regulations, see p 73 above.
5 Land Reform (Scotland) Act 2016 ss 40 and 41.
6 Donald Reid, 'The 2012 Act: a bold step forward?' (2017) 62 *Journal of the Law Society of Scotland* March/33, 34.

We are all adherents of a new religion: Cadastralism. No one has seen the cadastral map and lived. We make our sacrifices, praying that the gods will smile. Mystery and mysticism surround us: we hope our offerings are good enough; we gain confidence from our successes; but we are never certain. A rejection can come of the most apparently unblemished lamb. We long for certainty. We beg for second chances. We crave a guide who can see more clearly what will be the true, acceptable and worthy submission. In short, we need a castrologer.

The main point which Mr Reid goes on to develop from this sparkling beginning is one with which we have sympathy. With the push towards Land Register completion by 2024, there is a danger that assembling a public database of landownership is being prioritised over the main function of the Register, which is the protection of private property rights. The object, says Mr Reid, is 'to colour in the map of Scotland to show it as all registered by 2024, and take it to the teacher to get a prize for colouring in'. The result is 'to abandon quality control in favour of colouring in. It's a "cadastrophe" waiting to happen.'[1]

From this point of view, which we rather support, we now move to a different point of view, by which we are, by and large, rather puzzled. This derives not from Donald Reid but from a campaign which is being waged by some members of the Scottish Law Agents Society through the pages of the Society's journal, the *Scottish Law Gazette*.[2] The starting-point is a 'draft manifesto', prepared in March 2016, of issues in the law and legal practice that are in need of being addressed.[3] Among the items listed is the following:

Restoration of Function of the Land Register

After centuries of operation as the means of recording and registering rights in land in order to confer reality to these rights, Registers of Scotland has recently replaced that main objective with the new main objective of creating a cadastral map of Scotland. The Keeper's delivery of that objective has the effect of excluding previously recorded [rights] from the register. There is a real danger that these rights will be lost sight of. The aim of completing the map appears to result in significant losses or at least the accuracy of the information which is publicly available. These functions should now be separated and registration of rights be given as the main objective of the Land Register.

---

1 At p 35.

2 The issue discussed here is part of a larger initiative which is critical of the Land Registration etc (Scotland) Act 2012 and, perhaps especially, of the manner in which it is being handled by Registers of Scotland. With the issue of the *Scottish Law Gazette* for August 2017 there was issued a questionnaire which asked: 'Have you had any problems with the Land Register since December 2014?' By the time of the next issue, in October 2017, it was reported that responses had been received from less than 1% of the membership. Further developments are awaited. In the meantime it may be noted that the 2012 Act is one of the statutes which is to be considered by the Public Audit and Post-legislative Scrutiny Committee of the Scottish Parliament as part of its new remit of post-legislative scrutiny: see www.parliament.scot/parliamentarybusiness/ CurrentCommittees/105094.aspx.

3 Reproduced in (2016) 84 *Scottish Law Gazette* 1.

This takes up Donald Reid's point about completion of the Register being given priority over the registration of private rights but draws from it a different conclusion. Further details can be found in an article which appeared in the *Scottish Law Gazette* as well as in a national newspaper.[1] Only an extract can be quoted here:

> The conveyancing membership of the Scottish Law Agents Society is concerned about the new system of registration of property titles. This system came into operation in December 2014 by virtue of the Land Registration etc (Scotland) Act 2012. Many house and land-owners now find that long standing rights in property may be excluded from registration in the new system. This may result in the loss of legal recognition of established rights over land, including ownership of the land, rights of way, grazing, recreation and so on.
>
> We all had plenty of time to study the contents of the Act before it came into force. Nevertheless, its operation has taken many of us by surprise. We all knew, for example, that, from now on, the creation or transfer of property rights would be registered only if they were able to be added to a new cadastral map of Scotland. What many of us did not fully grasp was the meaning of the term cadastral or the significance of the government's objective to create a cadastral map of the whole of Scotland by 2024 …
>
> There was no mention until 2012 that the central register should take the form of a cadastral map. If the property rights which a person has acquired legitimately cannot be identified on the cadastral map, they will not be registered on the next occasion that the property is transferred. It follows from centuries of legal tradition that these rights may then no longer exist. We now see increasing numbers of conveyancing transactions in which sellers have sold their properties to purchasers who are, however, unable to register at least parts of these properties in the Land Register. Somewhere, between the seller and the buyer, some of the property rights have disappeared.

Finally, the pages of the *Scottish Law Gazette* mention various real-life cases in which registration was denied to property rights. For example:[2]

- *From Glasgow*, the exclusion from the registration of a title of a recorded right of exclusive use of an apartment located in the basement of a tenement building.
- *In the West of Scotland*, the exclusion from registration of newly built properties of rights in common land.
- 1st floor flat west end Glasgow including exclusive rights to substantial cellar area and common rights to other parts of basement per Sasines title recorded circa 1970. We sold on standard missives but Keeper rejected cellar and common rights from registration and other side raised issue of breach of missives.

Although this is not always made clear, it is assumed that these were all cases of first registration; for the problem of getting property mapped is, very largely, a problem that arises on first registration.

---

1 (2017) 85 *Scottish Law Gazette* 1. The national newspaper was *The Scotsman*.
2 (2017) 85 *Scottish Law Gazette* 1 and 36A.

Some comments

The anger and frustration lying behind the views just described are both palpable and understandable. But while the problems on the ground are real enough, the causes attributed to them are largely mistaken.

In the first place, the cadastral map is, by and large, simply a new name for something which has been with us since the introduction of registration of title back in 1979. The 1979 Act contemplated only individual title plans, so that the Land Register, when completed, would eventually involve about three million wholly separate plans, which might or might not dovetail. But in reality that is not what happened. Instead the Keeper created a single map on which title boundaries were entered, and title plans were in reality derivatives of the data on this single map – then called the Digital Mapping System ('DMS'). The DMS had no legal status. The 'index map', established not by the 1979 Act itself but by the Land Registration (Scotland) Rules 1980,[1] was in substance a particular form of the DMS. This DMS (index map) was the cadastral map *de facto* though not then so called. The 2012 Act gave it the status that it had had in reality though not in theory, and at the same time gave it a new name. As for the 'base map', that is the topographic dataset that underlies the cadastral map, and is provided by the Ordnance Survey. Thus the cadastral map, like its previous incarnation as the DMS (index map), shares the imperfections of the OS cartographic dataset.[2] If no one has seen the cadastral map and lived, as Donald Reid avers, it is because it is too big and not because it is new.

In the second place, the 2024 target for completion of the Register has nothing to do with the 2012 Act and was not in the minds of those responsible for the Act's creation.[3] The Scottish Government's announcement came out of the blue, in May 2014. Insofar as an origin for the target can be traced, it lies in the report of the independent Land Reform Review Group, published in the same month, which recommended 'that the Scottish Government should be doing more to increase the rate of registrations to complete the Land Register, including a Government target date for completion of the Register, a planned programme to register public lands and additional triggers to induce the first registration of other lands'.[4]

In any event, and thirdly, the requirement to map registered land comes, not from the 2024 target, but from the 2012 Act. Section 6(1)(a)(i) provides the legislative basis for the principle of 'no registration without mapping'. That principle may appear more prominent and pressing in the light of the 2024 target,

---

1 SI 1980/1412.
2 For imperfections, see eg (2017) 85 *Scottish Law Gazette* 1 ('From Kirkcudbrightshire'); J Keith Robertson, 'Ticking Timebombs at the Land Register' (2017) 85 *Scottish Law Gazette* 28, also at (2016) 62 *Journal of the Law Society of Scotland*, online edition: bit.ly/2xPgZLr; (2017) 62 *Journal of the Law Society of Scotland* May/6 (letter by Iain McDonald).
3 A much more leisurely progress was envisaged in Scottish Law Commission, *Report No 222 on Land Registration* (2010) paras 33.65–33.67.
4 Land Reform Review Group, *The Land of Scotland and the Common Good* (2014: www.scotland.gov.uk/Resource/0045/00451087.pdf) 27, 34.

and the resulting haste to complete the Register. But, even without the target, the issues would remain exactly the same.

Fourthly, the 'no registration without mapping' principle was not invented by the 2012 Act. On the contrary, it was already present in the 1979 Act.[1] Indeed the principle is intrinsic to the idea of a map-based Register.[2] It is true that the 2012 Act extended the principle to servitudes and certain other encumbrances.[3] It is also true that, in the early years of registration of title, Registers of Scotland did not always apply the principle consistently. From 2009 onwards, however, it was applied with full vigour.[4] As the Keeper said back in 2008:[5]

> [I]t is an essential requirement of the scheme of the Register that property is sufficiently described on the Ordnance map. An application for registration is not to be accepted unless it is 'sufficiently described' to enable the Keeper to identify it by reference to the Ordnance map. It is potentially misleading to say that the Keeper is given a discretion in this matter. In relation to each application he has to make a decision as to whether the land in question is 'sufficiently described'. The Keeper should not accept an application for registration of land that is not sufficiently described to enable him to identify it by reference to the Ordnance map.

Fifthly, the case which denied unmappable common areas a place on the Register – the second of the three examples quoted above – was decided on 20 November 2008, almost exactly six years *before* the coming into force of the 2012 Act.[6] Indeed it was this case which led to the tightening up of the Keeper's practice mentioned above.

Sixthly, an area of land either can be identified or cannot be identified. If identification is possible, the land can be mapped; if identification is not possible, then no right of ownership can arise in respect of it for, as Erskine said 250 years ago, 'the conveyancing of an uncertain subject is inept and ineffectual'.[7] Faced with a difficult title, an applicant for first registration must decide into which category his problem falls. If the second category applies, then the applicant has no right to the property and any application for its registration will, quite properly, be refused.[8] If, however, the first category applies, the remedy lies in the applicant's own hands. The property can be mapped and registration

---

1 Land Registration (Scotland) Act 1979 ss 4(2)(a) and 6(1)(a). The first of these provisions says that an application for registration must be rejected if 'it relates to land which is not sufficiently described to enable him [the Keeper] to identify it by reference to the Ordnance Map'. The second says that title sheets must contain 'a description of the land which shall consist of or include a description of it based on the Ordnance Map'.

2 Though there can of course be exceptions, as currently and to a limited extent for tenemental property: see Land Registration etc (Scotland) Act 2012 s 16.

3 Although only on first registration: see Land Registration etc (Scotland) Act 2012 ss 23(1)(d), 25(1)(c) and 28(1)(b).

4 See *Conveyancing 2009* pp 122–26.

5 This is the second of the Keeper's three principles which were articulated in *PMP Plus Ltd v Keeper of the Registers of Scotland* 2009 SLT (Lands Tr) 2, para 57.

6 *PMP Plus Ltd v Keeper of the Registers of Scotland* 2009 SLT (Lands Tr) 2; for a full discussion, see *Conveyancing 2008* pp 133–49.

7 Erskine, *Institute* II.3.23.

8 Land Registration etc (Scotland) Act 2012 ss 21(3) and 23(1)(b).

successfully accomplished. Admittedly this is easier to say than to do. A great deal of inconvenience, expense and frustration may be encountered along the way. And matters are not helped by various aspects of current RoS practice including the one-shot rule, the misguided principle of 'tell me don't show me',[1] and the sheer difficulty, as compared with the generous arrangements of former times, of finding someone who is willing to advise. 'We crave a guide', Donald Reid wrote, 'who can see more clearly what will be the true, acceptable and worthy submission'. Indeed in the absence of Mr Reid's mythical castrologer, a problem may not emerge until the application is rejected, unexpectedly and disastrously, many months after first being submitted.[2] None of this is in the slightest degree welcome; yet it is the price that must be paid for moving to a map-based system of registration from a system of registration in which descriptions of property were often vague and approximate.

Finally, what happens if the application in respect of the cellar, or common areas, or awkward triangle of land, is refused? It is said that 'Somewhere, between the seller and the buyer, some of the property rights have disappeared'. But that cannot be so. If the property was unidentifiable, no rights existed in the first place. And if the property was identifiable but unmapped, the right existed at the time of the application for registration and exists still even after the application is refused. Who then is its holder? If the property has been conveyed it belongs to the purchaser; if the conveyance has failed, it belongs still to the seller.[3] Could the property have been conveyed, notwithstanding the rejection by the Keeper? In some cases, at least, the answer is yes. For property of the kind we are discussing – cellars, common areas, and the like – is often a pertinent of other property, so that if the application for registration is accepted (eventually) in respect of the principal property then, on first principles, it carries with it, by implication, the title to the pertinent.[4] Of course the pertinent would remain, for the moment, unmapped and unregistered. But even this might change in the future when the new owner, rested and reinvigorated, was prepared and ready to try once again.[5]

---

1 For criticism, see K G C Reid and G L Gretton, *Land Registration* (2017) paras 8.10 and 8.11; Donald Reid, 'The 2012 Act: a bold step forward?' (2017) 62 *Journal of the Law Society of Scotland* March/33 ('I find it astonishing that the Government should be content, indeed proud, that the Keeper of this most important and valuable public register exercises no substantive quality control').

2 For complaint about rejections of applications for first registration 'many months, and sometimes over a year, after the application', see a letter by Ceri Williams in the *Journal of the Law Society of Scotland* for April 2017 (p 6). According to the RoS *Annual Report 2016–17* (2017) p 19, the target for turnaround of first registrations is (i) 20 working days if the property is in a research area and (ii) 6 months otherwise. In the year under review the first target was almost always met but the second target was met in only 63.5% of cases.

3 Or, if the seller's own title was bad, to whoever owned it before.

4 K G C Reid, *The Law of Property in Scotland* (1996) para 199. This rule applies most obviously to incorporeal pertinents such as the right to a servitude, but it is capable of applying to corporeal pertinents as well. In the 1979 Act the rule was made explicit, the effect of registration being defined in s 3(1)(a) as conferring a real right to the interest in land 'and in and to any right, pertinent, or servitude, express or implied, forming part of the interest'.

5 In such a case the correct procedure would normally be to seek rectification rather than registration.

LEASE OR LICENCE?

Introduction

Rights to use the land of another person

There can be many situations in which one person occupies the property of another. Some of these are non-contractual. The occupier may be a proper liferenter, or the beneficiary under a trust, or a squatter, or someone who believes he has a good title when in fact he does not – as where, for instance, a boundary fence is in the wrong place. And there are other possibilities too. If one broadens out 'occupation' to 'use of any type' then more types of case emerge, such as where Jenny crosses land belonging to Kate in pursuance of a servitude right of way, or of a public right of way, or of the right to roam. Turning from such cases to contractual rights, there are two cases: the lease and the licence.[1]

Contractual rights: lease or licence?

What is the distinction between a lease and a licence? The terms are often encountered, and the assumption tends to be that the distinction is settled and known to persons learned in the law, such as judges and, if we may mention them, law professors. Alas, it is not so. That leases and licences are very different things is, of course, true, but just what are the rules for distinguishing them is not settled.

Why does it matter whether a contract is classifiable as a lease or as some other contract? Part of the answer lies in the common law, which has a suite of rules that apply to leases but not to licences. For example, the doctrine of tacit relocation applies to leases but not to licences. More commonly, however, the reason why the distinction matters lies in statute. There are many statutes that apply certain rules to contracts that are contracts of lease but not to other contracts. This has been going on for quite a few years. For example, the Leases Act 1449, still in force, says that a contract of lease is (subject to certain qualifications) effective not only against the original landlord but against successors too. So, if the question arises as to whether a contract to occupy land affects an incoming owner, one has to know whether the arrangement is a contract of lease or some other contract.

It is sometimes said that if a contract is a lease, one result is that it is a real right – for instance under the 1449 Act. That is true almost always, but not quite:[2] there can be, and occasionally are, contracts that are (i) leases but (ii) not real rights. One example is a short lease that is not, to use an old-fashioned expression, clothed with possession; for a contract that gives a right to possess

---

1 Though terminology hereabouts is not straightforward. In *David Allen & Sons Billposting Ltd v Assessor for Clydebank* 1936 SC 318 Lord Pitman said that 'a licence to use a heritage is just a lease of heritage' (p 335). But this remark could be seen as substantive rather than terminological, reflecting a broader conception of the concept of lease. In that case a contract to use hoardings for advertising was held to be a lease of heritable property.

2 On this see Peter Webster, 'The continued existence of the contract of lease', in Andrew J M Steven, Ross G Anderson and John MacLeod (eds), *Nothing so Practical as a Good Theory: Festschrift for George Gretton* (2017) 119.

but where the tenant has not, or not yet, actually taken possession is not, or is not yet, a real right. Another example is a long lease that has not been registered in the Land Register (or, in older cases, the Register of Sasines). In other words, for a short lease the real right is obtained by possession, and for a long lease it is obtained by registration, and in either case it may be that the step of obtaining a real right has not been taken.

In most cases, of course, it is clear enough when an arrangement is or is not a lease. But not always, and some of the decisions are perhaps surprising. For instance in *Glasgow Tramway and Omnibus Co Ltd v Corporation of the City of Glasgow*[1] there was a contract between a private transportation company and Glasgow Council whereby the company could make use of tramlines for its trams, in exchange for payment. This was held to be a lease. An even odder case was *James Dunlop & Co v Steel Company of Scotland Ltd*[2] in which the right to take water in exchange for payment was held to be a lease. There are by contrast authorities that regard exclusive possession as a necessary feature of a lease, such as *Broomhill Motor Co v Assessor for Glasgow*[3] and *Chaplin v Assessor for Perth*.[4] In short, the authorities are conflicting.

In 1992 the Second Division reviewed many of the authorities in *Brador Properties v British Telecommunications plc*[5] and concluded that the Scottish concept of lease was considerably wider than the English concept.[6] On the view that a limited use of property, short of full possession, could be a lease in Scotland, the court decided that the leading English decision in this area, *Street v Mountford*,[7] was 'of no assistance'.[8] But it is arguable that the Scottish concept of lease, though clearly not the same as the English concept, is nearer than was indicated by Lord Justice-Clerk Ross in *Brador Properties*. In the case about to be discussed, the sheriff considered *Street* to be of considerable persuasive authority.

Because leases and licences have different legal consequences, the parties may well have definite views as to which type of contract they wish to enter into. Sometimes what they want is a lease, and sometimes a licence. Two examples will illustrate this. One is where the owner of residential property wishes to 'let' it but does not wish the contract to be a lease, because if it is a lease then the mandatory statutory rules about residential tenancies will apply, which may include security of tenure and rent control. So the contract is stated to be a licence, not a lease. The other is a contract in which solar panels are fixed to X's roof by Y, with Y making a periodical payment in return. The solar power company will wish the contract to be legally a lease, and indeed will usually intend it to

---

1 (1897) 24 R 628.
2 (1879) 7 R 283.
3 1927 SC 447.
4 1947 SC 373.
5 1992 SC 12.
6 Might this be because of the breadth of the Roman contract of *locatio-conductio*? We merely speculate.
7 [1985] AC 809.
8 At 19.

be registered in the Land Register (assuming that the duration is for more than 20 years). So the contract is stated to be a lease, not a licence.[1] Another area of contemporary uncertainty is whether there can be a lease of a buried pipeline or cable, ie of the pipeline or cable itself, or of the geometrical tube or cylinder that it occupies, without a lease of the ground itself.

Two key issues: intention and exclusive possession

In attempting to differentiate the two species, lease and licence, two issues are particularly important. One is the role of intention. To what extent does the intention of the parties matter? If a contract says loudly, both on the backing and in the body, 'this is a lease and definitely not a licence' (or conversely) what effect does that have? The second is the nature of the possession, in particular, whether exclusive possession is one of the hallmarks of a lease. On both issues *St Andrews Forest Lodges Ltd v Grieve*[2] is a significant contribution, containing a long,[3] learned, and carefully-reasoned judgment by Sheriff Simon Collins QC.

St Andrews Forest Lodges

The facts

Mr and Mrs Grieve had a limited liability partnership, Kincaple Lodge LLP, which owned a holiday park at Kincaple, Fife. The Grieves lived in the 'Lodge';[4] the rest of the holiday park was made up of 'cabins'. In 2014 Kincaple Lodge LLP went into administration. Early in 2015 St Andrews Forest Lodges Ltd (we shall refer to it as 'the company') bought the park from the administrators, the price being £650,000. The Grieves continued to live in the Lodge, and it was agreed between them and the company that they could continue to do so at a rent of £2,000 per month.[5] There was no written agreement, but there was some indication that what was intended was a 'holiday let', the significance of this being that a holiday let does not attract security of tenure.[6] There was discussion of the possibility that they would buy the Lodge, and in December 2015 missives were concluded for its purchase at a price of £435,000. Settlement was due in February 2016 but the Grieves failed to come up with the price. Settlement was rescheduled for March 2016 but again the Grieves failed to come up with the price, following which the company rescinded the contract. The Grieves had

---

1 On solar panel 'leases' see K G C Reid and G L Gretton, *Land Registration* (2017) para 20.5, and references therein.
2 [2017] SC DUN 25, 2017 GWD 14-224.
3 Indeed at about 16,000 words it is too long to do full justice to here.
4 It may be that Kincaple Lodge LLP leased the Lodge to the Grieves, but this issue is not discussed in the case, and if there was a lease it seems that it later came to an end.
5 To be precise, in fact they moved out briefly and then moved back in.
6 To what extent the parties intended the agreement to be a holiday let is unclear. It is not easy to reconcile what is said in paras 12 and 14 of the sheriff's findings in fact, the former suggesting that a holiday let was intended by both sides and the latter indicating that the Grieves did not have that intention. But it should be stressed that there was no written agreement.

paid a non-refundable deposit of £40,000 so they had incurred a substantial loss by failing to settle.

The Grieves continued to tender the £2,000 per month but the company eventually stopped accepting it and demanded that the Grieves should flit. The company then raised the present action for (i) declarator that the Grieves had no right or title to occupy the subjects, together with an order ordaining them to remove, and (ii) payment of various sums including (a) the accumulated 'licence' payments (= rent) until the time when the 'licence' had been terminated and (b) recompense for unlawful occupation thereafter.

The arguments

The pursuer argued that the arrangement was a licence and not a lease, or, *esto* it was a lease it was a holiday let and hence did not attract security of tenure. In support of his primary case, counsel for the pursuer argued as follows:[1]

> The agreement reached between the parties pursuant to which the defenders reoccupied the Lodge in March 2015 was, Mr Upton[2] submitted, a licence to occupy and not a lease. Therefore it could not be an assured tenancy within the meaning of section 12(1) of the Housing (Scotland) Act 1988, which provides that only a tenancy under which a house is let as a separate dwelling is for the purpose of the Act an assured tenancy. Here there was no lease, no let, and no tenancy. He submitted that the evidence showed that parties did not intend to create a tenancy, and that theirs was an agreement purely to facilitate a period of occupancy leading up to the purchase of the Lodge. An agreement could have all the hallmarks of a tenancy yet not be a tenancy if that was not what parties intended. In this regard Mr Upton relied on the decision of the Second Division in the case of *Scottish Residential Estates Development Co Ltd v Henderson* 1991 SLT 490. He accepted that there was agreement as to parties, premises, rent and duration, but that the absence of intention to create a tenancy was fatal to the agreement being a lease.

In other words, intention was decisive. There had been, at least on the part of the pursuer, no intention to enter into a lease. So there was no lease. There was a licence, and that licence had come to an end. Hence immediate eviction should ensue plus damages for unlawful occupation. Counsel for the pursuer relied in particular on *Scottish Residential Estates Development Co Ltd v Henderson*[3] where the role of intention had been stressed and the arrangement in question had been held to be a licence not a lease.

Counsel for the defenders placed reliance on the English House of Lords decision in *Street v Mountford*,[4] mentioned earlier, a case containing a much-quoted dictum of Lord Templeman: 'The manufacture of a five-pronged implement for manual digging results in a fork even if the manufacturer ...

---

1 Paragraph 5 of the sheriff's note.
2 Michael Upton, counsel for the pursuer.
3 1991 SLT 490.
4 [1985] AC 809.

insists that he intended to make and has made a spade.'[1] In that case there had been a contract for the occupation of residential property in return for rent, but the contract, which was headed 'licence agreement', contained a declaration signed by the occupier agreeing that the contract did not give her a Rent Act tenancy. The House of Lords held the contract to be a tenancy, thus engaging the provisions of the Rent Acts. Counsel also founded on a Scottish case, *Brador Properties v British Telecommunications plc,*[2] also mentioned earlier, where a contractual occupation right had been held to be a lease despite the apparent intention of the parties that it should be classified as a licence. That there was tension between the two Scottish decisions, both of the Inner House, namely *Henderson* and *Brador Properties,* could not be denied. Strikingly, in *Brador Properties* the earlier case was not mentioned.

Whilst numerous other authorities were cited to the sheriff, the three most important were those just mentioned.

The judgment (i): exclusive possession and the 'fifth cardinal element'

First, the sheriff discussed the question of whether exclusive possession is a necessary feature of a lease. On a consideration of the authorities the sheriff concluded that it is. He said:[3]

> The position today is therefore that the grant of exclusive possession to the occupier has been recognised as the 'fifth cardinal element'[4] of a lease in Scots law, and as an important feature which can assist in distinguishing a lease from a licence.

Strictly this argument works in the negative: if there is no exclusive possession then the contract is not a contract of lease. But the sheriff used it in a positive way: if there is a contract conferring exclusive possession then that, combined with other elements, is a pointer towards the contract being one of lease. As mentioned above, the question of exclusive possession in relation to leases is controversial, and a decision at the sheriff court level will not settle it, but it adds weight to that view. For what it is worth, we incline to the same view.[5]

The judgment (ii): the role of intention in the lease/licence distinction

What was the ratio of *Scottish Residential Estates Development Co Ltd v Henderson,*[6] the decision relied upon by the pursuer? That difficult question had to be tackled in the present case for, as a decision of the Inner House, it was binding on the sheriff. The case is brief. The facts are sparely reported, and the discussion from

---

1 *Street v Mountford* [1985] AC 809 at 819.
2 1992 SC 12.
3 Paragraph 29 of the sheriff's note.
4 The traditional four 'cardinal' elements of a lease are said to be parties, property, rent and duration.
5 By a curious coincidence, 2017 also saw the publication of an article on the question of exclusive possession in relation to leases: see Mitchell Skilling, 'The fifth element: should exclusive possession be considered an essential requirement for the constitution of a contract of lease in Scots Law?' (2017) 7 *Aberdeen Student Law Review* 1.
6 1991 SLT 490.

the bench falls short of a full exploration of the issues. What happened was that a company agreed with the defender that she could occupy a cottage on a temporary basis, until the company needed the property, and that during her occupation she would not have to pay rent. A letter to her, which she accepted, gave more details:

> Both the Cottage and walled garden will be available to you and your sons on a rent free basis, but it would be your responsibility to meet the costs of the rates and any repairs which you may find necessary from time to time. It would however be a condition of this general arrangement that your sons continue to cut the grass and generally maintain in good order the woodlands surrounding the walled garden area including where necessary keeping the walkways clear of vegetation.

And the defender confirmed: 'I … accept that I will have no legal rights to tenancy of the … Cottage except as detailed in your letter of 15th December 1976.'

When the company wished her to leave the cottage she declined, and the company sued to obtain possession. The Second Division found in favour of the company. Three possible *rationes* can be identified. (i) There was no rent, and without rent a contract cannot be a contract of lease. (ii) The period of occupation was to be at the will of the owner. In the language of Roman law it was a *precarium*, though that term does not appear in the case.[1] (iii) The parties had agreed that the contract was not a contract of lease. As to the first, the pursuer rather curiously said that the prestations incumbent on the defender *did* amount to rent. That concession seems dubious, and it is not clear whether it was accepted by the court.

The sheriff in *St Andrews Forest Lodges* doubted whether the defender in *Scottish Residential Estates* had been bound to pay anything that could be classified in law as rent, but equally he thought that this could not be relied on as having been the ratio of the decision. He also took the view that intention is not definitive as to the lease/licence distinction, and accordingly rejected the third possible ratio. That left the second. He accepted it. But that left him free to distinguish the earlier case, because in the present case the occupation had not been at the will of the owner.[2] As for what the Inner House had said about intention, he not only classified it as *obiter*, but in addition said he considered it to be wrong in law.[3]

---

1 Erskine, *Institute* II.1.23.

2 Paragraph 40 of the sheriff's note: 'That being the ratio of *Henderson* I am satisfied that there are grounds to distinguish it from the present case. In this case I am satisfied that the defenders' occupancy of the Lodge was for an agreed duration, namely the remainder of March 2015, and continuing on a monthly basis thereafter. The agreement was not that the defenders' occupation of the Lodge was to be at the pursuer's pleasure, terminable at any time.'

3 In *Henderson*, the court said (at 491–92): 'It was conceded before the sheriff by the solicitor for the defender that it was obvious from the terms of the offer letter that the pursuers did not intend to grant a lease to the defender. Counsel [for the defender] also conceded that the pursuers did not intend to give to the defender the security of a tenancy, but he submitted that in fact and in law the pursuers had done so. We find this to be a peculiar proposition because the intention of parties must be found from the words used in the relevant documents

It is not often that a sheriff court decision treats Inner House authority in such a way. But of course the sheriff had ammunition. One barrel of his shotgun contained other Scottish authority, and in particular *Brador Properties*, while the other barrel contained important English cases such as *Street*.

The sheriff also held, as a matter of fact after proof, that the parties had actually intended there to be a tenancy rather than a licence. So the conclusion that this had been a lease was based on both fact and law. The sheriff could easily have decided the point simply as a question of fact, but clearly he was interested in setting out his views of the law, and those who incline to agree with his exposition of law will be grateful.

The judgment (iii): a holiday let?

The pursuer pled, as mentioned above, that *esto* the contract was not a licence but a lease, it was a holiday let, and holiday lets do not attract security of tenure.[1] The sheriff had no difficulty in dismissing this argument:[2]

> A holiday let is simply a tenancy which, if it satisfies the terms of paragraph 8 of schedule 4 to the 1988 Act, will not be an assured tenancy. Critically, in my opinion, whether or not the terms of paragraph 8 are satisfied is a matter for the Court to determine in the light of the evidence before it. The tenancy does not become a holiday let just because one or both of the parties wish it so or describe it as such in a written agreement. The reality is that since March 2015 the defenders have occupied the Lodge as their only or principal home.

Conclusion

As will have been apparent from the foregoing discussion, we consider this to be an important case on the law of leases. It holds, in summary: (i) that exclusive possession is the fifth 'cardinal' element of a lease, (ii) that in the lease/licence distinction, intention is not determinative, and accordingly (iii) if a contract has all the characteristics of a lease then it is a contract of lease.[3] Are these propositions right in law, and (not quite the same question) will they gain general acceptance? To answer the first, and only the first, of these: with some hesitation we incline to think that they are probably right.

---

together, if necessary, with the inference to be drawn from the actings of parties thereafter.' In the present case the sheriff quoted this passage (para 41 of the note) and made this comment: 'With the greatest of respect to the judges of the Second Division, counsel's proposition was far from peculiar. Indeed it was the very proposition which the House of Lords had unanimously accepted five years previously in *Street v Mountford*, and has reaffirmed on more than one occasion since.'

1 Housing (Scotland) Act 1988 sch 4 para 8.
2 Paragraph 54 of the sheriff's note.
3 There is the converse issue: if a contract has the characteristics of a licence but is called by the parties a lease, which is it? The sheriff does not consider this, but the implication of his position is that, once again, intention is not determinative, and so in such a case the contract would not be a lease.

SERVITUDES

Access for external repairs

Access

Brydon v Lewis is not a new case.[1] But it has recently been recovered from the archives of the National Records of Scotland by that well-known conveyancing sleuth, Professor Roderick Paisley of Aberdeen University.[2] It was worth the effort because the case considers an issue on which there is virtually no authority. The issue is this: if repairs are needed to the outside of a building, and the building is hard up against someone else's land, is the owner of the building entitled to use the neighbour's land for the purposes of carrying out the repair – for example, by standing on it or placing on it ladders or scaffolding? Sometimes, of course, there is an express servitude in the title and, if so, that settles the matter. But often there is no express servitude. What then? Can access for repairs be taken or must repairs, rather, be carried out from inside the building – if that indeed is possible?

The facts of *Brydon v Lewis* were as follows. The pursuer and the defenders owned flats in a two-storey building in Edinburgh's Craigleith Road. The pursuer, Christina Brydon, owned the ground-floor flat, number 188. The defenders owned the flat immediately above, number 190, and also owned the garden ground immediately adjacent to the west gable wall of number 188. The west gable wall appears to have been the sole property of the pursuer.[3] Repairs were needed to that wall in order to deal with an outbreak of damp and dry rot. They could only be done from the outside, and hence by using the defenders' garden. The pursuer sought a declarator of servitude 'for the purposes of maintaining said west gable wall'. Although the split-off disposition of the pursuer's flat contained an express servitude of access to the flat itself, there was no servitude over the defenders' garden for the purpose of repairs. Nonetheless, argued the pursuer, such a servitude did exist: 'The pursuer having a duty both under the conditions of her title and at common law to maintain her west gable wall she is entitled to access for this purpose.'[4] By the time that the case went to debate, the defenders were willing to concede the existence of the servitude, and the declarator was granted without objection. On this point, therefore, the case is of limited value. The sheriff did, however, take the opportunity to endorse the pursuer's argument, saying that '[i]t is plain that there is a servitude right of access'.

---

1 *Brydon v Lewis*, 12 February 1958 (debate) and 26 August 1958 (proof), Edinburgh Sheriff Court. The NRS reference is SC 39/17, box 39/17, A1522/1957. The case was decided by Sheriff William Garrett QC.

2 A normal request is usually sufficient for the purposes of the National Records of Scotland but on this occasion a freedom of information request was needed, the request being made by John Bain of Macbeth Currie. The case is in fact briefly noted in D J Cusine and R R M Paisley, *Servitudes and Rights of Way* (1998) especially at para 17.11.

3 That appears to have been the case although it is not conclusively clear from the pleadings. But even if the wall had been common property, the pursuer would still have been an owner and the issues would be the same.

4 Condescendence 3.

The pursuer's case, as already mentioned, was that a person with an obligation to maintain a wall must be given the means of doing so in the form of the necessary servitude. Precisely why this should be so – why an obligation should give rise to a right, or indeed why others (such as the defenders) must concede the right even though they may not be among the beneficiaries of the obligation (though in this case they were)[1] – is not explained. In fact, it seems unlikely that the existence of the obligation to maintain is important. The truth is that Scots law is sufficiently pragmatic to concede access rights for repairs where there is no other reasonable way in which the repair can be carried out. The importance of getting a building repaired outweighs the temporary inconvenience of the owner of the land on which the ladder or scaffolding must be put. This flexible approach to property rights comes out of what appears to be the only other authority on this whole topic. This is a passage from the lectures of Baron David Hume, delivered to his students at Edinburgh University in academic year 1821–22:[2]

> [A]n owner's interest must yield sometimes to the immediate interest even of an individual where this is out of all proportion to the owner's interest in preventing the interference, or where the matter in question, though immediately concerning an individual, does at the same time, in its consequences, though remotely, concern the neighbourhood too … On the like [ie this] ground I think it may be maintained with respect to conterminous properties in a Burgh, which in many instances, owing to the crowded situation of the building, cannot be repaired without some temporary interference, as by resting ladders on the next area, or suspending a scaffold over the next area, that this slight and temporary inconvenience must be put up, from the necessity of the case.

Assuming such a right to exist, what is its juridical character? Hume himself gives none. Servitude, the attribution in *Brydon v Lewis*, seems a promising choice, although this would have to be a 'natural' servitude rather than one which was expressly created.[3] An alternative attribution is common interest.[4]

Obstructions to access

One other aspect of *Brydon v Lewis* is worthy of mention. Access to the gable wall was obstructed by a wooden hut close up to the wall and by a wooden lean-to, used for the storage of coal, which rested on the wall itself.[5] Accordingly, the

---

1 In respect that they owned the flat above and so had an obvious interest in the state of repair of the wall.
2 *Baron David Hume's Lectures 1786–1822* vol III (ed G Campbell H Paton; Stair Society vol 15, 1952) 206–07.
3 For natural servitudes, see D J Cusine and R R M Paisley, *Servitudes and Rights of Way* (1998) para 1.07.
4 See K G C Reid, *The Law of Property in Scotland* (1996) para 359(9).
5 Indeed one of the pursuer's craves was for damages for the cost of the repairs on the basis that the damp had penetrated from the lean-to. In this the pursuer was successful, the sheriff holding that, as the problem of damp had been drawn to the defenders' attention and the defenders had taken no action to deal with it, the defenders were liable to the pursuer on the basis of nuisance. This aspect of the case, however, is of no more than historical interest as the law of nuisance has been substantially rewritten in recent years through cases such as *Kennedy v Glenbelle Ltd* 1996 SC 95.

pursuer had ancillary craves (a) 'to ordain the defenders to remove all wooden structures from the west gable wall ... insofar as said structures interfere with the pursuer's access to the said west gable wall for the purpose of maintaining same', and (b) to interdict the defenders from erecting any structures 'so as to interfere with the pursuer's said servitude of access'.

At issue was the question of obstructions, and the responsibility for their removal. The defenders' position was that the structures, being on the defenders' own land, were perfectly lawful and that, while the pursuer could remove them temporarily in order to carry out the repairs, he must put them back when the repairs were completed. The pursuer's position was that the structures were unlawful and that it was the defenders' responsibility to remove them for good. The sheriff found for the pursuer.[1] Indeed that result necessarily followed from the characterisation of the access right as a servitude, for it is a basic principle of the law of servitudes that their exercise is not to be obstructed by the actions of the burdened proprietor.[2]

The implications are significant. If the decision is right on this point, it might seem to prevent owners from building on their land if this would obstruct a neighbour from taking access to repair the outside of the neighbour's building. On that view, the owner's land is sterilised and, depending on the configuration of the neighbouring building, sterilised in respect of a substantial area. For example, in *Brydon v Lewis* the entire length of the pursuer's west gable abutted the land of the defenders. But we doubt whether this can be the law. A right of access for repair will be exercised infrequently if at all. Against the slight chance that it might be needed, an owner should not be stopped from building. Indeed the erection of a sound and permanent building abutting the neighbour's wall might well, of itself, remove the need for any future repairs to the wall.[3] But there is a caveat. If the owner does build, and if the wall does need repaired, and if the repair can only be done from the outside – three big ifs – then the owner may have to make such provision as is necessary to allow the repair to go ahead.[4]

We should emphasise that we are talking here about the external walls of buildings and not about boundary walls. The rules for the latter are different. Assuming it to be built on the true boundary, a boundary wall is owned *ad medium filum* from each side; and each neighbour, owning the respective inner face of the wall, is free to build alongside that inner face in any manner he chooses provided the overall stability of the wall is not affected.[5]

---

1   'Even if the defenders had no responsibility for the damage to the pursuer's house they would, in my opinion, have been bound to remove obstructions like the hut and shed which were impeding the pursuer's access, provided that access was necessary to carry out repairs.' In the event, as the hut had now been moved and the lean-to demolished, the sheriff did not think it necessary to grant the craves.

2   See eg Cusine and Paisley, *Servitudes and Rights of Way* paras 12.93 ff.

3   As was the position in *Gray v MacLeod* 1979 SLT (Sh Ct) 17, 22–23.

4   Or may not: there may be considerations of personal bar or negative prescription which would relieve the owner of the obligation.

5   *Thom v Hetherington* 1988 SLT 724.

Access under the Tenements (Scotland) Act 2004

For tenements, some of the issues raised by *Brydon v Lewis* are now dealt with by the Tenements (Scotland) Act 2004. By s 17 of that Act the owner of a flat in a tenement is entitled, on reasonable notice, to take access over any other part of the tenement, including garden ground, where this is needed to carry out repairs.[1] This is both wider and also narrower than the common-law power that has just been described. It is wider because it allows access for repairs from inside the building as well as from outside, and to any part of the building and not just to external surfaces. But it is narrower because it gives no protection against obstructions. In that respect, at least, the common law remains of importance even in the context of tenements.

Interpretation

Traditionally, servitudes were so terse that there were few words that stood in need of interpretation. But elaboration is a growing trend in the drafting of servitudes, especially in a commercial context, with the result that interpretation is a topic of increasing importance. *Dunlea v Cashwell*[2] is the most recent example.

The rules of interpretation

The basic rules which apply to the interpretation of servitudes are well-established,[3] and were reaffirmed by the Sheriff Appeal Court in *Dunlea v Cashwell*.[4] Two are of particular importance. First, servitudes are strictly construed, in accordance with the presumption that land is free from burdens – the *praesumptio pro libertate*. Secondly, ambiguities are resolved in favour of the construction which is least burdensome to the burdened property. For this purpose, regard can be had to extrinsic evidence.

The first rule has often been glossed. The court in *Dunlea* quoted a well-known passage by Lord Reid in *Hunter v Fox*:[5]

> [T]here arises the question of what is meant by a strict construction. I can think of no stricter method of construction – and none was suggested in argument – than to ask whether a reasonable man with competent knowledge of the English language could have any real doubt about the meaning of the provision read in the context of the disposition.

Cusine and Paisley, however, warn against an over-strict approach:[6]

---

1 For background and discussion, see Scottish Law Commission, *Report No 162 on the Law of the Tenement* (1998) paras 10.10–10.21. An example is *Humphreys v Crabbe* [2016] CSIH 82, 2017 SCLR 699, where scaffolding was erected against the wishes of the owner of the garden ground.
2 [2017] SAC (Civ) 12, 2017 SCLR 675. The Sheriff Appeal Court comprised Sheriff Principal D L Murray (who delivered the Opinion of the Court), Sheriff Principal M Lewis, and Sheriff A L MacFadyen.
3 For a thorough analysis, see D J Cusine and R R M Paisley, *Servitudes and Rights of Way* (1998) ch 15.
4 Paragraphs 14 and 15.
5 1964 SC (HL) 95, 99.
6 Cusine and Paisley, *Servitudes and Rights of Way* para 15.15.

[T]he principle of strict construction does not mean that the most strict and narrow construction possible is put on the words used in any grant of servitude, so that the normal meaning of words is unnaturally constricted. The courts have indicated that they wish to give the words used their 'reasonable and fair construction' and that they will be construed in the context of the relevant deed, read as a whole, in the light of the surrounding circumstances, and subsequent exercise of the right.

Clear rules take one only so far, however. In reality, interpretation is often a matter of impression, and of what seems fair and reasonable to the reader. It is an art rather than a science, so that reasonable people may interpret the same words in different ways. Hence the dispute in *Dunlea v Cashwell*.

Dunlea: the facts

The appellants and respondents in *Dunlea* were the owners of two adjacent properties in Lochwinnoch, Renfrewshire, known, respectively, as Flax House and Mill House. Both were used for residential purposes. Access to Flax House was by a private road running through the land attached to Mill House. The properties appear originally to have been in single ownership and were separated by a disposition granted in 1987. The disposition contained an access servitude over the private road in favour of Flax House. As later entered on the title sheet for Flax House this read:

> A servitude right of access for both pedestrian and vehicular traffic over the part of the common access road tinted brown on the said plan; but declaring that the maintenance of the said common access road tinted brown and blue on the said plan shall be shared equally between the proprietor of the subjects in this title [ie Flax House] and the proprietor of the subjects lying immediately to the west of the said plot or area of ground in this title [ie Mill House] and further declaring that neither the proprietor of the subjects in this title nor the proprietor of the said subjects lying to the west of the said plot or area of ground shall use the said common access road for any vehicles other than vehicles required in connection with normal residential use of the said plot or area of ground in this title or the said subjects lying immediately to the west of the said plot or area of ground in this title.

The restriction of the road to 'vehicles required in connection with normal residential use of the said plot or area of ground in this title' will be noted.

Many years after the creation of the servitude the appellants, as owners of Flax House, obtained planning permission for the conversion of a derelict mill on their property into a two-storey dwellinghouse. There was nothing in the wording of the servitude to prevent the use of the road for the mill *once* the conversion works had been carried out. The point that this might amount to an unlawful increase in the burden of the servitude was raised in the course of the litigation but not pressed. In all probability, there would have been no unlawful increase: see *Alba Homes Ltd v Duell*.[1] The difficulty lay, not in post-conversion use, but in the act of conversion itself. Could the use of the road by construction

---

1 1993 SLT (Sh Ct) 49.

traffic be regarded as use 'in connection with normal residential use' of the Flax House property? Anticipating opposition from the owners of Mill House, the appellants asked the court for an answer. Their main crave was for declarator that they were:[1]

> entitled to exercise the said servitude rights as follows: by the pursuers' tradesmen and builders or their employees, together with their tools, plant & machinery, gear and effects having pedestrian and vehicular access to the Flax House Title Number REN 46779 over the access road or drive for the purposes of the development of the Flax House in accordance with the Renfrewshire Council planning consent reference number 13/0902/PP dated 20 March 2014.

Dunlea: the arguments

At first blush the appellants' case looked a little weak. What the servitude allowed was the passage of vehicles 'in connection with normal residential use', whereas what was being proposed was, not the use of an existing residence but the development of an entirely new one. Residential use was not the same as use for the purposes of development. Nonetheless, the argument put forward for the appellants had considerable force. Many different types of vehicle, said the appellants, were entitled in terms of the servitude to use the road. As well as ordinary cars this might include 'large vehicles associated with a house move; a scaffolding truck required to allow a builder safe access to the roof; a cement lorry for the floor of a new stand-alone garage; a royal mail delivery vehicle, a fire engine, an ambulance'.[2] But if vehicles were permitted in order to facilitate the repair and safety of the principal building on the property, they must equally be permitted to facilitate the repair and development of one of the other buildings. There was nothing in this which would defeat the purpose of the restriction. It continued to affect the appellants by preventing the use of the derelict mill for commercial purposes. The character and amenity of the area would still be preserved. But there was 'nothing in the context when the servitude was granted to suggest it was intended to prevent any redevelopment whatsoever of the remaining mill building'.[3]

Neither the sheriff nor, on appeal, the Sheriff Appeal Court was persuaded. As so often in matters of interpretation, however, their reasoning was entirely different. For the sheriff, the critical word in the phrase 'normal residential use' was the first one. Relying on a dictionary definition, he concluded that 'normal' use excluded ancillary use, and that use for development was excluded as being ancillary. The Sheriff Appeal Court had less confidence in dictionary definitions, varied as they were, and indeed placed little reliance on the word 'normal', regarding it as superfluous and unhelpful. In the court's view, this was a case where the words were ambiguous and so where, in accordance with the second rule mentioned above, interpretation 'must be done in the manner

---

1 Paragraph 3.
2 Paragraph 7.
3 Paragraph 8.

least burdensome to the burdened property'.[1] In resolving the ambiguity, the circumstances surrounding the grant of servitude were important. And what was of particular importance was the presence, in the same deed, of a separate servitude conferring a right of access for repair and maintenance. This was fatal to the appellants' case:[2]

> We consider that specification of this right decreases the scope to expand what may be thought to be ancillary to normal residential use, for we consider it must be appropriate to look at the words in the context of other provisions granted alongside the servitude in question. We conclude that the fact of a specific servitude being granted for maintenance and repair suggests that that is not included within the rights under the provision for 'normal residential use'. If the deed makes specific reference to a separate servitude to allow access for repair and maintenance we do not accept that an access right related to 'normal residential use' can be interpreted to permit access for construction traffic to develop an additional residential property on the subjects, even accepting as we do that the servitude relates to the whole subjects.

The argument is, perhaps, overstated. At this interval of time it is not possible to know the reason for including a separate servitude in respect of repair and maintenance. It might, for example, have been no more that the conveyancer's traditional desire to spell everything out, without the slightest intention of reducing the scope of the principal servitude. So while the second servitude is clearly important, it does not perhaps carry the full interpretative weight that the Sheriff Appeal Court sought to give it. The decision itself, however, seems correct. Although such cases are often marginal ones, it does appear that the use of the road for new construction was, on balance, beyond the scope of the servitude.

Installation of drainage pipes

The facts

No difficult issues of interpretation arose in *Pollock v Drogo Developments Ltd.*[3] On the contrary, it was apparent that the defender's activity with new drainage pipes went beyond the terms of any right of servitude.

The facts were these. By a disposition granted in 2008 the Scottish Ministers disponed some 50.5 hectares of a former hospital site, in Larbert, Stirlingshire, to the pursuers. As the land held back from the sale had development potential, the disposition reserved to that land a group of servitudes. Two were relevant for present purposes. One was the right 'to install and thereafter use, inspect, maintain, repair, renew, alter or enlarge services and utilities' underneath a stipulated service strip. The other comprised:

---

1 Paragraph 21.
2 Paragraph 23.
3 [2017] CSOH 64, 2017 GWD 14-221.

heritable and irredeemable servitude rights for all existing services including the main drain to the River Carron serving the Retained Property including the Larbert Hospital Development in so far as the same lie within the Disponed Property with right to use same and all necessary rights of access thereto for cleaning, inspecting, maintenance, repair, renewal, alteration and enlargement thereof ...

The first servitude was thus a right to install new services, the second a right to maintain and renew existing services.

In due course, the Scottish Ministers disponed to the defender part of the land that they had held back from the original sale to the pursuers. The defender installed two drainage pipes across and under the pursuers' land. Disputing the defender's right to do so, the pursuers raised an action for declarator of unlawful encroachment coupled with an order for removal of the pipes or, in the alternative, payment to them of the sum of £150,000. The case was heard by Lady Wise on the Procedure Roll.

The drainage pipes were not laid within the service strip. Hence there could be no question of the first of the two servitudes applying. As for the second servitude, it was true that the new pipes might be seen as replacements for the existing drainage pipes. The difficulty, however, was that, except to a small extent, the new pipes did not follow the line of the existing pipes. The question was whether that mattered.

Relocation of servitudes

There is a great deal of authority, not all of it consistent, as to whether the *burdened* proprietor has a right unilaterally to alter the route of a servitude.[1] Fortunately, the issue is seldom of practical importance, now that the Lands Tribunal has jurisdiction, quite frequently exercised,[2] to vary the route where it is reasonable to do so.[3] Very oddly, it seems to have been argued for the pursuers in *Pollock* that the Tribunal could vary the route even on the application of the *benefited* proprietor.[4] That, however, is not the case.[5] In practice it would be unusual for a benefited proprietor to wish to vary the route of a servitude except, as in the present case, by what looks like inadvertence. But such variation, where it is sought, rests wholly on the common law. If, therefore, the defender was able, in exercise of the second servitude, to lay replacement pipes along a different route from the pipes that were being replaced, that could only be because the common law allowed the defender to do so.

---

1 See Cusine and Paisley, *Servitudes and Rights of Way* paras 12.34–12.72.
2 See eg *Jensen v Tyler* 2008 SLT (Lands Tr) 39.
3 This is under the Lands Tribunal's standard powers to vary and discharge title conditions set out in part 9 of the Title Conditions (Scotland) Act 2003.
4 Paragraph 8: '[T]here was an established route for the variation of real burdens through the Land Court and if the defender's position was that some change in technical regulations had frustrated the operation of the parties' bargain there were options available to them. However, they had neither pled necessity nor sought to vary the burdens in the Land Court.' 'Land Court' is presumably a mistranscription of 'Lands Tribunal'.
5 In terms of s 90(1)(a) of the Title Conditions (Scotland) Act 2003, an application to the Lands Tribunal for the variation or discharge of a title condition can only be made by 'an owner of a burdened property or any other person against whom a title condition ... is enforceable'.

The common law, as it happens, provides almost no authority on the subject. Cusine and Paisley's view is that, where a servitude is indefinite as to route, as was the case with the second servitude in *Pollock*, the benefited proprietor can make his own choice. But the choice having been made, as was done in the present case by the laying of the original pipes, there is no further 'right unilaterally to vary the route'.[1] Cusine and Paisley continue:

> Unless the parties have agreed to the contrary, once exercised, the right to determine the route of the servitude is irrevocable without the consent of the servient proprietor and frees the remainder of the wider servient tenement from the possibility of being subjected to the exercise of the servitude.

Needless to say, no consent to a change had been obtained from the burdened proprietor, the pursuers in the present action.

The only authority given by Cusine and Paisley is a passage from Erskine's *An Institute of the Law of Scotland*, a work which was published, posthumously, in 1773. Erskine begins with the *civiliter* principle and develops from it a broader point:[2]

> As servitudes are limitations of the property, it is a rule, that they must be used in the way least burdensome to the servient tenement. Thus the servitude of a road, whether a coach or foot road, constituted through the grounds of another indefinitely, without describing through what particular part of the ground the road shall pass, must be continued in that line in which it has either been used before by the owner of the servitude, or which has been marked out for the road by authority of the magistrate; and the rest of the servient tenement is free.

The defender sought to explain this passage away as applying only to servitudes of way. Perhaps unsurprisingly, Lady Wise saw matters differently:[3]

> I cannot agree with that interpretation. In my view, the passage cited from Erskine articulates a general rule, consistent with the important presumption in favour of freedom of property, that servitudes must be used in the way least burdensome to the servient tenement. The passage goes on to give an example of the servitude of a road and confirms that where it is established along a particular route it must continue in that line. The use of the word 'thus' at the beginning of the second sentence of the passage narrated tends to support that interpretation ... In my view the defender had no entitlement to alter the established route of those existing services.

Personal bar

The defender's primary argument,[4] however, was of an entirely different nature. Even if the defender's actions in laying the pipes went beyond any right of servitude, the pursuers were personally barred from asserting their title. This was because, despite knowing of the defender's works, they took no steps to stop

---

1 Cusine and Paisley, *Servitudes and Rights of Way* paras 12.134 and 12.138.
2 Erskine, *Institute* II.9.34.
3 Paragraph 25.
4 Paragraph 12.

them and thereafter delayed by over 12 months in raising the present action.[1] This argument too was rejected by Lady Wise. Personal bar cannot operate where an objection is made,[2] and in the present case the pleadings showed ample evidence of objections on the part of the pursuers:[3]

> It seems to me that the difficulty with the defender's argument on personal bar is that, on the material before the court, the pursuers appear to have articulated strenuous opposition to the defender's proposed actings. While they threatened proceedings to prevent the laying of the pipes, they raised no action until the present one. However, a decision not to resort to litigation at a particular point is not tantamount to acquiescence. The pursuers were not silent on this matter. They raised their objections through proper channels and it was clear to both sides that there was a dispute about the interpretation of the disposition ... In my view the pursuers' objections, made at the material time, are sufficient to negate any suggestion of acquiescence.

With this conclusion too it is hard to disagree.

LEASES WITHOUT WRITING

Introduction

When is writing required in land transactions?

Generally speaking, rights relating to land need to be set out in a written document. Nowadays that can be done in an electronic document as well as in a paper document, but a written document, of one type or the other, is still needed. That has always been the law, though there have always been certain exceptions. The current law is set out in s 1 of the Requirements of Writing (Scotland) Act 1995, which, however, was far from a revolution: it represented an evolution of the existing law rather than a transformation of it.

Section 1 of the 1995 Act uses the distinction between personal rights, such as contracts, and real rights. As to the first, s 1(2)(a) says:

> A written document which is a traditional document complying with s 2 or an electronic document complying with s 9B of this Act shall be required for ... the constitution of (i) a contract or unilateral obligation for the creation, transfer, variation or extinction of a real right in land...

As to the second, s 1(2)(b) says:

> A written document which is a traditional document complying with s 2 or an electronic document complying with s 9B of this Act shall be required for ... (b) the creation, transfer, variation or extinction of a real right in land ...

---

1 Paragraph 17.
2 E C Reid and J W G Blackie, *Personal Bar* (2006) para 6–16: 'The relevant test is whether there has been sufficient notification to put the encroacher in bad faith, in the sense that the encroacher has been put on guard and can no longer legitimately assume that the owner will not object. In general terms, bar should not arise if it can be established that the encroacher has proceeded in the knowledge that the owner does not agree, or is unlikely to agree, even if the means of communicating dissent has been informal.'
3 Paragraph 27.

So unsigned missives, or wholly oral missives, would not be valid, nor would an unsigned or wholly oral disposition.

What about leases? Section 1(7) says: 'In this section "real right in land" means any real right in or over land… but does not include (a) a tenancy … if the tenancy or right is not granted for more than one year.' So a lease for six months can be oral, but a lease for six years cannot.[1]

Personal bar: general

Having laid down the rules just outlined, s 1 of the 1995 Act then provides, in subsections (3) and (4), an exception: a form of personal bar. In outline, personal bar requires (i) an agreement between the parties plus (ii) reasonable reliance on that agreement. This statutory form of personal bar applies to personal rights, but not to real rights. Thus an unsigned, or wholly oral, contract to sell land can be validated by personal bar, but an unsigned, or wholly oral, disposition could not. Thus Caspar could say to Dorothea, in front of ten witnesses and a camera recording the event, 'I Caspar hereby dispone to you Dorothea my house, "Dunroamin", Auchnashuggle, Fife, together with the whole parts, privileges, pendicles and pertinents effeiring thereto…' and no matter how much he and she might then rely upon that oral disposition, it would not help. In law there would be no disposition. Personal bar can validate contracts to grant a real right;[2] it cannot validate the grant of the real right itself.

Personal bar: leases

These rules apply to leases (except leases for a year or less). But there is a problem, which has long been recognised.[3] The contract/deed distinction works well in most cases. But leases are peculiar. A lease is itself a contract, and as far as common law is concerned it is only a contract. By statute it can have real effect, the two relevant statutes being the Leases Act 1449, which applies to leases of 20 years or less, and where the real right is obtained by possession, and the Registration of Leases (Scotland) Act 1857, which applies to leases for more than 20 years, and where the real right is obtained by registration of the lease in the Land Register. But it is the *contract* that operates as a real right. It is rather as if, in the sale of land, the *missives* were to be registered. Thus at first the missives would be effective only between the parties, and then, on being registered, they would take effect *erga omnes*. That is not what happens in sales of land. In sales of land there must also be a disposition. But it *is* what happens for leases. Of course, it sometimes happens that there are first missives of lease which are

---

1 In this discussion we do not seek to go into qualifications that are not relevant to the main issues. For instance s 1(7A) says that 'a private residential tenancy as defined in the Private Housing (Tenancies) (Scotland) Act 2016 is not a "real right in land" for the purposes of this section'. See also p 75 above.

2 'The contract … shall not be regarded as invalid' says s 1(3) which seems to mean simply: 'the contract is valid'.

3 See in particular Angus McAllister, *Scottish Law of Leases* (4th edn, 2013) ch 2; Robert Rennie (ed), *Leases* (2015) ch 3; Elspeth Reid and John Blackie, *Personal Bar* (2006) ch 10. These discussions all bring the problem into focus.

followed by a 'formal' lease, in the pattern of missives followed by disposition, but the similarity is somewhat misleading, for the 'formal' lease is also a contract.

So for leases, the personal bar rule in s 1 of the 1995 Act is problematic. On the one hand, a lease can be set up by personal bar (because it is a contract) and, on the other hand, it cannot be set up by personal bar (because it is a real right). As Lord Drummond Young put it more than a decade ago, in *Advice Centre for Mortgages v McNicoll*: 'On one hand, a lease is itself a contract for the creation of an interest in land. On the other hand, it creates an interest in land.'[1] No neat solutions exist, but until 2017 the prevailing view was that statutory personal bar cannot rescue a lease for more than a year that is not in formal writing. That too was the conclusion of the sheriff in the case about to be discussed, when the case was at first instance in 2016.

Gray v MacNeil's Exr

Conflict in South Uist

Donald MacNeil owned property in South Uist, including the Burnside Petrol Filling Station. His daughter Michelle and her husband John Gray helped him in the business. In 2004/05 the three of them, concerned that the petrol station was no longer trading satisfactorily, decided to add a chip shop to the site. This would require some capital to set up, and Mr Gray obtained a £11,000 loan from the Royal Bank of Scotland and grants from Western Isles Enterprise and Western Isles Council amounting to approximately £50,000 in all. He also attended a fish fryer course in Leeds.

The chip shop proved reasonably profitable, and matters went on satisfactorily until 2008, when relations between Mr Gray and his father-in-law began to sour. As time went on, relations between Mr Gray and Mrs Gray also began to sour, and they separated in 2011. In 2012 relations between Mr Gray and his father-in-law came to a crisis. The former accused Mr MacNeil of sexual offences and contacted the police.[2] The latter accused Mr Gray of having a 'female' in his house with him, which Mr Gray denied. In October 2012, following an alleged physical attack by Mr Gray on Mr MacNeil, the latter disconnected the chip shop's electricity supply with the result that Mr Gray could no longer operate the business. Subsequently, Mr MacNeil arranged for another relative (another Donald MacNeil) to begin trading in Mr Gray's place.

Action in the sheriff court[3]

Mr Gray then raised the present action against his father-in-law. The latter died during the course of the action, which was continued with the executor, Roderick

---

1 *Advice Centre for Mortgages v McNicoll* 2006 SLT 591 at para 19.
2 Material about certain members of the MacNeil family, material far too shocking to reproduce in these respectable pages, can be found by the inquisitive reader in such sources as www.thesun.co.uk/archives/news/785519/father-flash-rained-hell-on-family/ and www.dailyrecord.co.uk/news/scottish-news/dad-sex-shame-priest-father-flash-3722028.
3 2016 SLT (Sh Ct) 250: for discussion, see *Conveyancing 2016* pp 126–33.

MacNeil, brother of Michelle, as defender. One part of Mr Gray's claim was for the value of the equipment he had installed. In that respect he was successful. The other part of the claim was for damages for breach of the lease that he said he held. He said that his father-in-law and he had shaken hands on a 15-year lease. This was denied, and there was nothing in writing, but after proof, in which the decisive factor was the testimony of Mr MacNeil's daughter, and Mr Gray's estranged wife, Michelle, the sheriff found that such a lease had indeed been agreed.[1] The sheriff estimated that the damages for breach of the lease would be £141,117 plus interest, provided that there was a valid lease. But this lease had been oral, and a 15-year lease requires writing.

Mr Gray argued that, whilst admittedly there was nothing in writing, the agreement could be set up by statutory personal bar. But here he encountered the problem already discussed: the statutory personal bar rules in s 1 of the 1995 Act can set up personal rights but it cannot set up real rights, and a lease is both. The sheriff (Christopher Dickson), sitting at Lochmaddy Sheriff Court, gave a judgment in which he examined the problem in a careful and learned manner. Whilst the issue had been adverted to in previous cases, it had never had to be decided in a head-on way. So the sheriff was making legal history. He held, in line with the predominant view, that the statutory personal bar rules in s 1 of the 1995 Act cannot apply to leases. 'The verbal lease is accordingly invalid and the deceased was entitled to withdraw from it.'[2] Accordingly Mr Gray failed in this aspect of his case.

The appeal[3]

The pursuer appealed to the Sheriff Appeal Court, which gave its decision in May 2017. The court reversed the sheriff's decision and accordingly awarded £141,117 plus interest.[4] Why? It would be natural to assume that the appellate court took a different view as to how the statutory personal bar rules in s 1 of the 1995 Act should be interpreted in relation to leases. Not so. The issue of statutory personal bar disappeared at the appellate stage. The pursuer, now appellant, argued that the oral agreement was fully valid in itself, without the need to explore the possibility of saving it through personal bar:[5]

> The appellant conceded, on the basis the sheriff found that the parties had entered into an agreement, which they had understood or intended to be a lease, the sheriff was correct in his finding that the statutory personal bar provisions contained in subs 1(3) and 1(4) cannot be relied upon.

---

1 The sheriff held (finding in fact 8) that 'the rent for the forecourt shop would be that the pursuer would be responsible for the staffing and running costs of the petrol station business, save for the purchase of new fuel'. A contract cannot be a contract of lease unless there is a rent. Whether the deal described is indeed legally classifiable as 'rent' seems open to debate. But this issue was not ventilated.
2 Finding in fact and law 6.
3 [2017] SAC (Civ) 9, 2017 SLT (Sh Ct) 83, 2017 SCLR 666, 2017 Hous LR 47.
4 The sheriff's award of compensation in respect of the moveables was not discussed in the Sheriff Appeal Court, so presumably the defender did not cross-appeal that side of the case.
5 Paragraph 7.

The appellant's argument went on:[1]

> Although ineffective in constituting a lease, which creates a real right in land, as opposed to personal rights in land, the verbal agreement between the parties was effective to create purely personal rights and obligations between the pursuer and the deceased. On this analysis, the pursuer would have no right against any third party to whom the property was disponed, but would retain rights against the deceased for the breach by the deceased of his personal obligations, which would sound in damages.

The legislative basis of this view was the first two subsections of s 1 of the 1995 Act.[2] Subsection (1) set out the general rule that writing was not required for the constitution of a contract. Paragraph (a)(i) of subsection (2) qualified this general rule by requiring writing for the constitution of 'a contract … for the creation, transfer, variation or extinction of a real right in land'. On the appellant's argument, the contract being founded on was one concerned only with personal rights.

The court, in the course of a somewhat brief discussion, agreed with the appellant's approach:[3]

> We … agree with the submission made by the appellant that it is possible for the terms of the agreement as found by the sheriff to give rise to personal rights and corresponding obligations … An agreement constituting only a personal right in land does not require to be constituted in writing.

Accordingly the oral contract between Mr Gray and the late Mr MacNeil was valid. It did not, indeed, result in a real right. Hence it would not have been effective against third parties. But it was a good bilateral contract and hence breach of it gave rise to a valid damages claim.

Discussion

With respect, we do not find the approach of the Sheriff Appeal Court easy to interpret, but at all events we think that, however it is interpreted, it cannot be correct.

'An agreement' says the court, 'constituting only a personal right in land does not require to be constituted in writing.'[4] This, however, is stated too broadly for, as already mentioned, s 1(2)(a)(i) of the 1995 Act says that 'a contract … for the creation, transfer, variation or extinction of a real right in land' must be in writing. The court uses the phrase 'only a personal right in land'. An example would be missives, but missives of course must be in writing.

Possibly the court was taking the view that the agreement between Mr Gray and Mr MacNeil was an agreement for the occupation of the property that was not intended to be, or to lead to, a lease. In other words, on this view the deal was

---

1 Paragraph 8.
2 Paragraph 10.
3 Paragraph 21.
4 Paragraph 21.

not for a lease but for a licence.[1] In that case no real right would be in question. But there are two difficulties here. In the first place, that is not what the court actually says, at least in any clear terms. For instance the word 'licence' is not mentioned. In the second place, and more fundamentally, s 1 of the 1995 Act applies not only to real rights properly so called, but also to licences. Subsection (7), read short, says: 'In this section "real right in land" means any real right in or over land, *including any right to occupy or to use land*'; and by 'right to occupy or to use land' is meant a licence and not a lease, as is clear from the rest of subsection (7) which, in paras (a) and (b), distinguishes a 'right to occupy or use land' from a 'tenancy' (ie a lease).[2] Hence, when s 1(2)(a)(i) requires writing for the constitution of 'a contract … for the creation, transfer, variation or extinction of a real right in land', it requires writing for a contract for the constitution of a licence. The contract founded on by the appellant required to be constituted in writing.[3]

The appellant was of course correct in saying that rights to occupy land do not always bind third parties. That is true of licences. It is even true of some leases.[4] But it is a truth that makes no difference to the issue that was to be decided in *Gray v MacNeil's Exr.*

INCONSISTENCIES IN DESCRIPTIONS: STATEMENTS AS TO AREA

Introduction

Descriptions often have a statement of superficial area. This is more or less standard practice in Sasine deeds, including dispositions on first registration. On the Land Register, too, a statement of area must be given in the A (property) section of the title sheet if the extent exceeds a certain figure, which for registrations under the Land Registration (Scotland) Act 1979 was two hectares but which is now only half a hectare.[5] Inevitably, it sometimes happens that the area given is not wholly consistent with other elements in the description, such as a plan. Fortunately, discrepancies, when they occur, are usually small and so capable of being accommodated within those useful and comforting words 'or thereby'.[6] But not always.

1　For the lease/licence distinction, see p 155 above.

2　It is also clear from Scottish Law Commission, *Report No 112 on Requirements of Writing* (1988) para 2.18: 'The effect of a rule along these lines would be to require writing for agreements … to grant a licence to use land for more than a year.'

3　A stronger argument for the appellant would have been to revive the reliance on statutory personal bar which was a feature of the case at first instance. For if the appellant was seeking to establish the existence of a licence and not a lease, there could be no objection to making use of subsections (3) and (4) of s 1 of the 1995 Act.

4　The subject is a large one, but take a simple case. Sophronia owns land and grants to Theodore a 25-year lease. He takes possession but does not register the lease in the Land Register. The lease is a fully valid lease but it is not a real right because leases for over 20 years can acquire real status only through registration. Formal writing, however, is still needed.

5　Land Registration (Scotland) Act 1979 s 6(1)(a); Land Register Rules etc (Scotland) Regulations 2014, SSI 2014/150, r 12(1)(f).

6　On the meaning of 'or thereby', see D J Cusine (ed), *The Conveyancing Opinions of J M Halliday* (1992) 202.

What happens where the discrepancy is more substantial? Does the plan (or verbal description) prevail over the statement of area, or the statement of area over the plan (or verbal description)? On this question there has hitherto been relatively little in the way of authority. In 2017, however, the issue arose for decision in two different cases. And, obligingly, the cases between them cover the two situations where a discrepancy is most likely to matter. The first concerns the interpretation of the description, the second the question of whether the description is *habile* for the purposes of positive prescription.

Inconsistencies and interpretation

Veen v Keeper of the Registers of Scotland[1] concerned the former manse at Laggan, Newtonmore, Inverness-shire. When the manse was sold by the Church of Scotland General Trustees in 1976, the feu disposition described the property by means of (i) a plan, (ii) a traditional verbal description of the boundaries, and (iii) a statement as to area. (i) and (ii) were consistent with each other and disclosed an area of just over one acre. (iii), however, gave the area as being 1.65 acres. The buyer, Dr Robertson, took possession of the property to the extent defined by the boundaries, ie about 1.02 acres. When he died, his executor sold to Mr and Mrs Veen. This happened in 2005, and thus triggered first registration. The new title sheet followed the plan and verbal description. The title sheet was silent as to area. In 2010 the Veens applied for rectification, asking that the title sheet be 'rectified' so as to state that the area was 1.65 acres. The Keeper refused. Several years later the Veens appealed against that decision.

The issue to be determined was: what was the precise extent of the subjects conveyed by the Church of Scotland General Trustees in 1976? That was a question of interpretation. If the answer was an area of just over an acre, then the title sheet was correct. But if the answer was an area of 1.65 acres, then the title sheet was inaccurate and fell to be rectified – assuming, of course, that the Trustees in 1976 had owned that amount of land and more and so had a title to grant.

There has been a certain amount of case law over the years as to inconsistencies between different elements in a description. From those cases, Gordon and Wortley are able to extract two general rules, the first and more important of which is that:[2]

> In general it would seem that a verbal description of the boundaries will be regarded as controlling the extent of the land granted and as overruling other conflicting indications, but there is no doubt that the boundaries stated may be overruled if the description is so drawn that the boundaries stated have been made subordinate to something else such as a plan.

---

1   2017 GWD 17-276. This was a decision of the Lands Tribunal, the Tribunal comprising R A Smith QC and A Oswald FRICS.
2   W M Gordon and S Wortley, *Scottish Land Law*, vol I (3rd edn, 2009) para 3–08.

The primacy of verbal boundaries is also asserted by Halliday:[1]

> Where boundaries and measurements or plan (neither being stated to be taxative) conflict the boundaries, if clear, prevail, the measurements or plan being held to be demonstrative. So, if the boundaries are clear, a greater area specified by measurements which are not taxative will not convey more than that enclosed by the boundaries, nor will a lesser area in the measurements limit that within the boundaries.

In the hierarchy of descriptive elements, therefore, verbal descriptions come at the top and statements as to area at the very bottom.

Against this background, the interpretative issue raised by the 1976 feu disposition was easily solved. Even without the plan, it was clear that the verbal description prevailed over the statement as to area.[2] The plan simply reinforced that conclusion.[3] Citing the passage from Halliday quoted above, the Lands Tribunal had no difficulty in holding that it was the smaller area that was conveyed by the 1976 feu disposition, and hence that the title sheet was perfectly accurate.

There was also another reason for disregarding the statement as to area.[4] As already mentioned, the boundaries as disclosed by the plan and verbal description amounted to a little over an acre. If the feu disposition was now to be interpreted as conveying the full 1.65 acres, it was not clear from where the additional land was to come. It was true that the Church of Scotland General Trustees owned the surrounding land. But precisely which part of that land could be used to make up the shortfall in area, and on what basis? A statement of area does not, by itself, indicate boundaries. And while extrinsic evidence is competent in order to explicate a description,[5] there was no suggestion in *Veen* that extrinsic evidence might exist in respect of the supposed grant of 1.65 acres. Without it, the feu disposition would have failed to identify the property and, in view of that failure, would have been a nullity. This 'specificity principle' is an old one, as well as one grounded in common sense. As Erskine put matters in 1773, the property to be disponed must be described 'by its special boundaries or march-stones, or by its situation, or other characters, so that it may be distinguished from all others: for the conveyancing of an uncertain subject is inept and ineffectual'.[6] A conveyance of 1.65 acres, without further specification, is indeed inept and ineffectual.

---

1 J M Halliday, *Conveyancing Law and Practice* (2nd edn, 1997) para 33–13.
2 A well-known illustration is *Gibson v Bonnington Sugar Refining Co* (1869) 7 M 394.
3 The result might, however, have been different if the plan had corroborated the statement of area and not the verbal description, because a majority of descriptive elements would then have supported the larger area. That is certainly the view of Halliday para 33–13.
4 Paragraphs 26 and 31.
5 See *Murray's Tr v Wood* (1887) 14 R 856, where extrinsic evidence was used to identify land described merely as: 'All and Whole that piece of ground fronting Baker Street of Aberdeen, in the burgh and county of Aberdeen.'
6 Erskine, *Institute* II.3.23.

Inconsistencies and prescription

In *Veen* there had been no possession, indeed no identification, of the supposed additional land; hence there could be no question of positive prescription in favour of the Veens. Prescription, by contrast, was the main issue in the other case, *Munro v Keeper of the Registers of Scotland*.[1]

Camping for scouts

The facts of *Munro* were these. The owner of Borthwick Mains Farm in Gorebridge, Midlothian, a Mr Pringle, was a scoutmaster. In 1982 Mr Pringle sold a field to the Inveresk Scout Troop for £500. Title, which was recorded in the Register of Sasines, was taken in the name of trustees. The field was used by the scouts for camping. Over time, the scouts fell out with Mr Munro, who owned the immediately adjacent land. That land too had been broken off from Borthwick Mains Farm, the disposition being granted the year before the disposition in favour of the scouts.[2] At issue in particular was an area which the scouts used for camping but which, according to Mr Munro, was part of his property. On more than one occasion, the dispute finished up in the sheriff court, and Mr Munro was interdicted from entering the disputed area.

In 2015 the scouts disponed their field to Borthwick Campsite LLP. The disposition triggered first registration in the Land Register, and also the current dispute. The disposition bore to include the disputed area, and that area was included by the Keeper in the new title sheet made up for Borthwick Campsite LLP.[3] Unhappy about that, Mr Munro made the present application to the Lands Tribunal. His case was: (i) that the disputed area was included in the 1981 disposition of his own property; (ii) that it was not included in the disposition of 1982 in favour of the scouts; (iii) that accordingly the scouts had no title to include the disputed area in the disposition of 2015; (iv) that the disputed area should not have been included within the title sheet issued to Borthwick Campsite LLP; (v) that the disputed area continued to belong to him, Mr Munro; and (vi) that the title sheet was therefore inaccurate and should be rectified.

There was no dispute as to (i), and no real dispute as to (ii). In the 1982 disposition in favour of the scouts, the subjects were described both by plan and by statement as to area. The description read:

> ALL and WHOLE that area of ground extending to one acre or thereby Imperial Standard Measure delineated in red on the plan annexed and subscribed as relative hereto being the westmost part of enclosure Number 2069 on Ordnance Survey 1972 Edition Sheet NT 3758 which subjects are part and portion of the farm and lands of Borthwick Main, Gorebridge in the County of Midlothian.

1 2017 GWD 17-277. This was a decision of the Lands Tribunal, the Tribunal comprising Lord Minginish and A Oswald FRICS.
2 The disposition was in favour of Mrs Munro, but she later disponed the property to her husband.
3 It is hard to imagine this happening if the Keeper had checked the scouts' prior title, as would always have been done prior to 8 December 2014.

The land as shown on the plan amounted to 0.72 acres. It did not include the disputed area. It is true that the statement as to area promised 'one acre or thereby' and not merely three-quarters of an acre; but, as seen in the *Veen* case discussed above, in a matter of interpretation a plan will always be preferred to a statement of area. It was accepted on all sides, therefore, that the disputed area was not disponed to the scouts in 1982.

How, then, might the scouts have had title to dispone the disputed area in 2015? The answer, according to Borthwick Campsite LLP, lay in positive prescription. The area had been possessed by the scouts for longer than the prescriptive period of ten years. And if the 1982 disposition did not convey the disputed area, it was at least *habile* for the purposes of prescription. Hence prescription had run in favour of the scouts.[1] It was on the question of whether the disposition was *habile* for prescription that the case was fought.

A *habile* title?

A description which is inept to convey a particular area may still be *habile* in respect of that area for the purposes of positive prescription. The interpretative task is different in the two cases. In respect of the first, the task is to discover what the description really means. In respect of the second, the task is to determine whether, on *any possible* interpretation of the words used, the words can be read as including the targeted area. In the first case, the description must be interpreted in accordance with the rules that have already been discussed in the context of the *Veen* case. In the second case, those rules can be disregarded. The difference is captured in a well-known passage by Lord Justice-Clerk Moncreiff in *Auld v Hay* (1880) 7 R 663 at 668, which was quoted by the Lands Tribunal in *Munro*:

> A habile title does not mean a charter followed by sasine, which bears to convey the property in dispute, but one which is conceived in terms capable of being so construed. The terms of the grant may be ambiguous, or indefinite, or general, so that it may remain doubtful whether the particular subject is or is not conveyed, or, if conveyed, what is the extent of it. But if the instrument be conceived in terms consistent with and susceptible of a construction which would embrace such a conveyance, that is enough, and forty years' possession following on it will constitute the right to the extent possessed.

Was the description in the 1982 disposition *habile* to include the disputed area? The Lands Tribunal thought not.[2] The disposition contained a bounding description in which the boundaries were laid down by the plan. The disputed area lay outside these boundaries. Hence the disposition was not *habile* for the purposes of prescription. Accordingly the Tribunal held that 'Title Sheet MID162719 contains a manifest inaccuracy which requires to be rectified by the substitution of a title plan consistent with the boundary shown in the plan annexed to the 1982 disposition'.[3]

---

1 Prescription and Limitation (Scotland) Act 1973 s 1.
2 Paragraphs 25–29.
3 Paragraph 34.

That, certainly, is a possible view of matters. But another view is also possible. The 1982 disposition contained two distinct descriptive elements, namely the plan and the statement as to area. The two were in disagreement. The former excluded the disputed area. The latter, being necessarily vague, could be read as including it. Where two descriptive elements disagree, the rules of interpretation provide a hierarchy of significance, as we have seen, in which a statement as to area comes at the very bottom. But the rules of interpretation are not the same as the rules as to *habile* titles. And for the purposes of identifying a *habile* title, it is or may be sufficient if *either* of the contradictory elements is capable of including the targeted area. In matters of prescription, there is no reason for preferring one element over the other. That seems to have been the conclusion reached, by a majority, in the Inner House case of *Nisbet v Hogg* decided in 1950.[1] It is true that in a more recent case, *Trustees of Calthorpe's 1959 Discretionary Settlement v G Hamilton (Tullochgribban Mains) Ltd,*[2] it was held in the Outer House that the mere existence of contradictory descriptive elements was enough to prevent a description from being *habile* for the purposes of prescription. But this case seems inconsistent with *Nisbet v Hogg,* a decision which was binding on the Lord Ordinary.[3]

It is probably the law, therefore, that where two elements in a description are contradictory, either can be used as the basis for prescription. In *Munro* the description by plan excluded the disputed area, as we have seen, and so was not *habile* for the purposes of prescription. Thus far the decision of the Lands Tribunal is beyond reproach. But what of the other descriptive element, the statement as to? Of course it is true that, as the Tribunal said, 'the statement of area tells us nothing about where the boundaries are'.[4] But that is not infrequently the case with prescriptive titles. As Gordon and Wortley note, 'So far as the description of the land in which the interest in question is claimed, it is of course helpful if the title does expressly cover what is claimed, but it is not essential that this should be so.'[5] A purely general description is sufficient for prescription. If the plan is ignored, the description in *Munro* read:

> ALL and WHOLE that area of ground extending to one acre or thereby Imperial Standard Measure…being the westmost part of enclosure Number 2069 on Ordnance Survey 1972 Edition Sheet NT 3758…

It is hard to see why this should not be sufficient for the purposes of prescription.

The maintenance burden

Although the argument for Borthwick Campsite LLP made something of the statement as to area, discussed above, the main focus was on a different point. In disponing the field to the scouts, the 1982 disposition imposed the following real burden:

---

1 1950 SLT 289.
2 [2012] CSOH 138, 2012 GWD 29-599.
3 For discussion of this whole issue, see Reid and Gretton, *Conveyancing 2012* pp 151–55.
4 Paragraph 28.
5 Gordon and Wortley, *Scottish Land Law* para 12–34.

> In respect that I have erected at my own expense a stock proof fence along the southeast boundary of the subjects hereby disponed in order to separate the subjects hereby disponed from other parts of Borthwick Mains Farm which are presently owned by Mrs Jacqueline Mira Olive Massee or Munro it is declared that the maintenance of the said fence will be at the joint expense of my said disponees and their foresaids on the one hand and the said Mrs Jacqueline Mira Olive Massee or Munro and her executors and assignees whomsoever as proprietors of the adjoining subjects on the other hand.

The positioning of this fence, which marked the boundary between the field being disponed to the scouts and the property belonging to the Munros, was inconsistent with the boundaries as shown on the deed plan. Thus, argued Borthwick Campsite LLP, 'there was conflict between the dispositive clause and the plan, sufficient, at the very least, to give rise to ambiguity and therefore the measure of the right had to be decided by reference to possession and prescription. Put another way, the reference to the fence in the 1982 disposition rendered it habile to include the disputed area if regard could be had to where the fence had been erected.'[1] This argument too was rejected by the Lands Tribunal.

Implications for the Land Register

On the view taken by the Lands Tribunal, the 1982 disposition was not *habile* for the purposes of prescription. Hence, any possession on the part of the scouts counted for naught. And when the scouts came to dispone the disputed area to Borthwick Campsite LLP in 2015, they had no title to grant. No doubt Borthwick Campsite LLP was registered as proprietor in the Land Register. But, in the absence of title on the part of the scouts, such registration could achieve nothing. There is no Midas touch under the Land Registration Act of 2012. Mr Munro remained the owner of the disputed area.

It only remained to rectify the Register. Although the Keeper had already accepted that the Register was manifestly inaccurate, she had concluded that, because prescription was potentially running, she was prevented from rectifying the Register by s 81 of the 2012 Act.[2] The most she could do under s 81 was to mark Borthwick Campsite LLP's title as 'provisional'. For rectification to take place, s 81 required that the inaccuracy be judicially determined. The decision in *Munro* provided the judicial determination that was lacking. It was the very reason for Mr Munro's application.

SPECIAL DESTINATIONS: CONDUITS FOR LIABILITY?

Introduction

The law of special destinations is far from straightforward. A book could be written about it, especially when one considers that a branch of the subject

---

1 Paragraph 21.
2 On this provision, see K G C Reid and G L Gretton, *Land Registration* (2017) para 17.6.

was formerly the tailzie (entail), a special special destination; and when one looks from the branches down to the roots, one of those roots is the *substitutio fideicommissaria* of the *ius commune*. With that one delves into the subterranean network of comparative and historical European private law.

Special destinations have long provided, and continue to provide, a significant number of disputes coming before the courts. This series has, over the years, dealt with more than we can readily count, and 2017 produced yet another, *Machin's Tr v Machin.*[1]

Mr and Mrs Machin bought a flat, taking title equally between them and the survivor of them. Some years later Mr Machin died and his widow became his executor. It turned out that Mr Machin had extensive debts, and his widow decided that the only way forward was for his estate to be sequestrated.

Why Mrs Machin made this decision, and whether she received legal advice beforehand, is not known to us. We would note that there was formerly a rule that an executor was positively obliged to apply for sequestration 'within a reasonable period after he knew or ought to have known that the estate was absolutely insolvent',[2] but that provision no longer exists.[3] At all events, the decision to apply for sequestration perhaps proved not to be in Mrs Machin's best interests, as the sequel will show.

The sequestration took place about two years after Mr Machin's death. The trustee in sequestration then raised the present action, seeking payment from Mrs Machin of one half of the value of the flat (estimated as at the date of the death), being the half that she had succeeded to from her late husband by virtue of the special destination. The flat had, said the trustee, been worth £53,998, and so, he said, she had to pay to him £26,998. Mrs Machin defended the action both on the law and on the facts.

As to the law, she argued:[4]

That her late husband's one-half *pro indiviso* share of the flat never formed part of his estate on death, still less two years later at the date of sequestration, because it vested automatically in the defender on her husband's death. She denies any personal liability for her late husband's debts. She denies that any debts transferred to her upon acquisition of the deceased's one-half share.

As to the facts, 'the defender … denies that the deceased's estate was insolvent at the date of his death'. The sheriff (Stuart Reid) comments at this point: 'Though, interestingly, it was the defender, as the deceased's executrix, who applied for sequestration of the estate.'[5]

So what is the law in such cases? This question forms part of a larger question, that of how debt is handled on death. Of course it is a general principle in Scots

---

1 [2017] SC GLA 29, 2017 GWD 15-253.
2 Bankruptcy (Scotland) Act 1985 s 8(4).
3 It was repealed by the Bankruptcy and Debt Advice (Scotland) Act 2014, and the current primary legislation, the Bankruptcy (Scotland) Act 2016, contains no such provision. But it remains *competent* for the executor to apply for sequestration: Bankruptcy (Scotland) Act 2016 s 5.
4 Paragraph 5.
5 Paragraph 14.

law, as in other legal systems, that creditors come before beneficiaries. But the details can be complex, and we have a suspicion that not everything is as clear and settled in our law as ideally it should be. But this is not the place to embark on the large general issues: here only one issue was in question, namely the interaction between the rights of unpaid creditors and a person who has succeeded to property of the debtor by virtue of a special destination. And here one meets the fact that special destinations are amphibious beasts. They are part of the law of property, but they are also part of the law of succession. They are found in *inter vivos* deeds, but their effect is seen on death. Do they participate in the general principle that creditors come before beneficiaries? If Jack and Jill own a house with a survivorship destination, and Jill dies insolvent, does Jack take the property subject to her debts, or not?[1]

Prior authority

In *Barclay's Bank v McGreish*[2] title was held by husband and wife and the survivor. After the husband died, a bank sued the widow for money that he owed it. The bank failed. It was held that the widow took the property free of the debts of her late husband. But this decision was criticised, mainly on the basis that earlier authorities had not been drawn to the attention of the court, and it came to be reviewed by the Inner House in *Fleming's Tr v Fleming.*[3]

In the latter case, title was held by Mr and Mrs Fleming and the survivor. The husband was sequestrated. It seems that his trustee did not attempt to realise his one-half *pro indiviso* share. After some years the husband died, and now at last the trustee was roused to action. The trustee raised an action in which he sought (i) declarator that Mr Fleming's one-half share was vested in him, the trustee, and accordingly that he was entitled to division and sale of the property, or (ii) *esto* the one-half share was not so vested, but vested in Mrs Fleming, that the latter was liable to pay the trustee the value of the share to which she had succeeded.

The Inner House rejected the first argument. The fact that Mr Fleming had been sequestrated before his death did not, it was held, prevent the operation of the special destination. If the trustee had acted timeously, for instance by recording a notice of title in his own name, *qua* trustee, to Mr Fleming's one-half share, before the latter died, matters would have been different. In that case the operation of the special destination would have been precluded, for the simple reason that the one-half share would no longer have been owned by Mr Fleming at the time of his decease. Whilst sequestration vests the estate of the debtor in the trustee, that vesting does not necessarily, in and of itself, transfer the real right of ownership. It normally does so, it is true, for corporeal moveable property. But for

---

1 There is also the question of what happens if Jill is not actually insolvent, but nevertheless has extensive debts. The debts could be paid solely by her other assets. But should Jack have to chip in? We do not seek to explore that question here.

2 1983 SLT 344.

3 2000 SC 206.

heritable property it has long been settled that until (i) the trustee completes title in his own name, *qua* trustee, or (ii) a purchaser from the trustee completes title by registering the disposition in his favour, the real right of ownership remains in the debtor (albeit that his right to deal with the property is largely taken away by the sequestration). So the trustee's first argument failed.

But the second argument succeeded. Overruling *Barclay's Bank v McGreish*, and adhering to the earlier authorities that had not been drawn to the court's attention in that case, the Inner House held that someone who takes property under a special destination can be held liable by the creditors of the deceased, not, indeed, without limit, but up to the value of the property that has passed under the destination – in the typical case, a one-half share.[1]

The decision in *Machin's Tr*

Mrs Machin, therefore, faced an obvious difficulty: Inner House authority was against her. Her response was to attempt to distinguish it:[2]

> The defender's agent sought to distinguish *Fleming's Trustee* ... In *Fleming's Trustee*, the debtor had already been sequestrated prior to his death, with the result that his one-half *pro indiviso* share had vested in his trustee and already formed part of the sequestrated estate at death. In contrast, in the present case the deceased had not been sequestrated prior to his death, with the result that his one-half *pro indiviso* share vested in the defender upon his death, and never formed part of his sequestrated estate. It was submitted that, following his death, the deceased had 'zero rights' in the property. By virtue of the survivorship destination, he was automatically divested of his share.

In other words, the sequence of events was different. In the present case, unlike *Fleming's Tr*, the survivor had succeeded to the half-share of someone who, though he might have been in debt, had not been sequestrated. The sequestration had come later – and too late.

This argument was rejected by the sheriff, and, with respect, we think that he was right to do so. As he said:[3]

> The institute (Mr Machin) died long before his estate was sequestrated. Accordingly, his share devolved automatically to the substitute (the defender). But, according to long-established authority, the substitute also thereby incurred a personal liability to the unsatisfied creditors of the deceased institute, to the extent of the value of her succession. In contrast with *Fleming's Trustee* ... there is no need to analyse the substitute's real right as being 'burdened' by the deceased's debts. The substitute (the defender) has simply incurred a personal liability to the deceased's creditors by virtue of her succession under the special destination. That liability was enforceable directly against the defender at the instance of the deceased's unsatisfied creditors.

---

1 There is also the question of whether such a person can be asked to pay by the deceased's executor, but this raises issues that are outwith the scope of the present note.
2 Paragraph 17.
3 Paragraph 34.

The defender also invoked s 36(2) of the Succession (Scotland) Act 1964:[1]

> Where any heritable property belonging to a deceased person at the date of his death is subject to a special destination in favour of any person, the property shall not be treated for the purposes of this Act as part of the estate of the deceased unless the destination is one which could competently be, and has in fact been, evacuated by the deceased by testamentary disposition or otherwise ...

This provision had earlier been given a good deal of mileage in *Barclay's Bank v McGreish*. But as the critics had observed, this provision was relevant 'for the purposes of this Act'. As the sheriff commented:[2]

> The 'purposes' of the 1964 Act are to regulate rights of succession and, according to its long title, to amend the law in relation to the administration of deceased persons' estates. Nowhere can it be discerned that a purpose of the 1964 Act is to restrict the rights of third party creditors.

So the defender failed on the law. But she also had a plea as to the facts. She denied that her husband had been insolvent. That was a question, said the sheriff, that would have to go to proof. There was also a further issue as to whether, even if Mr Machin had been insolvent when he died, some of his debts might have negatively prescribed thereafter. The sheriff offered the following interesting remarks:[3]

> A separate and, perhaps, more intriguing question (given the passage of time between the death and the sequestration in the present case) is whether any of the deceased's debts as at the date of death may subsequently have been extinguished by prescription and, if so, whether the defender's personal liability to creditors would thereby be abated. This issue has not been addressed in the averments and was touched upon only fleetingly in the defender's submissions. Accordingly, I need not express a final view upon it. For what it is worth, my strictly preliminary thoughts are that the defender's personal liability to creditors (and, now, to the pursuer as trustee on behalf of the creditors) is essentially ancillary in nature, derived from the deceased debtor's primary obligation to his creditors. The defender's personal liability subsists only to the extent that the primary obligation (of the deceased's estate) to those creditors subsists. Death does not interrupt the operation of the prescriptive period. A debt subsisting at the date of death may nevertheless prescribe during the period of an executry, absent a relevant claim against, or relevant acknowledgment by, the debtor's executor or trustee. So, if some or all of the deceased's debts (so far as they may have existed at the date of death) no longer subsist (due, for example, to discharge by payment, compromise, prescription or otherwise) I would have thought that the defender's ancillary and derivative personal liability to the creditors may, in theory, likewise be abated.

---

1 Now, with some revision, s 28(1) of the Succession (Scotland) Act 2016. Had Mr Machin died after the 2016 Act came into force, the new wording would, we think, have made no difference.
2 Paragraph 27.
3 Paragraph 38.

BOUNDARY DISPUTES

Difficulties about the precise line of a boundary will not all disappear with the inexorable advance of registration of title. Although the cadastral map is a great deal better than no map, or plan, at all – the position, sometimes, in respect of Sasine titles – it falls some way short of perfection. It may, for example, be out-of-date or contain mistakes. And the scale at which the map is compiled can make fine judgments as to boundaries difficult or even impossible. The cadastral map is scaled at 1:1250, 1:2500 and 1:10,000 depending on whether the area is, respectively, urban, rural or moorland. Even on the largest of these scales (1:1250), 1 millimetre on the map is equivalent to 1.25 metres on the ground. In theory, it is possible to scale to 0.23 metres on such a map, but in practice the position is not always so clear-cut, and matters are not improved by the absence of written measurements. The area of the plot is given if it exceeds half a hectare (formerly two hectares),[1] but this is of limited help in calculating the position of individual boundaries.[2]

The absence of physical boundary features can add to the problems. But so too can their presence. A fence or other feature may be in the wrong place, or have been moved, or be new so that the feature on the ground is not the same as the feature shown on the cadastral map. Occasionally a fence or wall may be deliberately located slightly back from the boundary line. A natural feature, such as a hedge or line of bushes, might have increased in girth or grown out of control. All of these may be unreliable guides as to the precise position of the boundary.

Lane v Irvin Mitchell Trust Corporation Ltd[3] is an everyday example of the kind of difficulty that can result.[4] The pursuers and defenders were neighbours, the boundary between their properties consisting of a private road and a hedge. The road, which comprised a tarmac strip flanked by grass verges, was largely or wholly on the pursuers' land. The status of the hedge, which lay between the road and the defenders' property, was less clear. Often this sort of uncertainty is something that can be lived with, but only if each neighbour leaves the boundary alone. In the present case, the defenders did not leave it alone but removed a section of the hedge extending to some 30 feet. The present litigation was the result. The hedge, argued the pursuers, was wholly on their property. Accordingly, they sought declarator regarding the location of the boundary, damages for the cost of replacement of the section of hedge which had been removed, and interdict to prevent the defenders from removing any other part of the hedge. The case went to debate on the relevancy of the pursuers' pleadings. By the time of the debate the pursuers had departed from their initial position

---

1 Land Register Rules etc (Scotland) Regulations 2014, SSI 2014/150, r 12(1)(f).
2 For more on the use of measurements of area, see p 176 above.
3 29 March 2017, Dumfries Sheriff Court, unreported. For another aspect of this case, see p 11.
4 For earlier examples, see *Clydesdale Homes Ltd v Quay* [2009] CSOH 126, 2009 GWD 31-518; *Stuart v Stuart* 27 July 2009, Stonehaven Sheriff Court, unreported. For commentary on both cases, see *Conveyancing 2009* pp 176–77.

and only claimed the hedge as far as its mid-point. That, however, would still be enough to put the defenders in the wrong.

Both properties were on the Land Register, and both were properly aligned next to each other on the cadastral map.[1] In other words, there was neither overlap nor underlap: the boundaries dovetailed. Nonetheless, the precise location of the mutual boundary was unclear. In the A (property) section of the defenders' title sheet the property was described as:

> Raeburnhead Cottages, Kirkpatrick Fleming, Lockerbie DG11 3BA edged red on the Title Plan extending to 3.85 hectares in measurement on the Ordnance Map.

This brief verbal description said nothing about individual boundaries. On the title plan, the private road was represented by four parallel dotted (or 'pecked') lines, of which the inner pair was assumed to be the tarmac strip and the outer pair the grass verge on each side. The hedge, of course, was nowhere to be seen.

An oddity of the plan was the positioning of the red edging. Registers of Scotland policy here is quite clear:[2]

> The conventional method for referencing a cadastral unit is to give it a red edge following the *internal* edge of the boundaries of the cadastral unit. This method of referencing can be used to reference, for example, a detached or terraced house, a plot of garden ground, a large rural farm property, or a common drying green in a shared plot title sheet ... To help remove any ambiguity from the cadastral map, the red edge should only be 'flipped out' to follow the *external* boundaries of the cadastral unit in exceptional circumstances.

An example of such 'exceptional circumstances' is where 'the size or shape of the cadastral unit is so small or narrow that an internal red edge would look like a red fill when viewed or printed at the OS base map scale'. That could not be said to be the case in respect of the 3.85 hectares owned by the defenders. Nonetheless, if the red edging on the title plan was taken to follow the normal pattern of tracing the internal edge of the boundaries, the result would be to include within the defenders' property the whole of the grass verge on the defenders' side of the road. Not only would such a result be surprising, it would also give the defenders the entirety of the hedge.

The sheriff[3] concluded that, contrary to normal practice, the red edging must mark the *external* edge of the boundary, and hence that the grass verge was wholly excluded from the defenders' property. In this he received some encouragement in the form of a curiously equivocal letter from the Keeper which was sent in respect of the current proceedings:

---

1   See however the comments in para 23 as to the slight discrepancies in the title plans of the different properties.
2   Registers of Scotland, *Registration Manual* Further Guidance: Plans – mapping styles on the cadastral map (our emphases).
3   Sheriff Brian A Mohan.

Occasionally, the edging will be applied 'externally' to the boundary defining the subjects … For this reason it should not be assumed that the registered extent includes up to the outer edge of the red, but rather see the registered boundary as being the line (firm or pecked) to which the red edge has been applied.

In the end, thought the sheriff, the conclusion that the edging traced the external boundary edge was a matter of common sense.[1] That could be seen, not only from the boundary currently in dispute, but from one of the other boundaries, with a public road, where an internal tracing would result in part of the road being included within the defenders' property. That was most unlikely to be correct.

What then of the hedge? With the one clear feature on the plan (the red edging) having been discarded, there was almost no other material to work with.[2] Probably the hedge was part of the defenders' property. But in any event the pursuers had failed to aver a relevant case as to their ownership of the hedge. The action therefore fell to be dismissed.

It is hard not to feel sympathy for the pursuers' position. Given the vagueness of the respective title sheets, it was no easy matter to demonstrate ownership of the hedge. The sheriff may well have been correct in supposing that it fell within the defenders' property. But the sheer difficulty of determining this must have seemed unsatisfactory to both parties.

Finally, it is also unsatisfactory that users of the Land Register should be in any doubt as to the way that red edging is used. We would quote the Scottish Law Commission's 2010 report on land registration:[3]

> The red edge has a measurable thickness and users often are puzzled whether the boundary is the inner margin or outer margin or something in between. …[W]e consider that this is not a matter for primary legislation …. We make no specific recommendation, except that: The Keeper should ensure that the meaning of the red edge is reasonably clear to users.

PROPERTY TAXES IN SCOTLAND[4]

Introduction

2017 produced several milestones in the maturing of Scotland as its own tax jurisdiction. Notably, the 2017 Scottish draft Budget proposed significant income tax variations from the position in the rest of the UK, from 2018–19. While this is not of specific relevance to the taxation of land, income from land is one of the categories of income of Scottish taxpayers which will be affected by the newly differing rates (and thresholds). On the other hand, income from Scottish land for taxpayers not falling within the definition of Scottish taxpayers is unaffected by the new rules, one of the many inevitable anomalies of a partially devolved tax system.

---

1 Paragraph 20.
2 See, however, the rather inconsequential matters discussed at para 26.
3 Scottish Law Commission, *Report No 222 on Land Registration* (2010) para 5.38.
4 This part is contributed by Alan Barr of the University of Edinburgh and Brodies LLP.

In the meantime, developments and divergences continued for the main wholly devolved Scottish tax, land and buildings transaction tax, which affects all those dealing with Scottish land, whatever their taxpayer status. Among other developments were the first reported decisions on purely tax matters from a wholly Scottish tax tribunal; and that jurisprudential development is also illustrative of the need for those affected by Scottish taxes to maintain their Janus-faced regard for (at least) two systems of tax law.

At a UK level, developments in property taxes were less fundamental than in some recent years, although several existing measures moved further towards their full effects by gradual implementation. Relatively limited changes in property taxes occurred despite there being two full Budgets (the last one of Spring and the first one of Autumn) and also a general election (which event often gives rise to additional tax changes) in the calendar year. Brexit may have less impact on property taxes than in other areas, although VAT on land will bear watching in future years.

Land and buildings transaction tax

Additional dwelling supplement ('ADS')[1]

Before its introduction, ADS was forecast to raise some £23.5 million. In the event, its first complete year produced net receipts of some £81 million (slightly off-setting a shortfall in total, especially residential, LBTT receipts for 2016–17, as compared to prior estimates).[2] From the Scottish Government's point of view, it may thus presumably be judged to have been a success. This view may not be shared by the larger than expected number of taxpayers who ended up paying the supplement and still less by Scottish solicitors, essentially responsible for its administration. To a greater extent than with basic LBTT, difficult legal, administrative and valuation questions can arise in relation to potential ADS in what would otherwise be relatively straightforward transactions; and what can be perceived as anomalies continue to abound. But the eggs seem a little too golden for wholesale reform of this goose to be anticipated in the near future.

While the Scottish Government and Revenue Scotland appear to accept the desirability of curing various anomalies with ADS, only one was specifically addressed in 2017. This was in relation to certain 'family units' and the main residence relief generally available from ADS when a residence is replaced. The relief prevents ADS applying where all that is happening is that a taxpayer is replacing one residence with another, but may, in that process, come to own two residences at the time of the replacement, either permanently or on a temporary basis. However, the rules on counting ownership within 'economic units' (such as joint buyers, spouses and cohabitants) meant that, where only one member of

---

1 For an overview, see *Conveyancing 2016* pp 214–27.
2 See Land and Buildings Transaction Tax Statistics at www.revenue.scot/about-us/publications/ statistics/land-and-buildings-transaction-tax-statistics-0#overlay-context=about-us/ publications/statistics.

such a unit replaced a main residence, the relief did not apply. So for example a couple who each, separately, owned a dwelling could not qualify for the relief if they purchased a new dwelling together.

This anomaly was cured in part by secondary legislation, amending schedule 2A of the Land and Buildings Transaction Tax (Scotland) Act 2013.[1] This is aimed at ensuring that spouses, civil partners or cohabitants who jointly buy a main residence are considered to be replacing their main residence when their previous main residence is sold, even where that residence was owned by only one of them. This applies both to prevent ADS being charged at the outset when what will now be deemed to be the couple's main residence is sold before the purchase, and also to allow for repayment when that previous residence is sold after the purchase.[2]

But, not untypically, the revised relief is limited in scope. It only applies if there are no more than two joint buyers of the new main residence. More challengingly, it only applies if the property sold was the main residence of *both* the joint buyers. So in the not untypical situation of a couple buying a property to use as the first main residence which they will occupy together (having previously lived apart in their own respective dwellings), their new purchase will still be liable to ADS, unless by the time of purchase they have disposed of both of their previous properties. Their previous joint occupation of one such property as their main residence is a question of fact and degree and is vague enough to give rise to reasonable differing interpretations.

As matters currently stand, the introduction of the relief is not retrospective; it applies only in cases where the purchase transaction contract was entered into after 19 May 2017 and where the transaction completed after 29 June 2017. It was not possible to make the change retrospective by secondary legislation; but the Scottish Government has introduced a Bill to give retrospective effect to the extension.[3] Repayments of tax paid on the basis of the previous law will be permitted; the effect on those who have understandably but incorrectly *not* paid the tax when they should have done is unclear. One hopes that those sleeping dogs will be left to lie.

Rates of tax and first-time buyer relief

It was announced in the draft Scottish Budget for 2018–19 that the basic rates and thresholds of LBTT and ADS would remain unchanged at:[4]

---

1 See Land and Buildings Transaction Tax (Additional Amount-Second Homes Main Residence Relief) (Scotland) Order 2017, SSI 2017/233.
2 See Revenue Scotland, *LBTT Technical Bulletin 3* (28 December 2017; www.revenue.scot/sites/default/files/LBTT%20Technical%20Update%20-%2028%20December%202017_1.pdf) para 4; Revenue Scotland, *Guidance on Additional Dwelling Supplement* (www.revenue.scot/land-buildings-transaction-tax/guidance/lbtt-legislation-guidance) para LBTT10062A and examples 47A, 48A and 73A.
3 See Land and Buildings Transaction Tax (Relief from Additional Amount) (Scotland) Bill, introduced to the Scottish Parliament on 28 November 2017.
4 *Scottish Budget: Draft Budget 2018–19* (14 Dec 2017; www.gov.scot/Publications/2017/12/8959/3) Ch 2.

Table 1: rates of LBTT for 2018–19

Residential transactions		Non-residential transactions		Non-residential leases	
Purchase price	LBTT Rate	Purchase price	LBTT Rate	Net present value of rent payable	LBTT Rate
Up to £145,000	0%	Up to £150,000	0%	Up to £150,000	0%
£145,001 to £250,000	2%	£150,001 to £350,000	3%	Over £150,000	1%
£250,001 to £325,000	5%	Over £350,000	4.5%		
£325,001 to £750,000	10%				
Over £750,000	12%				

However, the Budget announcement also included a consultation on a first-time buyer relief. This followed the announcement of a similar relief for the rest of the UK in the Autumn Budget, introducing a zero-rate for first-time buyers on properties for a consideration up to £300,000 and relief where the consideration does not exceed £500,000.[1] The Scottish version is more restricted. Subject to consultation, this will increase the nil-rate band for first-time buyers for consideration up to £175,000. It is anticipated that this will take 80% of first-time buyers out of LBTT entirely.[2]

Technical guidance, confirmations and a change of view

Revenue Scotland published two further Technical Bulletins in 2017. The first merely presaged the change to main residence relief from ADS for certain economic units, dealt with above.[3]

The second dealt further with the ADS changes, but also included some further details.[4] Distinctly unwelcome was confirmation of a Revenue Scotland view on the availability of group relief in certain circumstances. This followed their response to a request for an opinion in a specific case. According to Revenue Scotland, this highlighted differences between LBTT and SDLT legislation in a transaction where a parent company transfers property to a subsidiary and the parent company grants security to a lender over the shares in the subsidiary. Their view is that the pledging of the shares constitutes an 'arrangement' under which a person (ie the lender holding the share pledge) could obtain control of the subsidiary but not the parent. Therefore, group relief is not available.

This view came as a shock to many, and would mean that a number of transactions thought to be free of LBTT should have been chargeable. Strenuous

---

1 See *Autumn Budget 2017*, November 2017, HC 587; www.gov.uk/government/uploads/system/ uploads/attachment_data/file/661480/autumn_budget_2017_web.pdf; Finance (No 2) Bill 2017–19 cl 41, inserting sch 6ZA into Finance Act 2003.
2 *Scottish Budget: Draft Budget 2018–19* p 25.
3 See Revenue Scotland, *LBTT Technical Bulletin 2* (22 May 2017; www.revenue.scot/sites/default/ files/LBTT%20Technical%20Update%20-%2022%20May%202017_0.pdf).
4 *LBTT Technical Bulletin 3*.

efforts were made for this position to be changed, as it puts Scotland (or, rather, property within Scotland) at a distinct disadvantage as compared to the rest of the UK.[1] It now seems likely that the law will be corrected.

Much more immediately welcome was a change of view in relation to pension fund *in specie* transfers. Previously, Revenue Scotland had expressed the view that the obligation to make pension payments represented consideration liable to LBTT, this being contrary to the view expressed in relation to SDLT by HMRC, this time on legislation with exactly the same wording.[2] They have now changed this view, following extensive representations. Transfers will still be considered to be land transactions, but debt in the form of the liability assumed to pay benefits to pension scheme beneficiaries will not generally be considered to be given as chargeable consideration in relation to such transactions. However, it is made clear that any actual money or money's worth consideration for the transfer will be chargeable to LBTT in the normal way. The change of view is retrospective and Revenue Scotland will consider claims to repayment of tax from any taxpayers who have paid LBTT on the basis of their previous view.[3]

The final and equally welcome announcement in the *Technical Bulletin* was in relation to early terminations of leases. It was announced that the early termination of a lease may give rise to a repayment if less rent has become payable than was originally included in the return, due to a reduction in the term of the lease.[4] This is a reflection of what might be expected in the LBTT system, which aims (primarily through the rules on three-yearly reviews of LBTT on leases) to make LBTT payable on the total amount of rent actually paid over the term of a lease. Earlier indications had been that there would be no repayment where a lease came to an end earlier than anticipated.

Scottish income tax

For 2017–18, in a slight change from its original proposals, the Scottish Government chose to maintain the *rates* of income tax on non-savings income (which includes property income) for Scottish taxpayers at the same level as in the rest of the UK, but froze the *threshold* at which the 40% rate commenced at the level (when combined with the increased personal allowance) as applied in 2016–17.[5] Thus the Scottish basic-rate band for that year was £31,500 rather than £33,500.

More fundamental changes for 2018–19 were heavily trailed. A wide variety of possible approaches, along with analysis of the manifesto proposals of all the main political parties, were published in advance of the Scottish Budget in a

---

1 See for example Law Society of Scotland *Comments: Scotland's Budget* (December 2017; www.lawscot.org.uk/media/359301/tax-comments-on-scottish-budget.pdf).
2 See Revenue Scotland, *LBTT Technical Bulletin 1* (2016; www.revenue.scot/sites/default/files/LBTT%20Technical%20Update%20-%20Oct%2016.pdf); *Conveyancing 2016* p 228.
3 *LBTT Technical Bulletin 3* para 2.
4 *LBTT Technical Bulletin 3* para 3; see also revised guidance at Revenue Scotland, *Guidance on Land and Buildings Transaction Tax* para 6017.
5 See Scottish Parliament, Scottish Rate Resolution, 21 February 2017; www.parliament.scot/parliamentarybusiness/report.aspx?r=10794.

detailed paper, with full assessments of possible overall revenue and individual impacts.[1]

In the end, the proposals in the draft Scottish Budget were for a system somewhat different from any of the models put forward.[2] They fell on the side of marginally reducing the tax burden for a significant number, whether compared to taxpayers elsewhere in the UK or (in particular and rather disingenuously) compared to the current year; while increasing it for others, generally those with higher incomes. In respect of the latter, it seems that pragmatism may have overcome (some) principles. There is to be no return to a 50% tax rate, on the realistic basis that this might well have led to a significant reduction in the overall tax take. This decision was heavily informed by technical advice from the Council of Economic Advisers.[3] The hope must be that those with higher earnings will not be driven by a relatively modest rise in their tax bill (especially in the highest rate) to attempt to cease being Scottish taxpayers at all.

In a move that is radical, at least in terms of structure, Scottish taxpayers will face five bands of income tax in 2018–19, for their non-savings income:

Table 2: rates of Scottish income tax 2018–19

Scottish income tax rates	Scottish Bands
A Starter Rate of 19%	Over £11,850 – £13,850
The Scottish Basic Rate of 20%	Over £13,850 – £24,000
An Intermediate Rate of 21%	Over £24,000 – £43,430
A (Scottish) Higher Rate of 41%	Over £43,430 – £150,000
A Top Rate of 46%	Above £150,000

An extended tax vocabulary is needed to incorporate the new bands – so for the Scottish taxpayer the equivalent to the UK rates of starting, basic, higher and additional are rates called starter, Scottish basic, intermediate, Scottish higher and top. Add to this possible zero-rate allowances for savings and for dividends, three further possible rates for dividends, and separate rates for capital gains tax, and it is very difficult to imagine how it could be made more complicated. The costs charged by HMRC for administering the changed Scottish rates are a work in progress, but it seems certain that the greater the divergence from the rates in the rest of the UK, the greater will be the cost of collecting and administering Scottish income tax.

The way that these bands are presented is a little confusing, because the figures include the proposed 2018–19 UK level for the basic personal allowance. The figure originally proposed at which the Scottish higher rate was to start was £44,273, that being based on an inflationary increase from the 2017–18 Scottish

1 See Scottish Government *The Role of Income Tax in Scotland's Budget* (2 November 2017; www.gov. scot/Resource/0052/00527052.pdf).
2 *Scottish Budget: Draft Budget 2018–19* pp 20–23, as revised by proposals issued on 31 January 2018.
3 *Scottish Budget: Draft Budget 2018–19* p 22.

higher rate threshold. In the event, political expediency as well, perhaps, as arithmetical convenience has produced a somewhat lower figure.

As noted, the Scottish rates will only affect the non-savings income (essentially that derived from employment, self-employment, pensions and rent) of Scottish taxpayers.[1] Those with savings and dividend income will pay tax at the UK rates, where those are different; and will benefit from the UK-specific allowances for such income. In deciding which rates to apply, savings income is treated as the highest part of income; and dividends are treated as being the highest part of savings income.

This produces anomalies. Scottish taxpayers within the starter-rate band may pay a higher rate on their taxable savings income than on their earnings, while those within the intermediate and higher-rate bands will pay at a lower rate (20% or 40%) on similar income.

Much was made in the Budget of the impact of the proposed new rates in relation to four policy tests – revenue raising, protecting lower earners, progressivity, and economic growth. In sheer arithmetical terms, assuming forecasts come true, the new structure will support the first three. In particular, a greater number of bands of tax must increase progressivity. The last test is much more nebulous and the Budget paper is most defensive about it, prompting the question of whether a greater tax take can ever be a stimulus to economic growth. Other tests could of course be set; and the addition to the complexities of the overall system cannot be welcomed. But the changes meet a new fundamental test – the Scottish Parliament has extensive tax-varying powers now and this is a significant use of powers long sought after. Thus far at least, the relatively modest overall and individual effects of the proposals are more akin to dipping a toe into potentially very hot water than a full-scale plunge into a high-tax society.

Other Scottish property taxes

Scottish landfill tax

Rates of Scottish landfill tax for 2017–18 were set by the Scottish Landfill Tax (Standard Rate and Lower Rate) Order 2017[2] at £86.10 per tonne (standard rate) and £2.70 per tonne (lower rate). In the Scottish Budget, it was confirmed that the rates here are to be increased to the planned UK rates for 2017–18, which are £88.95 (standard rate) and £2.80 (lower rate). The credit rate for the Scottish Landfill Communities Fund ('SLCF') is to be maintained at 5.6%, which exceeds the planned UK credit rate of 5.3%.[3] These credits support environmental and community projects.

Aggregates levy

Despite this levy being one of the taxes intended to be fully devolved,[4] on-going legal issues in relation to EU state aid mean that the Scottish version of the levy

---

1   A Scottish taxpayer is, essentially, one whose home is in Scotland.
2   SSI 2017/23.
3   See *Scottish Budget: Draft Budget 2018–19* pp 25– 26.
4   Scotland Act 2016 s 18, inserting s 80M into the Scotland Act 1998.

has still not been introduced. The Scottish Government has stated that it will work with the UK Government and other stakeholders, and conduct research in anticipation of the levy's eventual devolution.[1]

Non-domestic (business) rates

The report of the Barclay Review of non-domestic rates was published on 22 August 2017.[2] Almost all of the 30 recommendations have been adopted, in a response by the Scottish Government commencing in September 2017[3] and continuing in the Scottish Budget.[4] The recommendations accepted include:

- a business-growth accelerator, which will ensure that any rates bill rises due to improvements to or the expansion of existing properties will not take effect until 12 months after those changes are made to the property;

- a new relief for day-nurseries to support the increased provision of childcare;

- an expansion of fresh-start relief to include all property-types, not limited to listed property-types as recommended by Barclay, coupled with halving the period the property has to be empty to qualify from 12 months to six, and doubling the level of relief from 50% to 100% for the first year of new occupation; and

- a move to three-yearly revaluations from 2022, with valuations based on market conditions on a date one year prior.

The Scottish Government will also use the September 2017 rate for CPI (3%) rather than RPI (3.9%) to calculate the annual inflationary uplift in the business rates poundage for 2018–19. This produces a poundage figure of 48.0p, with the large business supplement set at 2.6p.

Scottish business will benefit from the new-growth accelerator which gives a 12-month delay before rates are increased when a property is expanded or improved and before rates apply to a new property. In addition, new properties will not be included in the valuation roll until they are occupied.

Penalties litigation

2017 marked the first reported tribunal decisions on purely Scottish tax matters. These were by the First-tier Tribunal for Scotland Tax Chamber;[5] they all concerned penalties (four on LBTT and one on Scottish Landfill Tax).

Anderson v Revenue Scotland[6] involved the late filing of a return for a lease. There was no tax due, and the penalty was fixed at £100. The taxpayer argued

---

1 *Scottish Budget: Draft Budget 2018–19* p 29.
2 *Report of the Barclay Review of Non-Domestic Rates* (www.gov.scot/Publications/2017/08/3435).
3 *Response to the Barclay Review of Non-Domestic Rates* (www.gov.scot/Resource/0052/00524630. pdf).
4 *Scottish Budget: Draft Budget 2018–19* pp 26–28.
5 The website, on which all decisions can be found, is http://taxtribunals.scot/.
6 [2016] TTFT 1.

that this was disproportionate and that he had the reasonable excuse of relying on his professional advisers. Unsurprisingly, but in some detail, both arguments were rejected.

Classic Land and Property Ltd v Revenue Scotland[1] was a more substantial case. A purchase transaction settled on 3 April 2015 (and thus just after LBTT was introduced), but the necessary LBTT return was not submitted until 17 February 2016. The consideration was £41,000 and thus, although within the zero-rate band for LBTT, the transaction was above the £40,000 reporting limit. The long delay in submitting a return led to a penalty of £900. A review requested by the taxpayer's lawyers was unsuccessful. The reason given for the delay was that there were substantial difficulties with the title to the subjects of the transaction. This was accepted; but it was not a reasonable excuse for failing to submit the return (which was in itself not problematic to do). The penalty was confirmed.

Watts v Revenue Scotland[2] involved a taxpayer who acted for herself. Her transaction settled on 8 January 2016, and the LBTT return was submitted 171 days late. Again, no tax was due, but the result of the late reporting was penalties totalling £890. The taxpayer claimed that it was reasonable for her to believe that, because no tax was payable, no return was due. She made the return as soon as she was made aware that this view was incorrect. She reluctantly accepted that the £100 initial penalty was reasonable, but asserted that the mounting £10 daily penalties were not. Again, these arguments were rejected. Future penalty recipients may perhaps take some comfort from the following statement by the Tribunal judges (emphasis added):[3]

> Although we have refused the appeal, we remind RS of its power under section 177 RSTPA to reduce penalties in the circumstances there set out and in particular section 177(5). It seems to us that the legislative existence of the power to impose daily penalties is intended to improve compliance. *It is not evident that the power to impose a daily penalty will necessarily achieve that perfectly appropriate goal where a buyer genuinely believes that he or she is not required to make a return, however wrong that belief actually is.* We say no more than that.

The most recent LBTT penalty appellant, in *Redwing Property Ltd v Revenue Scotland*,[4] met with more success. Here two adjoining properties were acquired about a month apart. The consideration for each was again below the LBTT zero-rate threshold, but above that for reporting. Again, there was no challenge to the initial penalties of £100; but an appeal was pursued against daily penalties which totalled £780 for each property. The failure to make returns was caused by the fault of an employee of the solicitors instructed by the taxpayer (and who subsequently left the firm). Her failure had only emerged after a review of her files following her departure. That circumstance had apparently led Revenue Scotland to remit the penalty in two other cases; and here the taxpayer relied on

---

1 [2016] TTFT 2.
2 [2017] FTSTC 1; the citation system for the Scottish First-tier Tribunal Tax Chamber apparently changed in 2017, but it remains the same appellate body.
3 Paragraph 23.
4 [2017] FTSTC 3.

that failure both as a reasonable excuse and as a special circumstance justifying remission of penalties by Revenue Scotland. The appeal met with limited success, as the Tribunal explained:[1]

> The circumstances relied on in these two appeals are unusual. However, they are not unique, even within the offices of Redwing's solicitors, where there were two similar cases several months previously. The fact that there had already been not one, but two similar events several months previously ought to have prompted swifter and more decisive action by the solicitors.
>
> On the other hand, on the evidence produced, there is no indication of culpability on the part of Redwing, as opposed to their solicitors, on whom they appear to have relied. Nonetheless, the scheme of LBTTA places the compliance obligations on the taxpayer, whether or not an agent is involved. It follows that a degree of diligence is required by the taxpayer in discharging the compliance obligations and taking reasonable steps to ensure that any agent is equally diligent.
>
> While the Tribunal was furnished with some evidence about the solicitors' failings, it was provided with no evidence about the extent of Redwing's engagement with the LBTT process. The Tribunal is, in effect, being invited to hold that the solicitors' organisational failings are special circumstances for the purposes of section 177 RSTPA. Standing the compliance obligation identified in paragraph 36, those organisational failings cannot justify the reduction of the penalties in their entirety.
>
> However, the Tribunal is satisfied that there would be significant unfairness in requiring Redwing to meet the whole of the penalty. It is clear from cases in other areas of, UK, tax law, this is a fact-sensitive consideration (compare *Hardy v HMRC* [2011] UKFTT 592 (TC) and *Blackman v HMRC* [2016] UKFTT 465 (TC)). The Tribunal is satisfied that, in the circumstances set out above, some reduction in penalty is appropriate. The penalty notice in each case will be varied so that the penalty in each case is reduced by one third, to £520.00.

The Tribunal in *Redwing* relied to a significant extent on the analysis of 'reasonable excuse' carried out in the landfill tax penalty case of *Straid Farms Ltd v Revenue Scotland*.[2] This involved a taxpayer who relied entirely on an employee who was due to be away on an extended holiday when a landfill tax return was due. She thus made the return early; unfortunately, this brought forward the date at which tax became payable, as it should have been paid when the return was made. Tax was thus paid late and a substantial penalty (£7,956) was demanded.

The following circumstances were said to lead to a 'reasonable excuse':[3]

(a) The unusual and unexpected circumstances of an employee's leave;
(b) The lack of understanding as to the obligation to pay the tax at the same time as the return is made;
(c) That payment was not deliberately withheld or delayed;
(d) That Revenue Scotland's online portal for submitting tax returns is particularly complex;

---

1 Paragraphs 35–37.
2 [2017] FTSTC 2.
3 Paragraph 20.

(e) That inaccuracies on Revenue Scotland's part resulted in confusion, stress and cost for the appellant; and

(f) Revenue Scotland delayed in issuing the penalty.

In considering what might amount to a reasonable excuse, the Tribunal drew on analogous law:[1]

> The test articulated by Judge Medd in *The Clean Car Company Limited v CEE*[2] has recently been approved in the context of Social Security legislation by Judge Rowland in *VT v SSWP*.[3] Judge Medd said:
>
> > '...the test of whether there is a reasonable excuse is an objective one. In my judgement it is an objective test in this sense. One must ask oneself: was what the taxpayer did a reasonable thing for a responsible trader conscious of and intending to comply with his obligations regarding tax, but having the experience and other relevant attributes of the taxpayer and placed in the situation that the taxpayer found himself in at the relevant time, a reasonable thing to do ... the question of whether a particular trader had a reasonable excuse should be judged by the standards of reasonableness which one would expect to be exhibited by a taxpayer who had a responsible attitude to his duties as a taxpayer ... such a taxpayer would give a reasonable priority to complying with his duties in regard to tax and would conscientiously seek to ensure that his returns were accurate and made timeously ... many other facts, may all have a bearing on whether, in acting as he did, he acted reasonably and so had a reasonable excuse.'
>
> Accordingly it is incumbent on the Tribunal to look at the appellant's individual circumstances and at the underlying cause.

While the Tribunal understood why the tax had been paid late in this case, the individual circumstances did not amount to a reasonable excuse.

However, the fact here was that the late payment had only arisen because the return had been made early. These were special circumstances which rendered the penalty levied disproportionate and unfair, in terms of (among other things) Article 1 to the First Protocol to the European Convention for the Protection of Human Rights and Fundamental Freedoms. The Tribunal stated:[4]

> The interests of the community would have been served if the appellant had simply filed and paid at the filing date. We cannot see that there is a fair balance in penalising the appellant for paying tax much earlier than the statutory filing date. The amount of the penalty in that situation is an excessive burden. The penalty, in these circumstances, is both harsh and unfair.
>
> Specifically and particularly, it does not reflect the clear compliance intention of the penalty regime to ensure compliance with the tax legislation by a hierarchy of penalties that are applied with care and which are proportionate.

Thus the penalty was reduced to £100, at the lowest end of the penalty regime.

---

1 Paragraphs 46–47.
2 [1991] VTTR 234.
3 [2016] UKUT 178 (AAC).
4 Paragraphs 107–108.

The developing jurisprudence on penalties will no doubt continue. The penalty regime in Scotland produces higher penalties and seems to be being more harshly enforced than would be the case elsewhere in the UK. While a number of appeals on LBTT appear to have proceeded on a slightly more sophisticated version of the playground argument that 'it isnae fair', this is perhaps not unreasonable when substantial sums of money are demanded when no actual tax is due. The balance between the need to ensure compliance and individual fairness seems to be tilted somewhat in favour of Revenue Scotland.

UK taxes on land

Residential property held for investment, and particularly in offshore entities, has been made subject to substantial new liabilities and tax increases in recent years. This process continued and was extended in 2017.

From April 2017, inheritance tax is charged on all UK residential property, even when held indirectly by a non-UK-domicile through a non-UK structure.[1] The main interests affected are partnerships and close companies. Interests in non-UK companies holding residential property are to be disregarded if they are below 5%, rather than the previously proposed level of 10%. There are also provisions affecting the creditor's interest in certain loans where those support the direct or indirect acquisition of UK residential property interests.

A major extension to the capital gains tax treatment of UK property held by non-residents was announced in the Autumn Budget. The tax has been charged on residential property on gains arising since April 2015. This is, for gains arising from April 2019, to be extended to all land and buildings.[2] This proposal, if enacted, will see commercial property fall into line with residential property and the UK's tax treatment of non-residents become aligned with elsewhere in Europe and most other countries in the treatment of land within their borders.

Additional rules will apply to tax 'indirect' disposals of UK land by non-residents – ie, the sale of interests in entities (such as companies or unit trusts) whose value is substantially derived from UK land. Corporate sellers will be subject to UK corporation tax; individuals and trustees will fall into the self-assessment regime and CGT. A major consultation on this measure was published immediately after the Autumn Budget.[3] It seems likely that the incredibly short deadline for reporting gains and paying tax on disposals of residential property (30 days from settlement) will apply to the new rules; and the consultation envisages a reporting requirement in relation to indirect disposals being imposed on certain advisors who are aware of the conclusion of the transaction and are unable to be sure that the transaction has been reported.[4] This is likely to be of considerable relevance to solicitors acting in relation to the Scottish aspects of company sales, for example.

---

1 Finance (No 2) Act 2017 s 33, sch 10, inserting sch A1 into the Inheritance Tax Act 1984.
2 *Autumn Budget 2017* (HC 587, November 2017) para 3.30.
3 HMRC/HM Treasury, *Consultation Document: Taxing gains made by non-residents on UK immovable property* (22 November 2017).
4 *Consultation Document* paras 7.12–7.15.

From 5 April 2017 there is a new £1,000 allowance for property income (as well as a similar relief for trading income). Individuals with property rents below £1,000 will no longer need to declare or pay tax on that income. Those with income above that level will have a choice whether to (i) calculate their taxable profit in the normal way by deducting their expenses; or (ii) deduct the relevant £1,000 allowance from the gross income.[1]

In the Spring Budget, a consultation was announced on rent-a-room relief, which was substantially increased in 2016. It seems that there will be proposals to ensure that it is targeted to support longer-term lettings – which seems likely to exclude those offering Airbnb and similar short-term lettings. This did not advance further during 2017, but was re-stated in the Autumn Budget.[2]

In relation to ATED[3], the Autumn Budget announced an increase by CPI inflation (3%) in the amounts chargeable for 2018–19.[4]

---

1 Finance (No 2) Act 2017 s 17, ch 3, inserting part 6A into the Income Tax (Trading and Other Income) Act 2005.
2 *Autumn Budget 2017* para 3.11.
3 Annual tax on enveloped dwellings.
4 See *Annual tax on enveloped dwellings: annual chargeable amounts* (www.gov.uk/government/publications/annual-tax-on-enveloped-dwellings-annual-chargeable-amounts-for-2018-to-2019/annual-tax-on-enveloped-dwellings-annual-chargeable-amounts).

❧ PART V ☙
TABLES

TABLES

CUMULATIVE TABLE OF DECISIONS ON VARIATION OR DISCHARGE OF TITLE CONDITIONS

This table lists all opposed applications under the Title Conditions (Scotland) Act 2003 for variation or discharge of title conditions. Decisions on expenses are omitted. Note that the full opinions in Lands Tribunal cases are usually available at http://www.lands-tribunal-scotland.org.uk/.

Restriction on building

Name of case	Burden	Applicant's project in breach of burden	Application granted or refused
Ord v Mashford 2006 SLT (Lands Tr) 15; *Lawrie v Mashford*, 21 Dec 2007	1938. No building.	Erection of single-storey house and garage.	Granted. Claim for compensation refused.
Daly v Bryce 2006 GWD 25-565	1961 feu charter. No further building.	Replace existing house with two houses.	Granted.
J & L Leisure Ltd v Shaw 2007 GWD 28-489	1958 disposition. No new buildings higher than 15 feet 6 inches.	Replace derelict building with two-storey housing.	Granted subject to compensation of £5,600.
West Coast Property Developments Ltd v Clarke 2007 GWD 29-511	1875 feu contract. Terraced houses. No further building.	Erection of second, two-storey house.	Granted. Claim for compensation refused.
Smith v Prior 2007 GWD 30-523	1934 feu charter. No building.	Erection of modest rear extension.	Granted.
Anderson v McKinnon 2007 GWD 29-513	1993 deed of conditions in modern housing estate.	Erection of rear extension.	Granted.
Smith v Elrick 2007 GWD 29-515	1996 feu disposition. No new house. The feu had been subdivided.	Conversion of barn into a house.	Granted.

Name of case	Burden	Applicant's project in breach of burden	Application granted or refused
Brown v Richardson 2007 GWD 28-490	1888 feu charter. No alterations/new buildings	Erection of rear extension.	Granted. This was an application for renewal, following service of a notice of termination.
Gallacher v Wood 2008 SLT (Lands Tr) 31	1933 feu contract. No alterations/new buildings.	Erection of rear extension, including extension at roof level which went beyond bungalow's footprint.	Granted. Claim for compensation refused.
Jarron v Stuart 23 March and 5 May 2011	1992 deed of conditions. No external alteration and additions.	Erection of rear extension.	Granted. Claim for compensation refused.
Blackman v Best 2008 GWD 11-214	1934 disposition. No building other than a greenhouse.	Erection of a double garage.	Granted.
McClumpha v Bradie 2009 GWD 31-519	1984 disposition allowing the erection of only one house.	Erection of four further houses.	Granted but restricted to four houses.
McGregor v Collins-Taylor 14 May 2009	1988 disposition prohibiting the erection of dwellinghouses without consent.	Erection of four further houses.	Granted but restricted to four houses.
Faeley v Clark 2006 GWD 28-626	1967 disposition. No further building.	Erection of second house.	Refused.
Cattanach v Vine-Hall	1996 deed of conditions in favour of neighbouring property. No building within 7 metres of that property.	Erection of substantial house within 2 metres.	Refused, subject to the possibility of the applicants bringing a revised proposal.
Hamilton v Robertson, 10 January 2008	1984 deed of conditions affecting 5-house development. No further building.	Erection of 2nd house on site, but no firm plans.	Refused, although possibility of later success once plans firmed up was not excluded.
Cocozza v Rutherford 2008 SLT (Lands Tr) 6	1977 deed of conditions. No alterations.	Substantial alterations which would more than double the footprint of the house.	Refused.

Name of case	Burden	Applicant's project in breach of burden	Application granted or refused
Scott v Teasdale 22 December 2009	1962 feu disposition. No building.	New house in garden.	Refused.
Rennie v Cullen House Gardens Ltd 29 June 2012	2005 deed of conditions. No new building or external extension.	Extension of building forming part of historic house.	Refused.
Hollinshead v Gilchrist 7 December 2009	1990 Disposition and 1997 feu disposition. No building or alterations.	Internal alterations.	Granted.
Tower Hotel (Troon) Ltd v McCann 4 March 2010	1965 feu disposition. No building. Existing building to be used as a hotel or dwellinghouse.	No firm plan though one possibility was the building of flats.	Granted.
Corstorphine v Fleming 2 July 2010	1965 feu disposition. No alterations, one house only.	A substantial extension plus a new house.	Granted.
Corry v MacLachlan 9 July 2010	1984 disposition of part of garden. Obligation to build a single-storey house.	Addition of an extra storey.	Granted.
Watt v Garden 4 November 2011	1995 disposition. Use as garden only.	Additional two-bedroom bungalow.	Granted but with compensation.
Fyfe v Benson 26 July 2011	1966 deed of conditions. No building or subdivision.	Additional three-bedroom house.	Refused.
MacDonald v Murdoch 7 August 2012	1997 disposition. No building in garden.	Erection of 1½-storey house.	Refused.
Trigstone Ltd v Mackenzie 16 February 2012	1949 charter of novodamus. No building in garden.	Erection of four-storey block of flats. Parking of two cars.	Refused.
McCulloch v Reid 3 April 2012	2011 disposition. No parking in rear courtyard.	Erection of two houses.	Refused.
Trustees of John Raeside & Son v Chalmers 2014 GWD 35-660	1989 disposition. Agricultural purposes only.	Erection of mews house in back garden.	Granted.
Sinton v Lloyd 11 June 2014	Instrument of sasine of 1813 prohibiting building.	Erection of new house and extension of existing house.	Granted.

Name of case	Burden	Applicant's project in breach of burden	Application granted or refused
MacKay v McGowan 2015 SLT (Lands Tr) 6	Feu disposition prohibiting building.	Erection of two-storey extension. Refused.	Granted in respect of new house (only).
Ferguson v Gunby 2015 SLT (Lands Tr) 195	1972 deed of conditions preventing alterations.		Granted.

Other restrictions on use

Name of case	Burden	Applicant's project in breach of burden	Application granted or refused
Church of Scotland General Trs v McLaren 2006 SLT (Lands Tr) 27	Use as a church.	Possible development for flats.	Granted.
Wilson v McNamee 16 September 2007	Use for religious purposes.	Use for a children's nursery.	Granted
Verrico v Tomlinson 2008 SLT (Lands Tr) 2	1950 disposition. Use as a private residence for the occupation of one family.	Separation of mews cottage from ground floor flat.	Granted.
Whitelaw v Acheson 29 February and 29 September 2012	1883 feu charter. Use as a single dwelling; no further building.	Change of use to therapy and wellbeing centre; erection of extension.	Granted subject to some restrictions.
Matnic Ltd v Armstrong 2010 SLT (Lands Tr) 7	2004 deed of conditions. Use for the sale of alcohol.	Use of units in a largely residential estate for retail purposes.	Granted but restricted to small units and no sale of alcohol after 8 pm.
Clarke v Grantham 2009 GWD 38-645	2004 disposition. No parking on an area of courtyard.	A desire to park (though other areas were available).	Granted.
Hollinshead v Gilchrist 7 December 2009	1990 disposition and 1997 feu disposition. No caravans, commercial or other vehicles to be parked in front of the building line.	Parking of cars.	Granted and claim for compensation refused.
Perth & Kinross Council v Chapman 13 August 2009	1945 disposition. Plot to be used only for outdoor recreational purposes.	Sale for redevelopment.	Granted.

Name of case	Burden	Applicant's project in breach of burden	Application granted or refused
Davenport v Julian Hodge Bank Ltd 23 June 2011	2010 deed of conditions. No external painting without permission.	Paint the external walls sky blue.	Granted.
Duffus v McWhirter 2014 GWD 34-647	2005 disposition prohibiting commercial use.	Commercial equestrian use.	Refused.

Flatted property

Name of case	Burden	Applicant's project in breach of burden	Application granted or refused
Regan v Mullen 2006 GWD 25-564	1989. No subdivision of flat.	Subdivision of flat.	Granted.
Kennedy v Abbey Lane Properties 29 March 2010	2004. Main-door flat liable for a share of maintenance of common passages and stairs.	None.	Refused.
Patterson v Drouet 20 January 2011	Liability for maintenance in accordance with gross annual value.	None, but, since the freezing of valuations in 1989, ground floor flats had reverted to residential use.	Variation of liability of ground floor flats granted in principle subject to issues of competency.
Melville v Crabbe 19 January 2009	1880 feu disposition. No additional flat.	Creation of a flat in the basement.	Refused.

Sheltered and retirement housing

Name of case	Burden	Applicant's project in breach of burden	Application granted or refused
At.Home Nationwide Ltd v Morris 2007 GWD 31-535	1993 deed of conditions. On sale, must satisfy superior that flat will continue to be used for the elderly.	No project: just removal of an inconvenient restriction.	Burden held to be void. Otherwise application would have been refused.

Miscellaneous

Name of case	Burden	Applicant's project in breach of burden	Application granted or refused
McPherson v Mackie 2006 GWD 27-606 rev [2007] CSIH 7, 2007 SCLR 351	1990. Housing estate: maintenance of house.	Demolition of house to allow the building of a road for access to proposed new development.	Discharged by agreement on 25 April 2007.

Applications for renewal of real burdens following service of a notice of termination

Name of case	Burden	Applicant's project in breach of burden	Application granted or refused
Brown v Richardson 2007 GWD 28-490	1888 feu charter. No buildings.	Substantial rear extension.	Refused.
Council for Music in Hospitals v Trustees for Richard Gerald Associates 2008 SLT (Lands Tr) 17	1838 instrument of sasine. No building in garden.	None.	Refused.
Gibson v Anderson 3 May 2012	1898 disposition. No building other than one-storey outbuildings.	Two-storey house.	Refused; burden varied to allow limited building.
Macneil v Bradonwood Ltd 2013 SLT (Lands Tr) 41	Mid-Victorian feus limited building at foot of garden to one storey.	1.5-storey houses.	Refused; burden varied to allow the proposed houses.
Cook v Cadman 2014 SLT (Lands Tr) 13	1876 feu prevented building.	Four additional houses.	Refused; burden varied to allow the proposed houses.

Application for preservation of community burdens following deeds of variation or discharge under s 33 or s 35

Name of case	Burden	Applicant's project in breach of burden	Application granted or refused
Fleeman v Lyon 2009 GWD 32-539	1982 deed of conditions. No building, trade, livestock etc.	Erection of a second house.	Granted.

Applications for variation of community burdens (s 91)

Name of case	Burden	Applicant's project in breach of burden	Application granted or refused
Fenwick v National Trust for Scotland 2009 GWD 32-538	1989 deed of conditions.	None. The application was for the complete discharge of the deed with the idea that a new deed would eventually be drawn up.	Refused.
Patterson v Drouet 2013 GWD 3-99	1948 deed of conditions apportioned liability for maintenance in a tenement on the basis of annual value.	Substitution of floor area for annual value.	Granted; compensation refused.
Gilfin Property Holdings Ltd v Beech 2013 SLT (Lands Tr) 17	1986 deed of conditions apportioned liability for maintenance in a tenement on a percentage basis rooted in rateable value.	Substitution of a more equitable apportionment.	Granted.
Stewart v Sherwood 7 June 2013	1986 deed of conditions	Addition of a prohibition on letting.	Refused.
Scott v Applin 16 May 2013	2005 deed of conditions.	Removal of requirement that the full-time manager should be resident.	Granted.
McCabe v Killcross 2013 SLT (Lands Tr) 48	Feu dispositions from 1976.	Altering apportionment of liability for maintenance following division of one of the flats.	Granted except in one respect.

Personal real burdens

Name of case	Burden	Applicant's project in breach of burden	Application granted or refused
Grant v National Trust for Scotland 8 August 2014	Conservation agreement from 1962 prohibited non-agricultural use.	Building of houses.	Granted in part.

Servitudes

Name of case	Burden	Applicant's project in breach of burden	Application granted or refused
George Wimpey East Scotland Ltd v Fleming 2006 SLT (Lands Tr) 2 and 59	1988 disposition. Right of way.	Diversion of right of way to allow major development for residential houses.	Granted (opposed). Claim for compensation for temporary disturbance refused.
Ventureline Ltd 2 August 2006	1972 disposition. 'Right to use' certain ground.	Possible redevelopment.	Granted (unopposed).
Graham v Parker 2007 GWD 30-524	1990 feu disposition. Right of way from mid-terraced house over garden of end-terraced house to the street.	Small re-routing of right of way, away from the burdened owner's rear wall, so as to allow an extension to be built.	Granted (opposed).
MacNab v McDowall 24 October 2007	1994 feu disposition reserved a servitude of way from the back garden to the front street in favour of two neighbouring houses.	Small re-rerouting, on to the land of one of the neighbours, to allow a rear extension to be built.	Granted (opposed).
Jensen v Tyler 2008 SLT (Lands Tr) 39	1985 feu disposition granted a servitude of way.	Re-routing of part of the road in order to allow (unspecified) development of steading.	Granted (opposed).
Gibb v Kerr 2009 GWD 38-646	1981 feu disposition granted a servitude of way.	Re-routing to homologate what had already taken place as a result of the building of a conservatory.	Granted (opposed).
Parkin v Kennedy 23 March 2010	1934 feu charter. Right of way from mid-terraced house over garden of end-terraced house.	Re-routing to allow extension to be built, which would require a restriction to pedestrian access.	Refused (opposed).
Adams v Trs for the Linton Village Hall 24 October 2011	Dispositions of 1968 and 1970 reserved a servitude of access.	Re-routing to a route more convenient for the applicant.	Granted (opposed).
Brown v Kitchen 28 October 2011	1976 feu disposition reserved a servitude of pedestrian access.	Re-routing to the edge of the garden.	Granted in principle (opposed) subject to agreement as to the widening of the substitute route.

Name of case	Burden	Applicant's project in breach of burden	Application granted or refused
Hossack v Robertson 29 June 2012	1944 disposition reserved a servitude of pedestrian access.	Re-routing to end of garden to allow building of conservatory.	Granted (opposed).
Cope v X 2013 SLT (Lands Tr) 20	Servitude of access.	Substitute road.	Granted (opposed).
ATD Developments Ltd v Weir 14 September 2010	2002 disposition granted a servitude right of way.	Narrowing the servitude so as to allow gardens for proposed new houses.	Granted (unopposed).
Stirling v Thorley 12 October 2012	1994 and 1995 dispositions granted a servitude of vehicular access.	Building a house on half of an area set aside for turning vehicles.	Refused (opposed).
Colecliffe v Thompson 2010 SLT (Lands Tr) 15	1997 disposition granted a servitude of way.	None. But the owners of the benefited property had since acquired a more convenient access, secured by a new servitude.	Granted (opposed).
G v A 26 November 2009	1974 disposition granted a servitude of way.	None. But the owners of the benefited property had since acquired a more convenient access (although not to his garage).	Granted (opposed) but on the basis that the respondent should apply for compensation.
Graham v Lee 18 June 2009	2001 disposition granted (a) a servitude of way and (b) of drainage.	None.	(a) was granted provided the applicants discharged a reciprocal servitude of their own, and compensation was considered. (b) was refused.
McNab v Smith 15 June 2012	1981 disposition granted a servitude of vehicular access for agricultural purposes.	None. But the owner of the benefited property could access the property in a different way.	Granted (opposed) but, because works would be needed to improve the alternative access, on the basis of payment of compensation.

Name of case	Burden	Applicant's project in breach of burden	Application granted or refused
Stephenson v Thomas 21 November 2012	1990 disposition granted a servitude of vehicular access.	None. But the owner of the benefited property could access the property in a different way.	Refused (opposed) on the basis that there were safety concerns about the alternative route and the benefited proprietors were proposing to revert to the original route.
McKenzie v Scott 19 May 2009	Dispositions from 1944 and 1957 granted a servitude of bleaching and drying clothes.	None. But the servitude had not in practice been exercised for many years.	Granted (opposed).
Chisholm v Crawford 17 June 2010	A driveway divided two properties. A 1996 feu disposition of one of the properties granted a servitude of access over the driveway.	None. But the applicant was aggrieved that no matching servitude appeared in the neighbour's title.	Refused
Branziet Investments v Anderson 2013 GWD 31-629	1968 disposition granted a servitude of vehicular access.	Narrowing the servitude to 5 metres so as to allow rear gardens for new houses.	Granted (opposed) except that at either end the width was to be larger.
Mackay v Bain 2013 SLT (Lands Tr) 37	Servitude of pedestrian access over the front garden of applicant's property (1989).	None.	Refused (opposed). The servitude was the only means of access to the respondents' front door.
Pollacchi v Campbell 2014 SLT (Lands Tr) 55	Servitude of vehicular access.	Re-routing to allow creation of garden.	Refused
Yule v Tobert 2015 GWD 39-620	Servitude of vehicular access over yard (1984).	None, but dominant proprietor wished to use access to allow teachers at his nursery to park.	Refused application to restrict servitude to residential purposes.
United Investment Co Ltd v Charlie Reid Ltd 2016 GWD 1-13	Servitude of vehicular access (1963).	Major redevelopment of site.	Granted (opposed) but subject to the possibility of compensation if loss in value to the benefited property could be shown.

CUMULATIVE TABLE OF APPEALS

A table at the end of *Conveyancing 2008* listed all cases digested in *Conveyancing 1999* and subsequent annual volumes in respect of which an appeal was subsequently heard, and gave the result of the appeal. This table is a continuation of the earlier table, beginning with appeals heard during 2009.

Aberdeen City Council v Stewart Milne Group Ltd
[2009] CSOH 80, 2009 GWD 26-417, 2009 Case (6) *affd* [2010] CSIH 81, 2010 GWD 37-755, 2010 Case (9) *affd* [2011] UKSC 56, 2011 Case (13)

Alexander v West Bromwich Mortgage Co Ltd
[2015] EWHC 135 (Comm), [2015] 2 All ER (Comm) 224, 2015 Case (71) *rev* [2016] EWCA Civ 496, 2016 Case (60)

AMA (New Town) Ltd v Finlay
2010 GWD 32-658, Sh Ct, 2010 Case (8) *rev* 2011 SLT (Sh Ct) 73, 2011 Case (1)

Argyll & Bute Council v Gordon
2016 SLT (Sh Ct) 196, 2016 SCLR 192, 2016 Case (78) *affd* [2017] SAC (Civ) 6, 2017 SLT (Sh Ct) 53, 2017 Case (73)

AWG Business Centres Ltd v Regus Caledonia Ltd
[2016] CSOH 99, 2016 GWD 22-407, 2016 Case (40) *affd* [2017] CSIH 22, 2017 GWD 9-131, 2017 Case (43)

Blemain Finance Ltd v Balfour & Manson LLP
[2011] CSOH 157, 2012 SLT 672, 2011 Case (69) *affd* [2012] CSIH 66, [2013] PNLR 3, 2012 GWD 30-609, 2012 Case (70)

British Waterways Board v Arjo Wiggins Ltd
12 May 2016, Fort William Sheriff Court, 2016 Case (15) *affd* [2017] SAC (Civ) 15, 2017 GWD 15-240, 2017 Case (17)

Brown v Stonegale Ltd
[2013] CSOH 189, 2014 GWD 2-27, 2013 Case (71) *affd* [2015] CSIH 12, 2015 SCLR 619, 2015 Case (85) *affd* [2016] UKSC 30, 2016 GWD 20-359, 2016 Case (73)

Chalmers v Chalmers
[2014] CSOH 161, 2015 SCLR 299, 2014 Case (22) *rev* [2015] CSIH 75, 2015 SLT 793, 2015 Hous LR 82, 2016 SC 158, 2015 Case (27)

Cheshire Mortgage Corporation Ltd v Grandison; Blemain Finance Ltd v Balfour & Manson LLP
[2011] CSOH 157, 2012 SLT 672, 2011 Case (69) *affd* [2012] CSIH 66, [2013] PNLR 3, 2012 GWD 30-609, 2012 Case (69)

Christie Owen & Davies plc v Campbell

2007 GWD 24-397, Sh Ct, 2007 Case (53) *affd* 18 Dec 2007, Glasgow Sheriff Court, 2007 Case (53) *rev* [2009] CSIH 26, 2009 SLT 518, 2009 Case (82)

Collins v Sweeney

2013 GWD 11-230, Sh Ct, 2013 Case (3) *affd* 2014 GWD 12-214, Sh Ct, 2014 Case (4)

Compugraphics International Ltd v Nikolic

[2009] CSOH 54, 2009 GWD 19-311, 2009 Cases (22) and (90) *rev* [2011] CSIH 34, 2011 SLT 955, 2011 Cases (21) and (74)

Co-operative Group Ltd v Propinvest Paisley LP

17 September 2010, Lands Tribunal, 2010 Case (36) *rev* [2011] CSIH 41, 2012 SC 51, 2011 SLT 987, 2011 Hous LR 32, 2011 Case (38)

Cramaso LLP v Viscount Reidhaven's Trs

[2010] CSOH 62, 2010 GWD 20-403, 2010 Case (58) *affd* [2011] CSIH 81, 2011 Case (57) *rev* [2014] UKSC 9, 2014 SC (UKSC) 121, 2014 SLT 521, 2014 SCLR 484, 2014 Case (31)

EDI Central Ltd v National Car Parks Ltd

[2010] CSOH 141, 2011 SLT 75, 2010 Case (5) *affd* [2012] CSIH 6, 2012 SLT 421, 2012 Case (4)

ELB Securities Ltd v Love

2014 GWD 28-562, 2014 Case (38) *affd* [2015] CSIH 67, 2015 SLT 721, 2015 Hous LR 88, 2015 Case (66)

Euring David Ayre of Kilmarnock, Baron of Kilmarnock Ptr

[2008] CSOH 35, 2008 Case (82) *rev* [2009] CSIH 61, 2009 SLT 759, 2009 Case (93)

Fortune's Tr v Medwin Investments Ltd

[2015] CSOH 139, 2015 GWD 34-552, 2015 Case (87) *affd* [2016] CSIH 49, 2016 SLT 923, 2016 Case (75)

Frank Houlgate Investment Co Ltd v Biggart Baillie LLP

[2013] CSOH 80, 2013 SLT 993, 2013 Case (61) *affd* [2014] CSIH 79, 2014 SLT 1001, 2015 SC 187, 2014 Case (65)

Martin Stephen James Goldstraw of Whitecairns Ptr

[2008] CSOH 34, 2008 Case (81) *rev* [2009] CSIH 61, 2009 SLT 759, 2009 Case (93)

Gordon v Campbell Riddell Breeze Paterson LLP

[2015] CSOH 31, 2015 GWD 12-216, 2015 Case (74) *affd* [2016] CSIH 16, 2016 SC 548, 2016 SLT 580, 2016 Case (63) *affd* [2017] UKSC 75, 2017 SLT 1287, 2017 Case (65)

Gray v MacNeil's Exr

2016 SLT (Sh Ct) 250, 2016 Case (37) *rev* [2017] SAC (Civ) 9, 2017 SLT (Sh Ct) 83, 2017 SCLR 666, 2017 Hous LR 47, 2017 Case (42)

Gyle Shopping Centre General Partners Ltd v Marks and Spencer plc

[2015] CSOH 14, 2015 GWD 6-127, 2015 Case (56) *rev* [2016] CSIH 19, 2016 GWD 10-205, 2016 Case (38)

Hamilton v Dumfries & Galloway Council

[2008] CSOH 65, 2008 SLT 531, 2008 Case (37) *rev* [2009] CSIH 13, 2009 SC 277, 2009 SLT 337, 2009 SCLR 392, 2009 Case (50)

Hamilton v Nairn

[2009] CSOH 163, 2010 SLT 399, 2009 Case (51) *affd* [2010] CSIH 77, 2010 SLT 1155, 2010 Case (44)

Hill of Rubislaw (Q Seven) Ltd v Rubislaw Quarry Aberdeen Ltd

[2013] CSOH 131, 2013 GWD 27-545, 2014 Case (11) *affd* [2014] CSIH 105, 2015 SC 339, 2014 Case (10)

Hoblyn v Barclays Bank plc

[2013] CSOH 104, 2013 GWD 26-533, 10313 Case (51) *affd* [2014] CSIH 52, 2014 GWD 30-376, 2014 HousLR 26, 2015 SCLR 85, 2014 Case (60)

Holms v Ashford Estates Ltd

2006 SLT (Sh Ct) 70, 2006 Case (40) *affd* 2006 SLT (Sh Ct) 161, 2006 Case (40) *rev* [2009] CSIH 28, 2009 SLT 389, 2009 SCLR 428, 2009 Cases (19) and (52)

Hunter v Tindale

2011 SLT (Sh Ct) 11, 2010 Case (16) *rev* 2011 GWD 25-570, Sh Ct, 2011 Case (19)

Jack v Jack

[2015] CSOH 91, 2015 Fam LR 95, 2015 Case (94) *affd* [2016] CSIH 75, 2016 Fam LR 177, 2016 Case (77)

K2 Restaurants Ltd v Glasgow City Council

[2011] CSOH 171, 2011 Hous LR 171, 2011 Case (20) *affd* [2013] CSIH 49, 2013 GWD 21-420, 2013 Case (5)

Kennedy v Dickie & More Holdings Ltd

[2015] CSOH 103, 2015 GWD 25-436, 2015 Case (3) *rev* [2016] CSIH 37, 2016 GWD 18-325, 2016 Case (4)

Kenwright v Stuart Milne Group Ltd

[2015] CSOH 86, 2015 GWD 22-389, 2015 Case (11) *rev* [2016] CSIH 45, 2016 GWD 20-351, 2016 Case (5)

Kerr of Ardgowan, Ptr

[2008] CSOH 36, 2008 SLT 251, 2008 Case (80) *rev* [2009] CSIH 61, 2009 SLT 759, 2009 Case (93)

Khosrowpour v Mackay

[2014] CSOH 175, 2015 GWD 1-8, 2014 Case (17) *rev* [2016] CSIH 50, 2016 Case (17)

L Batley Pet Products Ltd v North Lanarkshire Council

[2011] CSOH 209, 2012 GWD 4-73, 2011 Case (62) *rev* [2012] CSIH 83, 2012 GWD 37-745, 2012 Case (43) *rev* [2014] UKSC 27, 2014 SC (UKSC) 174, 2014 SLT 593, 2014 Case (39)

Liquidator of Letham Grange Development Co Ltd v Foxworth Investments Ltd

[2011] CSOH 66, 2011 SLT 1152, 2011 Case (64) *rev* [2013] CSIH 13, 2013 SLT 445, 2013 Case (47) *rev* [2014] UKSC 41, 2014 SC (UKSC) 203, 2014 SLT 775, 2014 Case (70)

Livingstone of Bachuil v Paine

[2012] CSOH 161, 2012 GWD 35-707, 2012 Case (12) *rev* [2013] CSIH 110, 2013 Case (9)

Luminar Lava Ignite Ltd v Mama Group plc

[2009] CSOH 68, 2009 GWD 19-305, 2009 Case (91) *rev* [2010] CSIH 1, 2010 SC 310, 2010 SLT 147, 2010 Case (77)

McCallum v City of Edinburgh Council

2016 GWD 24-450, 2016 Case (34) *affd* [2017] CSIH 24, 2017 SLT 466, 2017 Hous LR 42, 2017 Case (37)

McGraddie v McGraddie

[2009] CSOH 142, 2009 GWD 38-633, 2009 Case (60), [2010] CSOH 60, 2010 GWD 21-404, 2000 Case (48) *rev* [2012] CSIH 23, 2012 GWD 15-310, 2012 Case (38) *rev* [2013] UKSC 58, 2013 SLT 1212, 2013 Case (32)

MacQueen v MacPherson

3 October 2014, Oban Sheriff Court, 2014 Case (2) *rev* [2015] CSIH 60, 2015 GWD 26-449, 2015 Case (4)

McSorley v Drennan

May 2011, Ayr Sheriff Court, 2011 Case (14) *rev* [2012] CSIH 59, 2012 GWD 25-506, 2012 Case (6)

Mehrabadi v Haugh

June 2009, Aberdeen Sheriff Court, 2009 Case (17) *affd* 11 January 2010 Aberdeen Sheriff Court, 2010 Case (15)

Mirza v Salim

[2013] CSOH 73, 2013 GWD 17-348, 2013 Case (65) *rev* [2014] CSIH 51, 2015 SC 31, 2014 SLT 875, 2014 SCLR 764, 2014 Case (67)

Moderator of the General Assembly of the Free Church of Scotland v Interim Moderator of the Congregation of Strath Free Church of Scotland (Continuing)

[2009] CSOH 113, 2009 SLT 973, 2009 Case (96) *affd* [2011] CSIH 52, 2011 SLT 1213, 2012 SC 79, 2011 Case (77)

Morris v Rae

[2011] CSIH 30, 2011 SC 654, 2011 SLT 701, 2011 SCLR 428, 2011 Case (39) *rev* [2012] UKSC 50, 2013 SC (UKSC) 106, 2013 SLT 88, 2013 SCLR 80, 2012 Case (41)

Multi-link Leisure Developments Ltd v North Lanarkshire Council

[2009] CSOH 114, 2009 SLT 1170, 2009 Case (70) *rev* [2009] CSIH 96, 2010 SC 302, 2010 SLT 57, 2010 SCLR 306, 2009 Case (70) *affd* [2010] UKSC 47, [2011] 1 All ER 175, 2010 Case (52)

NRAM plc v Steel

[2014] CSOH 172, 2015 GWD 1-34, 2014 Case (63) *rev* [2016] CSIH 11, 2016 SC 474, 2016 SLT 285, 2016 SCLR 736, 2016 Case (62)

Orkney Housing Association Ltd v Atkinson

15 October 2010, Kirkwall Sheriff Court, 2010 Case (21) *rev* 2011 GWD 30-652, 2011 Cases (22) and (41)

Pocock's Tr v Skene Investments (Aberdeen) Ltd

[2011] CSOH 144, 2011 GWD 30-654, 2011 Case (40) *rev* [2012] CSIH 61, 2012 GWD 27-562, 2012 Case (36)

R M Prow (Motors) Ltd Directors Pension Fund Trustees v Argyll and Bute Council

[2012] CSOH 77, 2012 GWD 21-438, 2012 Case (44) *affd* [2013] CSIH 23, 2013 GWD 12-260, 2013 Case (44)

R & D Construction Group Ltd v Hallam Land Management Ltd

[2009] CSOH 128, 2009 Case (8) *affd* [2010] CSIH 96, 2010 Case (4)

Regus (Maxim) Ltd v Bank of Scotland plc

[2011] CSOH 129, 2011 GWD 27-600, 2011 Case (52) *affd* [2013] CSIH 12, 2013 SC 331, 2013 SLT 477, 2013 Case (43)

Rivendale v Keeper of the Registers of Scotland

30 October 2013, Lands Tribunal, 2013 Case (35) *affd* [2015] CSIH 27, 2015 SC 558, 2015 Case (29) and (84)

Royal Bank of Scotland plc v Carlyle

[2010] CSOH 3, 2010 GWD 13-235, 2010 Case (67) *rev* [2013] CSIH 75, 2014 SC 188, 2014 SCLR 167, 2013 Case (75) *rev* [2015] UKSC 13, 2015 SC (UKSC) 93, 2015 SLT 206, 2015 Case (91)

Royal Bank of Scotland v O'Donnell

[2013] CSOH 78, 2013 GWD 19-388, 2013 Case (59) *affd* [2014] CSIH 84, 2014 GWD 33-641, 2014 Case (54)

Royal Bank of Scotland plc v Wilson

2008 GWD 2-35, Sh Ct, 2008 Case (61) *rev* 2009 CSIH 36, 2009 SLT 729, 2009 Case (75) *rev* [2010] UKSC 50, 2011 SC (UKSC) 66, 2010 SLT 1227, 2010 Hous LR 88, 2010 Case (66)

Salvesen v Riddell

[2012] CSIH 26, 2012 SLT 633, 2012 SCLR 403, 2012 HousLR 30, 2012 Case (51) *rev* [2013] UKSC 22, 2013 SC (UKSC) 236, 2013 SLT 863, 2013 Case (50)

Schubert Murphy v The Law Society of England and Wales

[2014] EWHC 4561 (QB), [2015] PNLR 15, 2015 Case (78) *affd* [2017] EWCA Civ 1295, [2017] 4 WLR 200, 2017 Case (65)

Scottish Coal Company Ltd v Danish Forestry Co Ltd

[2009] CSOH 171, 2009 GWD 5-79, 2009 Case (9) *affd* [2010] CSIH 56, 2010 GWD 27-529, 2010 Case (3)

Sheltered Housing Management Ltd v Bon Accord Bonding Co Ltd

2007 GWD 32-533, 2006 Cases (24) and (35), 11 October 2007, Lands Tribunal, 2007 Case (21) *rev* [2010] CSIH 42, 2010 SC 516, 2010 SLT 662, 2010 Case (25)

@Sipp (Pension Trustees) Ltd v Insight Travel Services Ltd

[2014] CSOH 137, 2014 Hous LR 54, 2014 Case (42) *rev* [2015] CSIH 91, 2016 SLT 131, 2016 Hous LR 20, 2015 Case (51)

Smith v Stuart

2009 GWD 8-140, Sh Ct, 2009 Case (2) *affd* [2010] CSIH 29, 2010 SC 490, 2010 SLT 1249, 2010 Case (10)

STV Central Ltd v Semple Fraser LLP

[2014] CSOH 82, 2014 GWD 16-299, 2014 Case (61) *affd* [2015] CSIH 35, 2015 SLT 313, 2015 Case (59)

Tenzin v Russell

2014 Hous LR 17, Sh Ct, 2014 Case (51) *affd* [2015] CSIH 8A, 2015 Hous LR 11, 2015 Case (43)

Thomson v Mooney

[2012] CSOH 177, 2012 GWD 39-769, 2012 Case (63) *rev* [2013] CSIH 115, 2014 GWD 14-263, 2013 Case (74)

Tuley v Highland Council

2007 SLT (Sh Ct) 97, 2007 Case (24) *rev* [2009] CSIH 31A, 2009 SC 456, 2009 SLT 616, 2009 Case (48)

Van Lynden v Gilchrist

[2015] CSOH 147, 2015 SLT 864, 2015 Case (65) *rev* [2016] CSIH 72, 2016 SLT 1187, 2017 SCLR 351, 2016 Case (47)

Wright v Shoreline Management Ltd

Oct 2008, Arbroath Sheriff Court, 2008 Case (60) *rev* 2009 SLT (Sh Ct) 83, 2009 Case (74)

TABLE OF CASES DIGESTED IN EARLIER VOLUMES BUT REPORTED IN 2017

Gyle Shopping Centre General Partners Ltd v Marks and Spencer plc
[2016] CSIH 19, 2017 SCLR 221

Humphreys v Crabbe
[2016] CSIH 82, 2017 SCLR 699

Priya Properties Ltd v Inverclyde Council
[2016] SC GRE 81, 2017 Hous LR 19

Simpson v Hillcrest Housing Association Ltd
2017 Hous LR 2

Tock v Keeper of the Registers of Scotland
2017 GWD 12-183

William Tracey Ltd v The Scottish Ministers
[2016] CSOH 131, 2016 SLT 1049, 2017 SCLR 368

Van Lynden v Gilchrist
[2016] CSIH 72, 2016 SLT 1187, 2017 SCLR 351